Markets and power in digital capitalism

Manchester University Press

Markets and power in digital capitalism

Philipp Staab

Translated by Meredith Dale

MANCHESTER UNIVERSITY PRESS

Originally published in German as *Digitaler Kapitalismus*
by Suhrkamp Verlag Berlin 2019

First English-language edition published in 2024 by
Manchester University Press
Oxford Road, Manchester M13 9PL

www.manchesteruniversitypress.co.uk

British Library Cataloguing-in-Publication Data
A catalogue record for this book is available from the British
Library

ISBN 978 1 5261 7216 7 hardback

First published 2024

MIX
Paper | Supporting
responsible forestry
FSC
www.fsc.org   FSC® C007785

Typeset
by Cheshire Typesetting Ltd, Cuddington, Cheshire
Printed in Great Britain
by Bell & Bain Ltd, Glasgow

Contents

List of figures

List of tables

Preface to the updated English edition: politicising the market

This book first came out in German in autumn 2019. When I began preparing the text for publication in English, I was struck by the speed of change in the commercial internet. Companies have altered their names (Facebook to Meta), acquisitions have occurred, market shares and other company data had to be updated, and the political climate around big tech has shifted. Yet the broader analysis of digital capitalism still stands. Three years after its first publication, the historical dynamics, analytical concepts and potential trajectories I describe are, at least in my eyes, just as valid – maybe more so. The historic roots of digital capitalism remain by definition unchanged. And its manifestation – a highly financialised digital economy built on spectacular speculation – only snowballed during the global COVID-19 pandemic, which boosted investment in anything remotely digital and expanded the power of the digital networks. The economic turmoil accompanying the pandemic has left the basic structure of the digital economy fundamentally unchanged, along with the strategies pursued by its leading corporations. We still live in a society where control over digital platforms and ecosystems is exploited to literally privatise (actually: *propriatise*) entire markets, expand labour control and thus maximise profit extraction – at the price of growing social inequality.

What has probably changed most is that such developments are increasingly contested. New forms of labour organising in the gig economy, particularly the proliferation of wildcat strikes, are but the tip of the iceberg and, as I show in my updated reflections on social conflict in Chapter 6, probably not even the most important vector of contestation in digital capitalism. Political regulation, in particular within the European Union, poses a much greater threat to the power of big tech. Yet for the moment the platforms just keep on growing.

In order to capture these transformations, and to strengthen the analytical core of the theory laid out in the book, I have updated much of the economic data. I have also cut out certain passages relating to particularities that are of interest only in the German context. At the end of the book, as one of the principal additions, I address recent moves by the European Union to tighten political regulation – through the Digital Markets Act, the Digital Services Act and the Data Act – and contextualise these political contestations within my theory of digital capitalism.

Another significant development of the past three years is the volume of ambitious new scholarship exploring the question of how digital technologies are transforming capitalism. We can distinguish two main strands here: one that focuses on the 'capitalism' and one that places greater emphasis on the 'digital' (including alternatives like 'platform', 'informational', 'cognitive', 'cultural' etc.).

Authors thinking within rigorous Marxist categories tend to present the former as the only way to talk about technology and capitalism. Their concern often seems to be to insist that digital capitalism *is still capitalism*, not infrequently by discrediting alternative theories that build on assumptions outside of academic Marxism. Media scholar Christian Fuchs for example, as a leading and highly productive Marxist theorist of the political economy of digital technologies, captures much of the criticism of heterodox Marxist analysis in a recent volume entitled *Digital Capitalism*.[1] His main argument against Schumpeterian approaches like mine is their limited scope: that we address (digital) capitalism mainly if not purely as an economic system. What we 'bourgeois theorists' fail to understand, he argues, is that 'Marx spoke of the "capitalist society" … and "the capitalist mode of production" … This means that for Marx capitalism is both a type of the economy (*Produktionsweise*, mode of production) and a type of society (*Gesellschaftsformation*, a formation of society/societal formation)' (Fuchs 2022: 16). Class relations are essential to such takes on 'capitalism as a formation of society'. Fuchs continues in classical Marxist fashion: 'Workers are alienated from the conditions of production in class society because they do not own the means of production and the products of their labour. The logic of accumulation is not limited to the realm of the economy but extends into the political and cultural realms' (Fuchs 2022: 20).

I certainly agree with the basic assumption of that line of argument, that a theory describing a particular capitalist constellation must include an analysis of the class relations – or in less loaded terms, social inequality – as well as the interactions between the economic, political and cultural systems. However, to insist that the only possible route to achieving that is a fixation on Marx – sometimes adding a little Engels, Polanyi or Henri Lefebvre into the mix – seems to me an unnecessary and above all unproductive limitation on critical research. While Marx is without a doubt the most important theorist of capitalism, and laid the basic foundations for practically all critical research in the field, he is by no means the only source of inspiration for work conceptualising capitalism as more than an economic system.

Schumpeter, for example, expounded a very sociological theory locating the cultural origins of capitalism in the bourgeois family. And if we venture outside the orthodox Marxist framework, we discover drivers of social inequality in digital capitalism that challenge the Marxist preoccupation with class struggle. For example, by including cultural and political dynamics and employing social theory from various authors within and outside the Marxist spectrum, I uncover a transformation of citizenship in contemporary consumer society that would appear to shape social conflict in a way that prevents labour struggles from taking centre stage (see Chapter 6). A perspective on class relations is implicit here.

At the same time, the spectrum of conflict I observe is not limited to the contradiction between capital and labour. Examining how that particular conflict is demobilised in digital capitalism offers insights into other conflicts that have emerged as various segments of the political and economic elites fight for their respective visions of the digital economy, and that are of great relevance for the future of this particular capitalist constellation. I also address political trajectories within digital capitalism, analysing them from the perspective of Marxist theories focussing on the continuous struggle between capitalism and democracy (Streeck 2014) as well as within a framework concentrating more on the development of political and social rights.

This way, I think, an empirically and analytically much more sensitive and *explorative* analysis of the dynamics and conflicting trajectories of digital capitalism can take shape – one that takes inspiration from Marxist thinking while remaining open to new discoveries and aware of the many different ways we can make sense of the world. In this regard, my theory aligns with what one could call aspectological approaches to (digital) capitalism. These purposely remain open and sensitive to empirical transformations affecting economy and society. In terms of technological change and capitalist transformation, this strand of theory is not primarily concerned with identifying timeless features of capitalism (like private accumulation, capitalist labour process, class antagonism or alienation) over and over again. But that does not mean it necessarily neglects their existence. Instead we tend to treat those aspects as constants while examining how incremental changes transform the internal structure of a capitalist formation.

Aspectological approaches seek to identify potential vanguard phenomena in order to gain a more holistic understanding of the trajectory of capitalism. One could say they are theories in the subjunctive, striving for tentative generalisations and seeking orientation in an ever-evolving capitalist system. They are not static, but dynamic theories, which is one reason why Schumpeter is such an obvious choice as a frame of reference. As the theorist of 'creative destruction', he understood very well the problem of exploring the future on the basis of empirical observations restricted to the present and past: 'The best way of getting a vivid and realistic idea of industrial strategy is indeed to visualize the behavior of new concerns or industries that introduce new commodities or processes … or else reorganize a part or the whole of an industry' (Schumpeter 2003 [1942]: 89).

One very successful recent example of an aspectological approach to digital capitalism, striving to tease out its analytical core, is Shoshana Zuboff's opulent *Surveillance Capitalism* (2019). Zuboff's work represents a broader field of research on techno-economic change, which conceptualises the digital transformation under an implicit theory of data primacy. To Zuboff, like many others, data is first and foremost the by-product of digital communication. Whenever we exchange information, we leave traces that commercial entities exploit as a separate source of profit. The prime movers here are of course the giants of online advertising, Google and Facebook. According to Zuboff, the entire commercial internet can be understood as an enormous surveillance apparatus. And since capitalist imperatives are at work, the machinery of surveillance must expand constantly. So, she argues, more and more companies have begun to focus on extracting profit from data and monitoring, conceptualising this as a rapid expansion of surveillance capitalism. In this model, the function of smart washing machines, e-commerce platforms and household robots is to facilitate data gathering for the surveillance capitalists. Here, the essence of digital capitalism is the rise of an economic logic seeking to measure, influence and ultimately control our behaviour, rather than the resource-efficient production of goods and services (productivity).

The approach laid out in this book, by contrast, could be called the 'privatised markets' theory. The question of the larger economic project in which the data economy is embedded is, I would argue, central. An economy cannot consist exclusively of online advertising. My contribution is to propose that we are dealing with a project to establish privatised – or more precisely proprietary – markets.

The basis of these privately owned markets is formed by the platform companies of the commercial internet, which have in many cases established commercial monopolies (at least in the Schumpeterian sense) for their services, such as mobility, entertainment or home delivery. Each of these private markets, however, depends on socio-technical ecosystems run by a very small number of companies. The most important of these (at least in the West) are Google, Apple, Amazon and Facebook, around which the other platforms orbit like satellites.

These 'planets' or 'meta-platforms' increasingly control what we see and do online (and to an extent offline too). This position of power makes them gold mines in increasingly competitive consumer markets.

'Controlling users' attention' actually means 'controlling consumption' – or, in more abstract terms, 'controlling the demand side of the market'.

Surveillance capitalist advertising is thus one way of capitalising on consumer attention (capitalising on control of demand). There are others too (see Chapter 4). Such mechanisms are generally based on the various types of fees that the meta-platforms charge for their market function. The most obvious is naturally advertising revenue, but there are also more direct fees for market participation. Google and Apple charge 30 per cent of revenue for transactions in their app stores. Thus, the theory of privatised markets does not require far-fetched speculation about the end of individual self-determination and suchlike (as with Zuboff). It is much closer to theories positing a continuity of basic features of capitalism, as conflicts over control of markets have always been part and parcel of capitalist competition. I would, however, also argue that digital technology (and especially the emergence of the digital platforms) has facilitated a significant innovation in the capitalist system.

The crux of my theory of digital capitalism is the idea that the leading companies of the commercial internet (in the West, Google, Apple, Facebook and Amazon) do not really operate in markets whose pricing mechanisms they might distort. They *are* the markets, in the sense that in the economic space of the commercial internet they connect almost all the supply (apps, other software, content, goods and services sold online) to almost all the demand (everybody who has a digital device).

From this perspective, digital capitalism is essentially a programme for market control. As a result, social conflicts over digital capitalism must be conflicts over the shape, governance and – as Ralf Dahrendorf called it – 'the rationality of the market' (Dahrendorf 1979: 20). This conclusion takes us back to the fixation of certain Marxist thinkers on the question of class struggle. Class struggle is certainly an important driver of change within *digital* capitalism. But it only becomes a conflict over digital capitalism if it addresses the issue of privatised market ownership in some way. Seen this way, class struggle and labour conflicts are aspects of a broader sphere of contestation of digital capitalism. These contestations can be broadly divided into positions that are generally critical of the realities of digital market design and control, and positions that embrace those features. Today, the critical side is on the rise, coming from two different angles.

The first involves a grass-roots critique of digital market control, highlighting new and often rather unconventional labour disputes in the gig economy and in other fields controlled by privatised markets (such as Amazon). These contestations from below also include strategies like platform cooperativism (Scholz 2017), seeking cooperative self-organisation via digital platforms. Their basic normative position seems to be that digital markets should be democratically governed spaces ensuring fair redistribution to all stakeholders, and they are therefore critical of the possibilities of digital control epitomised by proprietary markets. The second model is contestation from above, as exemplified by the European Union's approach to platform regulation (addressed in Chapter 7). Here, we are dealing with political initiatives to develop an apparatus capable of reining in the power of the proprietary markets. Again, the normative frame of reference is 'good' (aka 'neutral') markets that are not controlled by any particular actor, instead embodying the infamous liberal ideal of the invisible hand.

On the other side, we have two very different modes of contestation featuring broadly affirmative perspectives on digital control. The first could be called the 'digital planned economy' or 'Walmart Socialism' (after Leigh Phillips and Michal Rozworski's *The People's Republic of Walmart* [2019]). This approach proposes using the power of digital market control to establish a socialist economy superior to contemporary digital capitalism. As proprietary markets are essentially cybernetic organisations engaged in constant and adaptive economic planning, their socialisation would open the door to a more just, equal and sustainable economy. That affirmation of digital control is shared by the fourth model: the 'punitive market society' is most notoriously represented by China's social credit system, on which I elaborate in Chapter 7. Here, the same techno-organisational model is applied to bolster social order by securing conformity and punishing dissent.

As different as these four models of contestation might appear at first glance, they certainly share salient features. They either advocate for the restoration of 'real' markets (as if those had ever existed) or for technocratic applications of digital market control. As a result, the politicisation of the market – instigated by big tech and increasingly contested from various angles – is stripped of its conflictual and thus progressive potential. We need to preserve and promote that politicisation, as it can point the way to an economy that escapes both the ideology of the market and the temptations of technocracy. The real innovation would be to advance freedom beyond both capitalism *and* commercial technocracy.

Note

1   The choice of the title itself speaks to the prominence the term *digital capitalism* has acquired. Much of the academic debate that Fuchs addresses originated in a book of the same title by the American historian Dan Schiller. Indeed, the original German title of this volume was *Digitaler Kapitalismus*.

We always plan too much and always think too little.
Schumpeter, 1946

1

Introduction: after neoliberalism

In early 2020, during the first Covid lockdown, I was approached by a leading German retailers' association. A senior representative wanted to discuss alternatives to the existing digital commerce. Bricks-and-mortar shops had just reopened but customers were not returning as expected. 'It was hard for us anyway', he told me, 'but we are playing a different game these days. There is no way around Amazon now.' I told him about the possibilities of bringing together stakeholders from different parts of the economy to create new networks of economic exchange. I even sketched out a proposal for a cooperative platform.

Nothing came of it, of course. The shops reopened properly and the strategists of the old economy went back to managing decline and dependency. But the pandemic had stripped away the mask. In today's economy the possibilities for avoiding the likes of Amazon, Alphabet/Google, Apple and Meta/Facebook are small, and shrinking. Capitalism has become digital.

One of the first to see this coming was the American historian Dan Schiller, who coined the term digital capitalism (Schiller 1999) to describe the central role of new information and communication technologies in the transformation of the global economy. Schiller saw the diffusion of digital technologies into all sectors of the economy as a metatrend, coinciding from the 1960s with the post-Fordist restructuring of capitalism. In terms of its empirical relevance and implications, he argues, 'digital capitalism … is comparable to "industrial capitalism"' as it emerged as a concept in the nineteenth century (Schiller 2014: 8). Accordingly, he wrote, the underlying technologies and all significant innovations were now digital. The mainspring of capitalist reorganisation was no longer the mechanical muscle of industrial manufacturing, but the digital networks of the information and communications technologies.

Schiller's first book (1999) revolved around the global expansion of information and communications technology. His argument there was that since the 1960s this sector had become the decisive vehicle for defending and expanding US hegemony. Control over technical standards, the construction

of crucial infrastructure and the resulting expansion of the US culture industry had, he argued, enabled the United States to preserve its hegemony within
its geopolitical sphere of influence. The leading players in this long epoch
were telecommunications firms like AT&T, the film industry and then in the
1990s the Microsoft/Intel duo ('Wintel', standing for personal computers
with Intel processors running Windows operating systems).

Schiller's fundamental observation is that these companies upheld US
global hegemony in two senses. Firstly their successes demonstrated that
American businesses dominated the decisive post-Fordist growth markets
and reinforced the country's geopolitical pre-eminence. Secondly – and
here Schiller is quite his father's son[1] – information and communications
technologies (ICT) had flooded the world with American media products
that globalised the American way of life and cemented its hegemony in the
cultural sphere.

In his second book, on digital capitalism (2014), Schiller lays out a much
broader tapestry. Now he sets out to demonstrate that other diagnoses
of the post-Fordist political economy can be subsumed into his concept.
Capitalism has become increasingly digital, even outside the ICT sectors, he
writes, because lean production, globalisation and the rise of the financial
markets are all based on digital technologies. In this understanding it is the
diffusion of particular technologies into all spheres of life and work that
makes capitalism digital.

Tautological metaphor or analytical category?

The problem for Schiller's readers, however, is that it becomes increasingly
hard to discern the actual essence of this new form of capitalism. What is
the actual analytical value, for example, of the observation that there are
chips in cars, and in the machines used to build them, that algorithms play
a huge role in the financial markets but also in computer games, that ever
more people use computers for their work, and that modern household
devices like washing machines can connect to the internet? For Schiller, as
a historian, this is not a central question. He simply follows connections
that lead him from the telecommunications sector into almost all spheres of
society and the economy. However, Schiller's process orientation manoeu-
vres him into a 'nominalist dead-end': the connection between the events he
describes and the structural transformation of capitalism remains unclear
(Pace 2018: 256). Worse, Schiller's concept ultimately appears tautological:
the digital in digital capitalism is the digital technology.[2]

As a sociologist I find this unsatisfying. To my mind the dissemination of
digital technologies into many or even most spheres of life and work only

becomes a relevant factor when it is connected with a hypothesis about the associated economic logic and societal effects. I am not interested in treating digital capitalism as a metaphor, as has become increasingly popular. It may be true that 'computers are everywhere',[3] but that does not make this an analytical statement capable of defining a specific form of capitalist economy.

Schiller's diagnosis of a historical trajectory involving a rather concentrated cluster of technologically ambitious telecommunications companies systematically growing and expanding to a point where the digital technologies become the foundational infrastructure of the highly developed economies is hard to fault. Nor would refuting Schiller be my objective. Instead I will argue that we are well into a phase where the successive diffusion of digital technologies into all spheres of life leads one to the emergence of a new concentration of economic power. The essence of the shift is not as diffuse as the omnipresence of computers might lead one to think. It lies in the commercial internet, whose leading companies have become the decisive interfaces for ever-growing numbers of economic processes; otherwise the ubiquitous computers would be little more than sophisticated calculating machines. If we are to understand the emergence, reproduction and effects of this concentration process in sociological terms, we must start by asking what it actually represents. Putting the question in those terms means swapping the descriptive breadth and precision of historiography for the analytical precision of sociology. What we are after is an analytical understanding of digital capitalism.

So what does the essence consist of, and what distinguishes the present moment from the situation when Schiller wrote his two books?

No unity of state and capital

I would argue that some of Schiller's central assumptions – which were certainly plausible at the time – have recently become questionable. The economic hegemony of the United States is no longer unchallenged, even in its erstwhile spheres of influence. The rise of China is widely cited as a central factor in the relative decline of US power. This applies in particular to the ICT sector and the commercial internet, and thus to the leading sectors of digitalisation. In hardware manufacturing, for example, Chinese enterprises dominate not only their own domestic market but increasingly also the markets of important emerging economies – in everything from consumer electronics to digital infrastructures (fibre optics, mobile networks etc.) (Kharpal 2017; S. Srivastava 2017; L. Y. Chen 2018; Iyengar 2018). And today most of the hardware marketed by the major US corporations is manufactured under contract in China (most prominently of course by Taiwanese-owned Foxconn) (Duhigg and Bradsher 2012; Barboza 2016) – without that meaning that the profits necessarily remain in China. Conversely, the Chinese market is to all intents and purposes closed to the major American internet companies. A mixture of economic protectionism and targeted state support for key digital enterprises – in particular the three leading companies of the Chinese-style commercial internet, Baidu, Alibaba and Tencent – has brought forth national conglomerates that are today among the world's most valuable companies. Tencent, for example, was the first Chinese internet company to make it into the elite club of corporations whose market value exceeds US$500 billion (Perez 2017; Staab and Butollo 2018).

The state whose investment enabled this growth has also heavily restricted the commercial opportunities of Western internet companies in China through a range of quasi-protectionist measures. Google abandoned China in 2010, ostensibly over its refusal to submit to censorship, and has since equivocated over the question of returning (and how to reconcile the concessions that would be involved with the progressive self-image of many Google staff). China blocked Facebook in 2009 following unrest in Xinjiang, on the grounds that it had served as the communication infrastructure for protesting Uyghurs – a charge that crops up pretty much everywhere when protests get out of hand or lynch mobs run wild. Amazon does retain a presence in China – whose population of 1.4 billion makes it the world's biggest internal market – although its market share is marginal. While Alibaba (55.9 per cent) and JD.com (16.7 per cent) account for the lion's share of the Chinese e-commerce market, Amazon shut down its domestic marketplace in China to 'focus on "cross-border" selling to Chinese consumers' (eMarketer 2019; Kharpal 2019). As they seek to expand internationally, the Chinese internet companies have also become direct competitors of their Western counterparts. In India, Amazon and Alibaba fought a bitter price war for the e-commerce market (M. Srivastava 2021). The ride-hailing platforms Uber and Didi Chuxing compete indirectly in Brazil – even though Uber actually owns a stake in Didi.[4]

In light of the aspect of US hegemony that Schiller highlights, it is more important to understand the structural interests behind the rise of regional leading companies and key industries. Schiller's theory of digital capitalism securing economic and cultural hegemony implies a certain unity of state and economy in the affected spheres. Only if leading companies served the interests of a specific state (and vice versa) could that promote the latter's hegemony. While that may have been true for the history of the ICT sector, as I lay out in Chapter 2, it is no longer the case today. The investing state is certainly no longer the decisive supplier of capital to the established sectors of the digital economy, especially the commercial internet. The private venture capital driving the growth and global expansion of the internet companies is largely outside political control (which functions indirectly if at all). While sovereign wealth funds pursue strategic political interests by lending to key industries or investing in research, venture capital is politically comparably uncontrolled. It is therefore no surprise that practically all the leading Chinese digital enterprises are in large part foreign-owned[5] (Jia 2018) and that the volume of American venture capital invested in Chinese businesses has grown steadily for decades.[6]

At the same time the US administration has blocked particular investments and acquisitions by Chinese companies on grounds of national security.[7] In other words, there is no great unity of state and capital, no 'Stamokap 2.0'[8] (Lovink 2017) enabling the state to pursue national interests across the globe on the back of private venture capital. Despite the undeniable confluence of the key enterprises of digitalisation with the national security state and their acquired role as an arm of the 'anti-terror' apparatus, there is no denying that the state had for a long time abandoned any idea of active economic policy in today's key sectors of digitalisation. What we are dealing with now is not digital hegemony but digital capitalism.

Concentration through diffusion

The essence of the matter is that the diffusion of digital technologies into all spheres of life, work and business leads not to a decentralisation and democratisation of economic and political power but to its concentration. In the consumer-driven commercial internet a very small number of very large companies control access to goods, services and infrastructure. The giant 'meta-platforms' – Google (Android), Amazon, Facebook and Apple (iOS) (together 'GAFA') – have become 'gatekeepers' (Dolata 2015) of the commercial internet, on which even corporations and governments are more or less dependent. From this core, threads extend out into every aspect of economic activity and private life.

To my mind this form of concentration of power, which has turned the 'meta-platforms' (Nachtwey and Staab 2020) into decisive power structures, has not been adequately analysed. There is increasing discussion about the monopolistic character of these companies, among critical academics and increasingly also in politics and civil society. Two theories are widely cited to explain this phenomenon: network effects (C. Shapiro and Varian 1999) and the low and falling marginal costs of digital goods (Rifkin 2014).

Specific supply-side scale effects involving systemically low marginal costs operate in the commercial internet. The platforms' digital products often incur (very) high development costs, while the marginal cost of each additional unit is extremely small (think software or MP3 files). This permits companies to sell large volumes at relatively low unit prices or even to give their products away to generate long-term customer relationships, and lends systematic advantages to larger firms. The larger the firm, the greater the cost and speed advantages in developing new products, and the greater the diversity of the portfolio.

Specific network effects also operate on the demand side, where the utility of digital products often grows with the number of users. The more people using an Android smartphone, the better the traffic data supplied by Google Maps. Facebook is the poster child for this phenomenon, its attractiveness growing absolutely with the number of 'friends' users find there. Achieving a critical mass of users makes it increasingly appealing for others to adopt the system. When demand for a successful product crosses a certain threshold a self-amplifying process comes into play: the strong become stronger and the weak weaker, in a classic example of the 'Matthew effect' (Merton 1968). Scale and network effects occurring in combination encourage the concentration of power and the emergence of winner-takes-all markets where smaller players are left behind or become absolutely dependent on the meta-platforms to reach potential users of their products.

Schumpeter in the internet

That widely discussed criticism of the meta-platforms is also cited as a 'plus' in almost every pitch for investment in digital businesses. In fact the critical narrative of the dangers of monopolisation reproduces the sector's self-image – but reverses the pros and cons (Reitz 2017). In certain respects the Silicon Valley 'superstructure' has long begun to respond to criticism of concentration and monopolisation tendencies. For example Peter Thiel, PayPal founder, early Facebook investor, legendary venture capitalist (and notorious for his interest in parabiosis and support for Donald Trump) (Bercovici 2016; Jacobs 2016; Cuthbertson 2018), lauded the era of 'creative monopolies' in his famous Stanford start-up class of 2012 (Thiel 2014). Contrary to the expectations of conventional economic theory, he argued, the creative monopolies did not stifle innovation and undermine consumer interests. Instead, he said, networking everything was unlocking historically unprecedented efficiency gains, from which consumers could only benefit. Thus, Thiel posits, scale and network effects benefit contemporary 'consumer citizens' (Streeck 2012).

The Austrian economist and chronicler of capitalism Joseph Schumpeter can, in a sense, be regarded as the intellectual godfather of this thesis, which has become a tenet of faith in Silicon Valley. Schumpeter enjoys enormous popularity in the West Coast internet economy, principally on account of a particular reading of his theory of entrepreneurship (Schumpeter 2021 [1934]). Many of today's digital entrepreneurs see their slogan 'Move fast and break things' as a modern version of Schumpeter's theory of creative destruction.

Another reason for Schumpeter's popularity might well be that his second major work, *Capitalism, Socialism and Democracy* (2003 [1942]), adopted a comparatively monopoly-tolerant position, at least in the context of the political and academic debate in the United States at that time. The power of the large industrial corporations he investigated could be compared to the leading companies of digital capitalism today, although the circumstances are entirely different. The leading companies of Schumpeter's industrial monopoly capitalism were operating in an economy of scarcity, and the consensus at that time was that they were failing to make full use of their capacities in order to maximise profits: keeping supply artificially scarce and the standard of living unnecessarily low. It was also argued that the leading companies were failing to promote technological innovation, because they were more concerned about securing their profits than advancing their products and production methods in the interests of consumers.

Schumpeter made short shrift of that theory, which he believed was detached from reality. In a world of systematic scarcity, ensuring that the economy actually supplied its maximum output was naturally a priority. He demonstrated that the widely discussed dangers were not in fact empirically realised in the first half of the twentieth century. Schumpeter began by fine-tuning the – then as now overtly political – concept of monopoly, which tended to express public and political misgivings over the concentration of economic power in the hands of a few major industrialists rather than the strict literal sense of the 'single seller' of a particular product (Schumpeter 2003 [1942]: 101). The relationship between these was one of 'monopolistic competition' (Schumpeter 2003 [1942]: 79).

In a second step, Schumpeter demonstrates that the enormous productivity of economically rational monopolies was a decisive condition for the explosive growth of affordable mass commodities. Schumpeter certainly saw the risks involved in controlling consumer prices, but believed they had been dispelled by the aforementioned 'monopolistic competition'. Nevertheless, he argued, capitalism would be brought down by its own success. Although rational production ensured an ever-growing supply of industrial mass goods, it extinguished the entrepreneurial function as consumer-oriented middle classes succeeded the bourgeois family (which Schumpeter identified as the social origin of entrepreneurialism) and employed managers took the place of risk-taking owners. As such the leading companies of his era guaranteed prosperity but relied on rational planning rather than creative destruction. This, he believed, would ultimately lead to the death of capitalism.

Contrary to the tech entrepreneurs who so like to quote from chapter 7 of *Capitalism, Socialism and Democracy*, Schumpeter's arguments supply no intellectual justification for their actions. What reading Schumpeter does tell us is that the problematic debates on which he was commenting were not dissimilar to today's timorous criticisms of digital monopolies. Today's commercial internet is also dominated by 'monopolistic competition' rather than the logic of the 'single seller', and again controlling consumer prices is not decisive for the profits of the leading companies.

At the same time, however, we are dealing with new processes of concentration of economic power, which necessitate a rejigging of the coordinates of any analysis of capitalism orientated on today's leading companies. While an analysis of that nature can borrow a specific perspective on capitalism from Schumpeter, it will come to quite different conclusions about the central problems, agents, mechanisms and effects. Digital capitalism cannot be conceived as a problem of scarcity, but only in terms of a logic of superabundance. Its leading companies are not rational producer monopolies, but proprietary markets. Its dynamism is driven more by rent-seeking than by entrepreneurial logic. The objective is not to maximise production but to derive profit from goods that are actually superabundant. The outcome of this constellation is not the death of capitalism, but a radicalisation of its fundamental traits, especially social inequality. Under these conditions, Schumpeter is not the prophet of economic advancement through a concentration of economic power ultimately leading to socialism, but a source of intellectual and practical criticism of digital capitalism.

Markets in private ownership

The starting point for such a critique must lie in an analysis of the leading companies of digital capitalism and their interconnectedness with the contemporary political economy. In this perspective the beating heart of digital capitalism is a system of proprietary markets.

A combination of low marginal costs, systematic network effects and – last not least – the structural importance of private venture capital undoubtedly goes some way to explaining the concentration of power in the commercial internet. These factors are needed to explain how the rise of the leading companies came about in the first place. But above all, any analytical concept of digital capitalism must answer the question of what characterises the digital monopoly of the present age and whether we are merely dealing with a reincarnation of the classical monopoly capitalism described by Schumpeter and others.

At first glance there appears to be ample evidence for the latter. The classical monopolisation processes of the industrial age were often based on so-called 'natural monopolies', with which the leading companies of digital capitalism at first glance apparently share much in common. As far as their material preconditions are concerned, natural monopolies have extremely high fixed costs and comparably lower variable costs. Telecommunications, utilities and railways all required costly infrastructure, while the actual goods and services were comparatively cheap to produce and provide. The resulting scale effects created often insurmountable obstacles to rivals (Nachtwey and Staab 2015).

One could argue that the same also applied to all the digital business models, which depend on a global infrastructure (core routers, submarine cables, data centres and much more). But did the establishment of a search engine like Google really demand investment comparable to the first transcontinental railroad, for example? Probably not. The infrastructure for the internet already existed (within the existing telephone system) when Google's search algorithm was programmed, if not in its present form. There was no need to lay track and build stations, 'just' to index the connections between different locations. The leading companies of the commercial internet successively became relevant providers of material infrastructure with relevant fixed costs only *after* their rise, a point to which I will return in greater depth in Chapter 4. At this juncture it is sufficient to note that the leading companies of digitalisation are neither natural monopolies nor suppliers of goods burdened with high fixed costs. What they do, essentially, is exploit 'first-mover dividends' secured by the relevant patents and the combination of effects described above.

In other words, the leading companies of the commercial internet are not natural monopolies in the classical sense. They also differ systematically in another respect – and this is the central argument of the present volume – from the 'monopolies' discussed by Schumpeter and others. Classical monopolies operate in markets; the leading companies of digital capitalism *are* markets. That distinction is central to any systematic theory of digital capitalism, and has far-reaching implications.

Classical monopolies dominate their sector as the leading or only supplier of a particular product or service, allowing them to control prices. Given that this can be detrimental to customers, competition authorities are supposed to ensure that companies do not abuse their market power.

The leading companies of the commercial internet, on the other hand, are no longer really operating in markets whose mechanisms they might distort, or at least that is not the crux of the matter. In a very comprehensive sense *they are the market*. What that means is illustrated by the example of the most advanced representative of the GAFA group: Google's search engine does not operate within a conventional market. Its users do not pay to search, so they are not customers. Nor is there a pricing aspect for the providers of information whose websites are displayed in the results list (the exception being the paid spots at the top of the list). Facebook is much the same. The customers of these platforms are entities that pay to advertise. Here Google and Facebook do indeed possess a degree of price control. But the decisive factor is the size of the user base, because advertisers are paying for reach. In order to acquire and retain users, the services are almost completely cross-subsidised out of advertising revenues, which can hardly be described as harmful to the consumer.

Google's history reveals how the company has systematically expanded its range of services to integrate more users into its network. After starting out as a plain search engine it has added one application after another, often through acquisitions: cartography (Maps), free e-mail (Gmail), social network (Google+)[9] and cloud storage (Drive) to name but a few. But the decisive milestone was the purchase of Android Inc. in 2005 and the launch of the first Android operating system for mobile devices, complete with app store, in 2008. Today Android holds about 72 per cent of the smartphone operating system market (Statcounter 2022). The operating system and app store serve as the basis for various in-house services, but also as a place where third parties can offer their own products. This brings producers and consumers together. This is a market with a consistent and systematically growing range of products and services. The heart of the meta-platform is not the search engine or any of the numerous applications; it is the *proprietary market*, which is essentially identical with the company as a whole.

In comparison to the classical producer monopolies that Schumpeter analysed and to an extent defended, the power of the market owner is manifested in various forms of control – over information, access, performance and prices – vis-à-vis both the producers and the consumers. These forms of control, which I discuss in greater detail in Chapters 4 and 5, form the basis for effective enforcement of the system of commission on which the profit model in proprietary markets is based. As the example of Google's app store illustrates, access control means firstly that the market owners are free to choose which producers they grant access to their private market and on what terms. These terms, secondly, regulate the distribution of revenues via a commission model. Google's app store for example charges 30 per cent commission on all transactions.

This combination of access control and commission is the key to understanding proprietary markets. Exclusive control over access allows market owners to charge whatever commission they choose, while they exploit the mechanism of supply and demand to secure other systematic advantages. If it so chooses, a platform can create competing products of its own that are cheaper at least by the share of commission. Amazon is notorious for this strategy.

In one sense or another the logic of the proprietary market applies to all the GAFA companies – without it being possible to reduce any of them entirely to this. Facebook is first and foremost a social network, but has also become a kind of market for information and a widely used source of news (Shearer and Gottfried 2017). Amazon earns exorbitant revenues through its cloud division Amazon Web Services, but is also the GAFA company where – through its e-commerce platform – the logic of capitalising on market ownership is most strongly and consistently pursued. Amazon exemplifies the push to expand the proprietary market model from the narrower sphere of the commercial internet to the entire world of material things. Here Amazon has to reckon with considerably higher fixed costs, which explains why it – or strictly its e-commerce business – has a significantly lower rate of profit than Google, Apple or Facebook. At first glance Apple appears to be the most similar to a conventional manufacturer, because it derives the overwhelming bulk of its profits from the sale of digital devices. In fact Apple was also a pioneer of the proprietary market with its iPod and iTunes store. Today its app store is not only the quintessence of a comprehensive proprietary market, but also a rapidly growing and increasingly important source of profit. In other words, my argument is not that the leading companies of the commercial internet can be reduced to their role as proprietary markets. They are all much more than that. Nevertheless, the factor of market ownership remains decisive for a proper understanding of digital capitalism. No analytical exertion is required to understand how profits are made with hardware (Apple), advertising (Google, Facebook) or infrastructure leasing (Amazon Web Services). That occurs in markets whose functions are known and understood. If we want to find parallels to companies seeking to become markets themselves, we must look to early or 'proto-capitalism' (Kocka 2016), such as the state-backed trading monopolies of mercantilism (more on this in Chapter 7).

The central argument of this volume is that the shift from classical monopoly strategies to the logic of proprietary markets is firstly poorly understood and secondly represents the analytical heart of a development that subsumes numerous phenomena that are widely discussed under the label digitalisation. Thirdly, the ultimate end point is for digital capitalism to become the dominant production model.

From Wintel to GAFA

The proprietary market model also presents, as I lay out in detail in Chapter 4, a qualitatively new development in the history of the ICT sector. The GAFA complex is qualitatively different from the first quasi-monopoly of the digital age, the Microsoft/Intel duo.

Wintel's dominance of the PC market began at the end of the 1980s when Microsoft's Windows emerged as the standard operating system of the PC age and the company developed a systematic partnership with the chip manufacturer Intel. From that point on, the two were able to impose relatively strict conditions on the hardware manufacturers: no smoothly running operating system without an installed Intel chip, no Intel chips without Windows compatibility. Wintel was accused of illegal anti-competitive practices, and the European Court of Justice imposed record fines on both companies (Wilkens 2004; European Commission 2008, 2009; Spiegel online 2008). In that respect there was already a form of market control at the point where the digital economy was born. But in the Wintel model this was restricted to the PC sector, where Wintel's market power allowed it to secure a comparatively large share of the profits in the new PC market.

In that sense Wintel was both 'bigger' and 'smaller' than the GAFA complex. When the leading companies of the commercial internet are labelled as monopolies today it is frequently overlooked that their ability to set prices through control of relevant sub-markets is in most cases considerably less comprehensive than it was for Wintel in the PC market. Today we are dealing with true monopolies only in specific sub-markets. Google, for example, has a quasi-monopoly on internet search, with a global market share of about 93 per cent in January 2023; Facebook (Meta) has a global market share of almost 70 per cent in the social networks (Statcounter 2023a, 2023b). But they stand in direct duopolistic competition in the online advertising market, where they still generate the lion's share of their revenues (92.5 per cent for Google/Alphabet, 97.5 per cent for Facebook/Meta).[10] Nor does Amazon hold as clear a monopoly as Wintel still maintains today in the PC market. Amazon does possess an impressive share of the e-commerce market in many countries (especially in North America and Western Europe): estimated 51 per cent in the United States, about 54 per cent in Germany and more than 30 per cent in the United Kingdom in 2021 (Bartnik 2021; Davidkhanian 2021; HDE 2021; PYMNTS 2022; Strugar 2022). But Amazon's share of sales seldom exceeds 50 per cent, even though there is often no competing platform with a comparably universal range of products. Amazon also faces sometimes extremely fierce competition from firms like Alibaba (China) and Flipkart (India). Apple also has a significant share of the global hardware market, but is by no means without competition.

On the other side of the equation, Wintel is restricted to a specific part of the ICT sector and dwarfed by the GAFA group. As of October 2017, the GAFA companies together had over three times the revenue of the Wintel duo: 'If you compare GAFA in their current dominance with Wintel in their period of dominance, you see not a 3× difference in scale but a 10× difference' (B. Evans 2017: n.p.). They have established 'socio-technical ecosystems' (Dolata 2015), characterised by a steadily growing spectrum of products and services. That has effects on both producers and consumers. As already touched on above, the proprietary markets wield enormous power over producers. An app that does not appear in the Google and iOS app stores does not really exist. And the fact that there are two stores and thus two markets does not significantly lessen the market power of either, because most apps depend on interoperability. The same can be said of Amazon's Marketplace, which has become indispensable for small and medium-sized internet vendors.

In recent years more and more goods and services have been sucked into the maw of the proprietary markets. As a result, the market owners have acquired even tighter control over ever-broader profit sectors. Where Wintel earns disproportionately in the PC market, the GAFA companies have long since eaten up large parts of the rest of the economy: from the entertainment and media industries through apps and online gaming to basically all hardware and consumer goods. One sector after another is drawn in: employment services, mobility services, grocery retailing etc.

The overarching objective of socio-technical ecosystems is to bind consumers systematically into the respective proprietary markets. One means is to remove any necessity to leave the system, by making all relevant goods available through a single ecosystem; another is to increase the 'switching-costs' for changing ecosystem (Dolata 2015). Herein lies the key to the accumulation of power in the commercial internet. To date we have largely been dealing 'only' with meta-platforms as proprietary market-*places*. If consumers do not like the conditions of a particular marketplace they can in principle switch to another and must normally expect no worse than a certain loss of convenience. The advent of socio-technical ecosystems changes this, and with it the analytical character of the companies concerned. From their users' perspective they become what we generally describe as *the* market: the universal venue for economic transactions.

After neoliberalism: privatisation of the market

If we are seeking to understand a specific historical variant of capitalism, *the market*, as the superordinate instance for organising and ordering economic activities, is not only central in practice, but also in theory (Fligstein and Dauter 2007; Aspers 2015). At first glance the centrality of the market idea to the concentration of power in the commercial internet might appear to be the logical continuation of the developments of recent decades. Was the expansion of the market into one new sphere after the other not the decisive characteristic of the formation generally referred to as *neoliberal*, which came to dominate most economies from the early 1980s? The market as politically established competition (Baccaro and Howell 2017) between 'national competitive states' (Hirsch 1995), as an instrument for disciplining labour (Sauer 2010; Brinkmann 2011), as a tool for opening up new growth in the sphere of public and private services (Butterwegge, Lösch and Ptak 2017) – no set of ideas has been more central to understanding the reorganisation of global capitalism since the 1980s, although this does not in itself say anything about the actual conditions of competition in actually existing neoliberalism.

What that narrative omits is that the process of imposing the market followed very different trajectories in different countries and institutions, and achieved very different results (Baccaro and Howell 2017). This occurred because, to cite a fundamental tenet of economic sociology (Sparsam 2015), markets are always socially constituted and institutionally secured, and therefore all different. Simply equating neoliberalism with expansion of the rule of the market neglects two other factors that are crucial to the shape of contemporary digital capitalism. Firstly, China can certainly not be subsumed into a narrative of the universal imposition of the free market. Despite its rapid integration into the global economy since the opening under Deng Xiaoping in 1978, China must be characterised as a system *sui generis* that – in the sense of a 'state capitalism 3.0' (ten Brink and Nölke 2013) – combines market elements with state control mechanisms in a manner entirely of its own. China's agnostic relationship to the market and its tradition of state management also go some way to explaining why it has brought forth the few companies capable of challenging the GAFA group. It follows that the highly selective and by no means universal topography of market forms supplies the key to understanding the geopolitical reconfiguration that is currently under way in global capitalism, and in particular in its digital leading sectors (see Chapter 8).

Secondly, the narrative of the universality of the market obscures the systematic difference between the model of market ownership and the ideological heart of neoliberalism, the idea that *the market is neutral*.

There is certainly no shortage of critiques of the neoclassical assumption that the role of the state should be restricted to protecting private property and guaranteeing public security. Adding yet another to the pile is not my interest here. It is, however, important to understand that the function of the state in the various iterations of neoliberal theory very definitely extends further than the aforementioned 'night-watchman' tasks (Lassalle 1862), and that the liberalisation of recent decades was in a very fundamental sense a politically driven project. Even libertarian thinkers like Friedrich August von Hayek – and adherents of the Freiburg School (Fleischmann 2019) – insist on a formal legal and institutional framework to secure the neutrality of the market. Neoliberalism as an ideological system, as a legitimiser of economic and political action (Boltanski and Chiapello 2003) and as a formation materialising in organisations is characterised by a specific conception of the market as a neutral place of exchange. The widely criticised policies of the institutional trinity of global neoliberalism – World Trade Organization (WTO), International Monetary Fund (IMF) and World Bank – were always built around absolutely practical concerns to dismantle trade barriers and create neutral markets.

Clearly digital capitalism, whose greatest innovation appears to be a system of proprietary markets, differs substantially from the neoliberal economic and social order that we have come to regard as normality. While advocates – from the right and the left – of the losers of neoliberalism wage battle with a politically heterogeneous group defending the neoliberal order, the leading segment of the capitalist transformation has long abandoned the idea of free, neutral markets and is in the process of expanding its economic practice to ever larger segments of the economy. The political acceptance and promotion of the leading companies of the commercial internet represents yet another aspect of the closing of the neoliberal epoch. A system of proprietary markets is well on the way to replacing it.

If this succeeds and the logic of proprietary markets – cloaked as digitalisation – becomes dominant, that would represent a development comparable only with the 'great transformation' described by Karl Polanyi (2001 [1944]). That process, beginning in the late eighteenth century, was when capitalism really took off on its quest to subject the very last corners of society to its mechanisms and imperatives. This was the first time the modern nation state played its dual role as enabler and shaper of socio-economic change on a grand scale. The economically most developed nation states experienced the culmination of their transformation into 'market societies' before the First World War, when the idea of the self-regulating market became the paradigm of global capitalism under economically liberal governments and the gold standard. This formation came tumbling down in the crash of 1929. The various shades of neoliberalism that emerged after 1945 under the Keynesian post-war consensus responded by conceding the state a stronger regulatory role backed by national and international institutions and cushioning the free market with a welfare state safety net. Their intention was to make the market society more resilient through a 'liberalism plus' and to enhance its attractiveness in the scope of system competition with 'actually existing socialism': in other words, shoring up liberalism and its three pillars – liberal state, free market, market society – rather than fundamentally transforming it.

Privatised mercantilism

If we understand neoliberalism as the second coming of classical liberalism, it becomes clear that a system of proprietary markets differs systematically from both classical liberal and neoliberal capitalism. To avoid any misunderstanding, I am certainly not arguing that the system of proprietary markets already dominates the entire economy. We are living in the smoking ruins of neoliberalism, in a kind of 'interregnum' (Gramsci 1999 [*c*.1930]: 556), where the old is not yet quite dead, the new not yet fully developed. My methodological argument is that turning our attention to the pioneering sectors of this latest transformation of capitalism offers a glimpse of the future. In this respect my theoretical approach is to seek a tentative generalisation.

As I lay out in greater detail in Chapter 4, the developments can only be comprehended against the backdrop of a complex political economy that accounts for specific crisis phenomena of global capitalism. Economics and economic sociology (Engels 2009) treat markets as instances for distribution of goods. It follows that enterprises constituted as proprietary markets differ systematically from traditional producers. The latter produce something; the former generate profits through their efficient distribution of goods produced by the latter. This makes commercial internet platforms inherently consumption-centred organisations. Their attraction – for producers and consumers alike – consists in enabling a relatively frictionless, and for their users extremely convenient, form of consumption. Nobody has to traipse to the record shop now that music streaming is available on any smartphone. Nobody needs to brave the Saturday shopping crowds now that an army of modern delivery boys bring purchases to the door. Today stressed-out commuters can order groceries for immediate delivery before they are even off the Underground (Staab 2016).

But what does it say about contemporary capitalism if its strongest suit is rationalising the distribution of goods rather than their cost- and resource-efficient production? The first thing to note is that the proprietary market model is the latest attempt to remedy the central economic problem of post-Fordist capitalism. The growth crisis of the highly developed capitalist economies has dragged on since about the mid-1970s, when the motor of Fordism – the combination of efficient mass production with equivalent mass consumption – began to misfire. The productivity dividends of the second Industrial Revolution – the Taylorist reorganisation of production – were basically exhausted, while the modern consumer markets were exhibiting the first signs of saturation. Whole societies had been equipped with the durable goods of modernism – refrigerator, washing machine, television set, household by household. Private demand collapsed, decimating the economic growth Fordism required to reproduce itself. In Chapter 4 I go into greater detail on the historical sequence of strategies seeking to address the consumption problem of post-Fordism. But what all these responses share in common – from expanding public and private (consumer) debt to the various varieties of Keynesianism – is the attempt to cure weak demand by boosting consumption. The economic promise of the proprietary markets of the commercial internet today lies in the same vein, this time addressing weakness of demand by rationalising consumption.

Yet if we examine the logic of proprietary markets, it is clear that such a system is fundamentally a zero-sum game. Markets are, as I said, instances for the distribution of goods, not their production (even if the companies concerned do also dabble in the latter). Producers generate their profits through the difference between a good's sale price and the variable and fixed costs incurred in its production (where labour is generally crucial). Proprietary markets, on the other hand, extract profits as rents from market ownership. Their position at the interface between producers and consumers enables them to cream off commission on market transactions while enjoying relatively low fixed and variable costs. What this means essentially is that in a system of proprietary markets, economic profits are merely transferred from producers to market owners who, to cite Mariana Mazzucato, are primarily interested in extracting – rather than creating – value (2019).

This systematically changes the logic of accumulation of wealth in society. Whereas efficient use of labour is the decisive factor in a production-based economy like Fordism, in a system of proprietary markets it is the appropriation of economic rent from market ownership. The latter represents a crisis-proof source of economic profit because a proprietary market on which, as described above, producers and consumers depend to find each other, can maintain constant or increasing profits even when sales fall, through its control of access via the terms of use and level of commission.

If its core model makes the economy of digital capitalism a zero-sum game, it is clear just how far such a system has diverged from the foundations of the market society whose emergence Polanyi described and whose second coming we have had the privilege to experience since the 1980s. The idea that all market participants benefit from the organisation of economic transactions via the market is axiomatic for (neo)liberalism.

In a sense, proprietary markets represent the return of an idea that shaped the early capitalist, pre-liberal epoch in Europe. The mercantilism of that age was based on an understanding of world trade as a zero-sum game: a favourable balance of trade was the central objective of the mercantilist state. In this perspective prosperity could only be achieved at the expense of other parties. Positive trade balances were regularly extracted by brute force, especially in the scope of imperialism. The state granted and protected trade monopolies like the British East India Company, which was even granted the right to raise its own troops by the crown (Wallerstein 1998 [1980]).

The big difference between the system of proprietary markets and classical mercantilism lies in the respective roles of the state. The state promoted the early trade monopolies and benefitted from their profits. In that respect the trading companies were monopolies by grace of the absolutist state. The proprietary markets of the commercial internet, by contrast, are private enterprises, and have drawn growing criticism for practices including tax avoidance and fragmenting the democratic sphere. All the while, their profits flow unabated and the GAFA companies have become the world's most valuable. So the state must be regarded as the big loser from this development. A *privatised mercantilism* has emerged within (neo) liberal capitalism. It combines proprietary markets with the contours of a rentier society and concedes only a very restricted role to the state, while itself penetrating ever further into the social realm.[11] If neoliberalism meant the penetration of the market into ever new spheres, then digital capitalism is the capture of the market itself by a small number of private enterprises.

Understanding digital capitalism

In the following chapters I will examine the privatised mercantilism of the leading companies of the commercial internet in five dimensions that are central to any analysis of capitalism. Chapter 2 describes the role of the state in creating and developing the commercial internet. It transpires that the roots of digital capitalism can be traced back to the Keynesian 'entrepreneurial state' (Mazzucato 2018) of the Cold War and the end of the economic boom at the beginning of the 1970s, and that the rise of digital technologies is intimately bound up with various macro trends of capitalist reorganisation. But the path that ultimately led to the digital capitalism of the present age was not finally set until the neoliberal deregulation of the 1980s and 1990s.

Chapter 3 explores the logic of capital, especially the rise of private venture capital that is inseparably bound up with the commercial internet.

The narrative of growth and profit – like the warning of monopolisation tendencies – rests not only on the economic workings of digital production, such as low marginal costs and network effects, but crucially on the specific logic of this form of economic capital. Its growing importance must be placed in the context of a systematic shift from income to wealth (Piketty 2014), whose importance for the history of the commercial internet cannot be overstated. The growth of the platforms would be inconceivable without the relative superabundance of private venture capital, which is associated with very specific economic and social effects.

Chapter 4 describes the dimensions of market and organisation, which in my understanding of digital capitalism successively come to mean the same. The paradigm for the organisation of the digital companies is the platform: in other words the market. The rise of a system of proprietary sub-markets and ever more powerful meta-platforms has specific consequences for the distribution of wealth that are also of great importance for the restructuring of work. In particular four control technologies employed by proprietary markets metastasise into ever broader spheres of the economy. Chapter 5 investigates the phenomena of algorithmic management as filiations[12] of social and economic control that penetrate into ever broader parts of the economy. Chapter 6 draws together the dynamics of capital, market/organisation and labour and considers their relevance to social inequality in digital capitalism. As will be seen, my findings point not only to a successive radicalisation of social inequality but also to a specific constellation of social conflict. Chapter 7, finally, reviews the options open to us and considers whether a good digital society is possible.

Notes

1 His father was the legendary media critic Herbert Schiller, who saw the media as the central instrument legitimising the military/industrial complex of his age (H. Schiller 1989, 1996).

2 As Jonathan Pace shows, the same applies to the concept of 'informational capitalism', prominently advanced for example by Christian Fuchs (2010). Here too, the new role of information in capitalism merely demonstrates that its fundamental structure has not changed: 'Fuchs arrives at the same logical quagmire as Schiller, albeit through a different route. If information technology has *not* transformed the forces of production, why purvey the structural concept of informational capitalism at all? Why not simply refer to informational production, informational commodities, and informational labor?' (Pace 2018: 257).

3 Channelling Robert Solow's (1987) famous observation on the productivity paradox of computerisation: 'You can see the computer age everywhere but in the productivity statistics.'

4 Didi owns a major stake in Brazil's leading platform 99, while Uber received a stake in Didi in return for handing over its Chinese operations.

5 The Japanese Softbank – to which we will return in greater detail below – owns 27 per cent of Alibaba; Yahoo owns another 15 per cent. In the case of Tencent, South African media group Naspers holds 33 per cent, J.P. Morgan Chase another 6 per cent. Almost all the most important Chinese internet companies are also listed on the American Nasdaq; all their IPOs (initial public offerings) have been managed by Western banks (Jia 2018).

6 Venture capital investment in Chinese businesses involving at least one US investor reached a ten-year high in 2017 with US$24.7 billion (the figure in 2007 was just US$1 billion) (Klein 2018).

7 In 2018 US President Donald Trump vetoed Singapore-based Broadcom's planned takeover of US-based chip manufacturer Qualcomm on the grounds that the deal could leave key technologies under Chinese control. Another example of the new US response to growing geopolitical tensions is the protracted conflict over Huawei's network infrastructure (Armbruster 2018).

8 Referring to the fusion of surveillance state and capitalist interests that Lovink regards as typical of the commercial internet. The term alludes to the twentieth-century Marxist-Leninist theory of fusion of the imperialist state with big business.

9 Google shut down Google+ in April 2019.

10 Author's calculations using data from the two companies' annual reports for 2018.

11 For example in the health sector ('smart health') and urban infrastructure ('smart city') programmes.

12 In the sense of a parent/child relationship.

2

The roots of digital capitalism

In order to identify the core aspects of digital capitalism we must describe it, on the one hand, as an effect and legacy of the progressive insertion of digital information and communications technologies into capitalist processes since the 1960s. On the other, we must systematically distinguish today's *digital* capitalism from the 'merely' *digitalised* capitalism that has increasingly characterised the highly developed economies over the course of the past seven decades. In digitalised capitalism, whose evolution Dan Schiller (1999, 2014) describes so brilliantly, information and communications technologies successively enhanced traditional processes of accumulation. Microchips and semiconductors became standard components of industrial machine tools, PCs found their way into offices and homes, communications infrastructures were connected to the internet. Ideally the new technologies boosted productivity by enabling comprehensive networking of previously isolated activities (Dyer-Witheford 1999) – whereby the question of productivity gains soon provoked a debate within economics that continues to this day (Solow 1987; Gordon 2016).

It was a long time before the new technologies really affected the logic of profit-making. In the best case manufactured products could be produced more efficiently as machines became more capable and factories more networked; administrative activities were also expedited. But the way profit was generated remained fundamentally unchanged: goods were traded, with traders competing with one another in a neutral market context.

Seeking innovation

The Fordist growth combo began losing momentum around the end of the 1960s, at different times in different national contexts. On the one hand, the dividends from the successive conversion of manufacturing industry to Taylorist methods had gradually been exhausted (Streeck 2012). The rapid productivity gains achieved since the 1930s tailed off from the early 1970s. The average annual growth rate of West German labour productivity fell from 7.3 per cent in the 1950s to 3.2 per cent in 1980 (Giersch, Paqué and Schmieding n.d.). Similar developments were seen in other industrialised countries. In the United States annual growth in labour productivity fell from 3.6 per cent between 1948 and 1953 to 1.4 per cent between 1973 and 1980 (Sprague 2017). In the United Kingdom it shrank from an average of 3.1 per cent between 1950 and 1973 to 1.7 per cent between 1973 and 1990, the fall in France in the same period was from 5.1 to 2.9 per cent, and in Japan from 7.7 to 3.0 per cent (Broadberry and O'Mahony 2005: 31).

At the same time, the consumer markets that were so crucial for Fordism were exhibiting the first signs of saturation. By now most Americans, Europeans and Japanese already owned a fridge, a fitted kitchen and a car. Demand collapsed. In an environment of declining productivity gains, businesses shied away from drastic price reductions. Instead they applied downward pressure on wages, which only tended to exacerbate the demand problem.

These first manifestations of a crisis of Fordism served as the starting shot for an incremental transformation of the highly developed economies, a search for new innovation and growth paths. This coincided with the beginnings of the digitalisation of capitalism. Digital network technologies became essential elements of this transformation, through networking, decentralisation and control.

Firstly, it now became possible to establish more closely integrated value chains, which produced economies in planning, coordination and logistics,[1] and also opened up possibilities to access labour in other parts of the world increasingly efficiently. Advancing networking optimised the interfaces between companies and consumers. Consumer behaviour became increasingly important for strategic business decisions (Dyer-Witheford 1999: 20), and was integrated directly into the process using advances in market surveillance. At the same time the expansion of self-service systems building on the new technologies made it possible to get consumers to carry out tasks that were previously paid work (Staab 2016). In this sense the labour process was considerably expanded, by connecting its increasingly fragmented parts and managing them ever more efficiently.

Secondly, the labour process was decentralised through new technologies associated with very concrete cost benefits. On the one hand the transfer of particular tasks to self-service systems operated by 'working customers' (Voß and Rieder 2005) enabled labour cost savings. On the other, network technologies were used to outsource infrastructure elements, for example by buying in software or external computing power. Today's cloud computing, where ever larger parts of business, the state and the public rely on digital infrastructure services supplied by companies like Amazon, Google and Microsoft, represents a direct extrapolation of this early trend.

Thirdly, by the early 1980s businesses had discovered the potential of network technologies to generate profits through market control. A whole generation of management gurus already believed it was possible to make users dependent on proprietary software through exclusive access to particular services (Parsons 1983; McFarlan 1984). Warren McFarlan (1984), for example, pointed to two possibilities for generating profits through market closure. On the one hand, businesses used digital technologies to create market entry barriers by implementing exclusive customer communication channels that were not open to rivals:

> A successful entry barrier offers not only a new service to appeal to customers but also features that keep the customers 'hooked.' The harder the service is to emulate, the higher the barrier for the competition. An example of such a defensible barrier is the development of a complex software package that adds value and is capable of evolution and refinement. (McFarlan 1984: 99)

On the other, they employed software lock-in strategies to increase the cost of switching to a different system. The point of this was to familiarise the customer with a particular system to a point where its use infiltrated their routines: 'Finally, the customer will have to spend too much time and money to change suppliers' (McFarlan 1984: 99).

Today, proprietary systems like iOS, Android and the associated app stores represent examples of extremely successful application of this principle. Apple and Google genuinely do control consumers' access to the mobile commercial internet via their operating systems. Amazon's e-commerce platform applies the same logic, only here it is a great deal more obvious how market control strategies also affect producers. As the share of book sales processed through its proprietary marketplace has grown, Amazon has been able to dictate successively tighter terms to the book trade (Leisegang 2014). Vendors of other goods find themselves systematically undercut by Amazon's in-house products; effectively, Amazon controls the prices in its own marketplace.

Networking, decentralisation and control using the new digital information and communications technologies drove the macro-trends of the capitalist reorganisation that emerged in response to the collapse of growth rates. This applies in particular to four factors: the increasing technical rationalisation and *automation* of work; the *globalisation* of value chains and markets; public investment and the *commodification* and privatisation of public goods; and finally the *financialisation* of the economy. These four aspects explain the astonishing rise of the information and communications technologies over the course of the second half of the twentieth century.

They generated ever-growing demand for digital technologies and chan-nelled investment into the sector. The digital owes its position as the beating heart of modern capitalism to those processes of automation, globalisation, commodification and financialisation (D. Schiller 2011).

Automation

Wage restraint was one strategy for responding to the collapse in demand at the end of the Fordist boom. From a narrow managerial perspective this initially appeared to make sense: to respond to stagnating or falling sales by cutting variable costs, which in concrete terms generally meant cutting wages or other labour costs. One way to reduce long-term labour costs was to invest in machinery, to introduce ever new automation technologies, especially in industrial manufacturing.

The technologies implemented from the 1970s differed markedly from their predecessors. Firstly, their technological basis changed: waves of technological development drove a shift from (electro)mechanical to micro-electronics, especially in the guise of the personal computer (Bahrdt et al. 1970; Weltz and Lullies 1983). In particular, the strategy of systemic rationalisation expanded beyond industry to prove the rule that digital network technologies metastasise incessantly to penetrate throughout the economy and society. By the 1980s – and this is the second point – IT systems were no longer used just to optimise manufacturing processes or individual office tasks. Now systemic rationalisation enabled 'the integra-tion of entire functional complexes from consultation and sale through to filing and data management' (translated from Deutschmann 2001). This also brought lasting change to service occupations that had traditionally been regarded as resistant to automation.

What was special about this development was that rationalisation processes were no longer focussed on isolated tasks, as technology was increasingly used to create transparency throughout the production chain, to integrate workflows, and thus to increase the planning and steering capacities of management. The strategy was radicalised in the lean produc-tion programme (Holweg 2007; Womack, Jones and Roos 1990; Jürgens 2017). This comprehensive networking of manufacturing and supply chains was rolled out from the late 1980s and set off another wave of digitalisa-tion in manufacturing. Like the roughly contemporaneous experiments and innovations under the label of 'computer-integrated manufacturing' (CIM) and the programme for a fourth Industrial Revolution (Industrie 4.0) dis-cussed since 2011, these revitalisation strategies ensured constant demand for digital products (both hardware and software). This was associated with growing research and development spending, funded not least by the state (see below), which also contributed to the rapid rise of the digital sector.

Globalisation

The demand for digital technology was further amplified by processes discussed since the 1990s under the label of globalisation. In economic terms globalisation processes serve two principal objectives (Osterhammel and Petersson 2007): to expand markets and reduce labour costs. Businesses responded to the emerging growth crisis by establishing production facilities outside their home regions in order to open up new markets. Producing at or close to the target market reduced transport costs and often offered a means to avoid high import tariffs. This allowed less saturated markets to be tapped. This strategy was pursued by Volkswagen from the 1950s, with its expansion into South America (Brazil, Argentina). It is followed today by Western manufacturers in China, the world's largest internal market. At the same time this strategy was always also about tapping new sources of cheap labour. For a long time the scope of both these benefits remained limited: the price of profiting from cheap labour in a particular region was high transport costs. But producing for the market in the place where cheap labour was available required growing local purchasing power (meaning rising wages). And the effect of wage rises on labour costs threatened to wipe out any comparative advantages.

Both developments were really gathering steam at the very moment when modern ICT was eviscerating the barriers of space and time (Harvey 1991): the digital technologies of the late twentieth century made it possible to globalise and network the division of labour. The culmination of this development is the production of Apple's iPhone, which involves nine firms in seven countries and more than thirty-seven global component suppliers, while the product itself is sold in almost every country on earth.

The enormous efforts of industrial enterprises to boost growth by transnationalising their value chains and globalising their markets also ensured constantly growing demand for digital equipment. So globalisation was and remains the handmaid of the digital sector.

Military Keynesianism, commodification, privatisation

But the true starting point, as Mariana Mazzucato (2018) describes so impressively, lay in an entrepreneurial state, namely in the United States, during the Cold War. Under military Keynesianism, the United States invested in key technologies both to keep pace with its superpower rival and to stimulate demand through public investment.

The most important and certainly most widely discussed example of this dynamic is the development of the internet. The predecessor of today's internet emerged through cooperation between the US Defense Advanced Research Projects Agency (DARPA) and several American universities, in particular MIT. As so often, it was the state – rather than private venture capital for example – that stepped in as the initial risk-taking investor. It was also the state that enabled the later commercialisation of the resulting technologies and unleashed the associated growth stimuli. Many of the technologies that later appeared in the personal computer also came out of DARPA programmes (Abbate 1999).

The role of the military was not restricted to funding research. The vision of an 'electronic battlefield' (Klare 1972) was already in the air during the Vietnam War, and Ronald Reagan's Strategic Defense Initiative (SDI, the 'Star Wars' programme) also generated enormous demand for digital military technology (Mosco 1989; D. Schiller 2011). The same story continues to the present day, with the US military still shouldering the bulk of public investment in digital technologies. In 2019, for example, the Pentagon invested almost US\$38 billion in information technology, representing more than 40 per cent of the US government's entire IT budget (IT Dashboard 2019). The enormous and continuing significance of the national security state as a source of demand for digital products and innovations is also reflected in bitter bidding wars, for example between Amazon and Microsoft, for lucrative contracts with the Pentagon and the CIA. High-value start-ups like the ominous Palantir often owe their spectacular growth to military and intelligence contracts (Ruttan 2006).

If we look back to the origins of this dynamic we find that the original internet – the Arpanet – was no great exception: DARPA and the military complex were in good company. The 'proactive risk-taking' state also brought forth programmes like the Small Business Innovation Research (SBIR) programme, the Orphan Drug Act and the National Nanotechnology Initiative (Mazzucato 2018). In the United States these and other funding sources not only provide enormous resources for pure research but also '20–25 per cent of total funding for early-stage technology firms. … Thus, government has played a leading role not only in the early-stage research … but also in the commercial viability stage' (Mazzucato 2018: 55).

The state has also supported digital innovation in the consumer electronics sector, playing a key role in the enormous success of today's digital behemoths. Google's original search algorithm, for example, was developed with funding from the National Science Foundation (Mazzucato 2018: 27). All twelve key technologies in Apple's iPhone originate from publicly funded research (Mazzucato 2018: 100 ff.). The digital assistant Siri, for example, was originally conceived to assist battlefield communications – rather than making hairdresser appointments and the other mundane purposes it serves today.

The fundamental institutional structures are strikingly similar in other leading industrialised countries.[2] But the really decisive factor in the American entrepreneurial state was the 'spinoff culture' (Mazzucato 2018: 82), typical of the US technology sector, in the sense of the institutional and legal framework for capitalisation.

The investing state of digitalisation represents an especially impressive example of the commodification and privatisation of public goods. Products whose development was funded with public funds are essentially public property. But if public research is subsequently privatised we are certainly entitled to ask what benefit the public receives in return. Normally the state would share in the success of such firms through tax revenues. That brings us to the heart of Mazzucato's critique, because businesses like Apple, Google, Amazon and Facebook pay almost no taxes despite their enormous profits and cash reserves, and despite growing public pressure.

Aside from these justified objections, to which I return in Chapter 6, the analytical abstraction reveals that we must understand the American entrepreneurial state in relation to a larger privatisation of public goods – generally subsumed under the label neoliberalism – that also contributed to the digitalisation of capitalism in other spheres. This includes the liberalisation of the telecommunications markets, which took off internationally in the 1990s. As well as sucking billions into the pockets of the now profit-seeking network operators, it also spurred great investment in digital infrastructures (D. Schiller 2011).

The regulatory element of the investing state

Kenji Kushida (2015) shows how different liberalisation strategies in the telecommunications sector formed the starting points for different national and regional digitalisation paths. He also underlines how the rise of the leading digital companies was contingent to the extent that it unfolded on foundations that could have been very different. Kushida explains the rise of the internet giants – in particular Google and Apple – in terms of the marketisation strategy applied in the US telecommunications sector, which was systematically different from the approaches followed in the European Union and Japan. The latter two, Kushida argues, had chosen a different form of regulatory policy and therefore taken different paths to the application of modern digital technology. Wherever it occurred, the objective of liberalising the telecommunications markets was to introduce competition into hitherto monopolistic markets as a mechanism to reduce consumer prices and promote investment. In Europe and Japan in the 1980s, state-owned telephone companies controlled the market; in the United States AT&T held a practically unchallenged private monopoly. AT&T was broken up in 1984 after a protracted anti-trust process; the Japanese and British state telephone companies were privatised in the mid-1980s; Germany and France followed in the 1990s.

The different liberalisation strategies ultimately generated path dependencies that can be followed through to the rise of the leading companies of digital capitalism. A succession of phases can be identified: initial liberalisation of the respective market, followed by growth in the mobile telephony sector and finally the rise of the internet as the central technology of mobile communications (Kushida 2015: 52). Germany and France missed the leap into mobile telephony through their comparatively late liberalisations. Even after privatisation their former state monopolies maintained close ties to their mostly domestic suppliers and concentrated their core business in network operation and fixed-line telephony. This created an opening for Nordic firms like Eriksson and Nokia, which were quick to occupy the emerging mobile telephony gap and subsequently expand globally. Mobile phone manufacturers were the winners of the European liberalisation path, in particular Nokia which dominated this market through the late 2000s (Kushida 2015: 55). They in turn concentrated on their flourishing mobile telephony businesses and missed out on the advent of mobile internet, which was presaged by the first Blackberrys and accelerated rapidly after the launch of the iPhone in 2007.

In Japan the telephone companies initially came out on top and rode the successive innovation waves. Despite a liberalisation in the mid-1980s the Japanese telecommunications market remained effectively closed to foreign competition through into the 1990s. In this context the privatised NTT was not only able to defend its strong position, but even – backed by massive investment in research and development and a benevolent public sector – to expand it. Equipment manufacturers also remained dependent on the telephone company, which was able to secure a large slice of the growing profits in mobile telephony. Hardware manufacturers and network operators formed a highly innovative pairing and accomplished pioneering work in the transition to what was at the time the most technologically advanced mobile telephony market. But Japanese firms paid a high price for their relative isolation from the global market when their technological ecosystem proved difficult to internationalise in the 2000s (Kushida 2015: 56).

This phase of globalisation of the telecommunications markets is crucial for understanding the situation today, as it was the major American corporations that came out best placed to exploit the global transformation. Investment and demand stimuli from the state and other economic sectors was not the only reason why companies like Google and Apple were in the starting blocks at this point. The break-up of AT&T was also crucial. This meant that – unlike in Japan – there was no telephone company waiting to pounce on the new growth sectors. The break-up also created a fragmented and innovative hardware manufacturing scene out of AT&T's extensive research and development network. With no mobile telephony pioneers waiting in the wings – unlike the Nordics – US firms were unable to profit from the transition from fixed line to mobile. This relative weakness and the fragmentation of the American market created initial advantages in the next phase, when American companies led the pack on internet infra-structure and the business models associated with the new technology. The ground for the hostile takeover of the mobile telephony sector by the com-puter industry (West and Mace 2010; Pon, Seppälä and Kenney 2014) was prepared by an investing state and demand for digital technologies from other sectors. It led to a rapid global restructuring of the information and communications landscape, in the course of which the proprietary systems of Google, Apple and Amazon in particular have been able to accumulate economic power on a hitherto unimaginable scale.

Economic macro-trends and the investing state

The history outlined in this chapter underlines the central role of the proactive state. The beginnings of leading companies of the commercial internet ultimately lie in an investing state that drove developments through Keynesian demand stimulation and investment in research. Yet, para-doxically, the rise of the GAFA complex also began with a radical move against the era's dominant information and communications monopoly. The American entrepreneurial state's investments unfolded in a context of proactive regulatory policy to enforce the neutrality of the relevant markets.

This historical perspective on the rise of the commercial internet reveals a very different story from the one the sector itself likes to tell (starring free-minded inventors working in their garages). The roots of the development that gave us the leading companies of the commercial internet lie not solely in the innovative culture of Silicon Valley but also in contingent measures of national regulatory policy. The origins of digital capitalism are found not in the relative isolation of the San Francisco Bay Area, but in the systematic connection with the decisive macro-trends of the restructuring of Fordist capitalism. For the transition from a digitalising global capitalism to a truly digital capitalism, which developed a life of its own as the commercial internet, another element is decisive. This is the connection between the digital sector and the financial markets, to which we now turn.

Notes

1 Logistics costs are decisive in the lean production paradigm. Digital control of supply processes allowed warehouse capacity to be reduced.
2 In Germany, for example, important funding for applied research comes from the Federal Ministry of Education and Research (BMBF), in combination with various more or less industry-oriented organisations such as the various Fraunhofer Institutes and the Max-Planck-Gesellschaft.

3

Financial capitalism online

The most important external growth impulse for the digital sector and the leading companies of the commercial internet occurred in the 1990s and early 2000s.[1] The media – not uninfluenced by consultants, PR flaks and the leading companies themselves – tend to present the rise of the internet giants as a simple tale of intrepid entrepreneurs on the US West Coast. In fact the most recent wave of digital expansion is systematically bound up with the 'finance-driven capitalism' (Windolf 2005) of the past thirty years. This connection is crucial to understanding the universe of the commercial internet, its major planets and the satellites orbiting them. The financialisation of the economy since the 1980s forms a crucial background to any historical understanding of digital capitalism, with the filiations between the financial sector and the internet economy revealing the economic programme behind the rise of the leading companies of the commercial internet.

At this juncture it is analytically productive to return once again to Schumpeter. As the theorist of 'monopolistic competition' he was working in an age when economic scarcity represented a real problem. If monopolies reduced output to increase prices, prosperity would suffer, giving grist to the mill of the critics of the big businesses that Schumpeter admired. Apologists for today's commercial internet like to cite Schumpeter's observation that this did not in fact occur. In fact that is only plausible if digital capitalism shares the fundamental premise of its industrial predecessor – essentially an economy of scarcity – where improving the efficiency of production of goods and services really does generate benefits for consumers.

However, influential commentators (Rifkin 2014; Mason 2016) reject the idea that we are today – under conditions of advanced digitalisation – still dealing essentially with problems of economic scarcity. They point out that an increasingly digital capitalism inevitably encounters the challenge of transforming goods that are actually available in abundance into tradable capitalist commodities. Digital capitalism, they argue, is by nature an economy of superabundance, so the digital has a tendency to undermine capitalism. As I will argue in the following, both drawing on and sharply criticising such theories, digital capitalism shares the trait of superabundance with the very sphere where capitalism has not retreated but experienced its latest major expansion: the financial markets. The analogies and connections between the digital economy and the financial sector indicate that the rise of a digital economy of superabundance must systematically transform the premises of any economic and sociological analysis of digital monopolies.

Economies of superabundance and the prophets of post-capitalism

The rise of the internet has long been associated with utopian hopes, not only among the management gurus mentioned above but even in left-leaning activist circles. John Perry Barlow's 1996 'Declaration of the Independence of Cyberspace' is a seminal document of cyber-activism. Speaking as the voice of an imagined internet community, Barlow calls for the internet to remain an autonomous space outside state jurisdiction, arguing instead for self-government. He connects his demand for freedom from state power to a call for liberation from capitalist production in a manner that anticipates more explicitly economically-minded intellectuals:

> Your increasingly obsolete information industries would perpetuate themselves by proposing laws, in America and elsewhere, that claim to own speech itself throughout the world. These laws would declare ideas to be another industrial product, no more noble than pig iron. In our world, whatever the human mind may create can be reproduced and distributed infinitely at no cost. The global conveyance of thought no longer requires your factories to accomplish.

In other words, a world of superabundant goods has no place for capitalism. More recently, writers including Jeremy Rifkin (2014) and Paul Mason (2016) have laid out detailed visions proclaiming a decentralised internet coordinating respectively a more democratic economy (Rifkin) or the coming of 'postcapitalism' (Mason). Aside from the contestable belief that individuals connected via the internet can act as an effective collective, the arguments of the prophets of post-capitalism rest essentially on a single characteristic of the digital: the relative superabundance of digital and digitalised goods.

As data, they argue, digital goods are nothing more than rows of digits, information. Once such products (websites, music and video files, search algorithms etc.) exist they can be reproduced at extremely little additional expense (marginal cost). There is therefore no easily identifiable limit to the total volume of production, and certainly none that corresponds to the obvious resource-dependency of a farmer or manufacturer. To put it in the terms of economic discourse, the production of digital products is assumed to be infinitely scalable: the quantity produced does not depend to any relevant extent on the availability of resources or capital, as is the case in other sectors. What one consumes is not necessarily therefore unavailable to others. According to Rifkin and Mason (see also Elder-Vass 2016), this potential 'non-rivalry' of goods challenges the foundations of classical models, such as Lionel Robbins's widely accepted axiom of 1932 that economic activity is characterised by scarcity. Only scarce goods can be traded for profit, as required in capitalism. Nobody will pay money for something that is available in abundance. The concept of 'economy' describes in a very fundamental sense 'the social practice of employing the world's scarce resources to secure material production' (translated from Sahr 2013: 7) – or as Robbins (1932: 75) puts it: 'Economics is concerned with the disposal of scarce goods with alternative uses.' If a thing is not scarce – and cannot be made artificially scarce – it is fundamentally unavailable to the capitalist market. Thus non-rivalry and infinite scalability (economists also speak of a 'highly elastic' supply) by definition present a threat to profit-seeking enterprise itself. If goods can be produced and distributed more or less without cost – in other words they are no longer scarce – it is no longer possible to assign them an economic value or to obtain profits through their control and sale.

In formal terms, this structural problem affects all actors trading in digital goods. A business like Facebook, for example, can open its service – a communication platform – to additional users without (relevant) additional costs. Of course it makes a difference if traffic from ten users is passing through its server farms, or from two billion. In fact, by 2018 the information and communications technologies were responsible for about 8 per cent of global electricity consumption (Andrae 2019). Nevertheless, the marginal costs of each additional unit are negligible.

Rifkin (2014) and Mason (2016) are certainly aware of the fundamental possibility of stopping the systematic fall in market prices by establishing effective monopolies. Mason for example writes:

> The equilibrium state of an info-tech economy is one where monopolies dominate and people have unequal access to the information they need to make rational buying decisions. Info-tech, in short, destroys the normal price mechanism, whereby competition drives prices down towards the cost of production. (Mason 2016: 110)

But, like Rifkin, he does not regard this as a realistic option. Instead both identify a second aspect of the digitalised economy as a systematic obstacle to accumulation: the decisive means of production are available to the users of digital goods themselves, in the form of laptops and other digital devices. This hampers profit extraction, they say, because people are able to bypass the digital monopolies – which represent the only possibility to generate profits where marginal costs tend to zero – and produce their own products in do-it-yourself networks.

Additionally, they say, the so-called sharing economy places ever more distribution channels in the hands of their users. This enables a systematic decentralisation and democratisation of production through what Benkler (2006) calls 'commons-based peer production', and thus opens the door to new post-capitalist systems of production and distribution (Mason 2016: 120 ff.).

Both also argue that the rise of the internet of things (meaning the ubiquitous dissemination of digitally networked hardware) and further automation of production will bring zero marginal costs, falling prices and new means of production and distribution to a significant portion of the economy. This leads them to conclude that comprehensive digitalisation endangers the profit principle, because economic scarcity is no longer a given. In this scheme digitalisation of the economy is the gravedigger of capitalism, because – to put it in a nutshell – you can't make money from digital and digitalised goods.

Follow the money

So what does all that mean for the spectacular financial success of the internet giants? Since 2016 the GAFAM five (including M for Microsoft) have regularly occupied the first five positions in the list of the world's most valuable companies (Ovide and Molla 2016; PwC 2021). Apple has topped the list almost continuously since 2012 (PwC 2021: 7), although the years 2018 to 2020 witnessed a close three-way race with Amazon and Microsoft where each occupied first place for a time; currently Apple is neck and neck with oil giant Saudi Aramco (Feiner 2019; PwC 2021; FXSSI 2022; Wearden 2022). Two of the GAFAM group's Chinese counterparts, Alibaba and Tencent, joined the top ten in 2017. By 2016 – and this is central to the argument laid out here – the market capitalisation of the leading technology companies reached almost US$3 trillion, overtaking the entire financial industry and making it the last great growth (and crisis) sector of global capitalism.

In other words, the diagnosis of a post-capitalist infection of the digital economy stands in stark contrast to the volume of capital flowing into it. We are looking at a clear divergence between the empirical finding – that this has been a highly attractive field of investment for decades – and the theory that immateriality of the products automatically means the end of economic profit (post-capitalism). The discrepancy in fact runs even deeper, with the financial system itself operating on a very similar material basis to the digital economy: it also ultimately produces non-rival and potentially infinitely scalable products and is therefore – exactly like the digital economy – confronted with the threat of superabundance of these goods. Yet financial capitalism, unlike the digital capitalism of the internet companies, is widely regarded as hyper-capitalism – and certainly not any kind of post-capitalism.

The rise of the financial sector

While some observers regard the digital economy as a potentially subversive sphere where the rules of capital accumulation are somehow less valid, nobody would dream of saying that about the financial system. The latter's profits have been growing faster than the economy as a whole for years. In the 1950s and 1960s the financial sector accounted for just 10 to 15 per cent of profits generated in the United States. Its share grew in the 1980s and 1990s to over 20 per cent and exceeded 30 per cent for some years after the turn of the century. The figure dropped to barely more than 7 per cent in the crisis year of 2008 but bounced back to almost 31 per cent the next year; since then it has fluctuated around 27 per cent (author's calculations using data from BEA 2018a, 2018b, 2018c).

The lure of the financial markets, whose steady growth since the late 1970s was only briefly occluded by the crisis of 2008, is crucial for understanding digitalisation. At first glance the digital economy and the financial system might appear very different. But financial products – loans, shares, receivables, derivatives – share the (im)materiality of software and other digital goods. They are in the first place, as for example Aaron Sahr (2017a) has demonstrated, nothing more than data stored electronically: 'A keystroke then turns that into "reality"' (Wray 2012: 64). Here, likewise, no additional resources are required to create one hundred derivatives rather than one. And given that such obligations tend to be parked in complex structures located partly or entirely offshore to evade accounting and regulation, there is not even any need for equity.

This becomes even clearer in the case of the book money that banks create 'out of nothing' (Werner 2014) through a simple accounting operation known as 'balance sheet extension' (Huber 2015). In other words, to produce new capital all they need is demand and an electronic accounting system. Money-creating credit is therefore a 'free' – infinitely scalable – product within the existing economic order (Sahr 2017b). It is fundamentally superabundant.

Nevertheless, the financial system has plainly developed strategies for dealing with this problem. The massive accumulation of capital in the digital economy suggests that the same also applies there. Has the digital sector copied the trick of capitalising on superabundant goods from the financial world? There are certainly clues in the historical development of the financial sector that lead directly to the rise of the commercial internet. Historically the two sectors are intimately bound up together, while the structural similarities are so obvious that one could say that the internet giants learned their profit-making from the financial markets.

Historical filiations

Financialisation and digitalisation are not discrete, separate developments. The rise of the financial sector depended heavily on digital technology, in which it has invested enormous sums since the 1970s to develop products and expand capacity.

In sociology and political science 'financialisation' describes a shift in patterns of capital accumulation in the developed OECD economies since the late 1970s, an increase in the relative importance of the financial markets compared to agriculture, industry and non-financial services (the so-called real economy) (Table 3.1). Financialisation processes involve non-financial companies, states and individuals accumulating increasing

Table 3.1 Indicators of financialisation

Indicator	1980	1990	2000	2010	2020
Global financial assets (trillion US$)	12	56	119	219	469
Global traded derivatives (trillion US$)			107.9	663.3	582.1
Financial investments as proportion of US commercial assets* (%)	25.36	32.81	45.49	47.79	
US corporate debt* (trillion US$)	2.01	4.73	9.61	13.16	24.34
US household debt (trillion US$)			5.51	11.71	14.56
US state debt (% of GDP)	31.16	56.04	54.26	91.61	129.19

* In the non-financial sectors.

Sources: Lund et al. 2013: 2; Davis 2014: 49; calculations using data from Bundeszentrale für politische Bildung 2017; Financial Stability Board 2021: 7; BIS 2022; Board of Governors of the Federal Reserve System (US) 2022; Federal Reserve Bank of New York n.d., 2022; Federal Reserve Bank of St Louis/US Office of Management and Budget 2022.

amounts of debt to finance their investments and current spending while at the same time generating ever more income from financial investments (Krippner 2011). In the United States the share of financial income in the profits of non-financial companies more than doubled between 1980 and 2007 (Lin and Tomaskovic-Devey 2013).

The expansion of financialisation is attributable to three factors, which can only be sketched briefly here. Firstly the OECD economies have experienced a process of successive deregulation since the 1970s. The options for configuring financial products (such as interest rates) have been successively expanded, while the dismantling of restrictions on transnational movement of capital prepared the ground for tax havens. Enormous amounts of capital are today stashed away in these hyper-liberal offshore financial centres (Palan and Nesvetailova 2014; Zucman 2014). Secondly, the process greatly expanded the use of derivatives. These are innovative financial products used to calculate, hedge, fragment and distribute risks (certain aspects of the derivate business are discussed in greater detail below). Together with new mathematical models, this creates the impression of a secure investment climate, which in turn generates new demand for financial investments. The third factor is the ability of private banks to create money, which has been practically unconstrained since the end of the gold standard (Ingham 2004; Postberg 2013; Sahr 2017a). This permits banks to create money through simple accounting operations – independently of deposits and enforceable central bank regulation – by lending (Werner 2014; Pettifor 2017; Sahr 2017b). Since the 1990s this new money has flowed largely into the financial system rather than into the real economy (Huber 2015).

The untrammelled flow of capital from the digital money-creating machinery of the banks into the financial system was an important driver of financialisation. At the same time, the financial sector – equipped with fundamentally superabundant resources – channelled ever larger sums into the technology sector. This drove rapid expansion of the digital economy, which has become one of the most important growth motors in the OECD economies (OECD 2013, 2015, 2016).

Digitalisation in dollars

The revenues of the world's hundred largest telecommunications companies doubled in the first decade of the twentieth century (OECD 2013: figure 1.4). The total value of globally traded ICT goods grew by 12 per cent between 2008 and 2015, driven above all by Chinese exports, whose value grew by almost half in the same period (OECD 2017b: 124). The value of exported ICT services increased by almost 50 per cent just between 2010 and 2016, bringing its share of all globally traded services to over 10 per cent (OECD 2017b: 127).

In the EU, ICT sector 'value added' has more than tripled since the mid-1990s, while value added in the economy as a whole grew by less than half (Mas et al. 2018: 13). The value added by the US digital economy has also more than doubled since 2005 (BEA 2021).[2] The average annual growth rate of the US digital sector between 2005 and 2019 was 6.5 per cent, or about 3.6 times that of the US economy as a whole (BEA 2021). According to OECD data, the ICT sector contributed 7.25 per cent of the value added in the American economy in 2020 (OECD 2021). That comes close to the figure for the financial and insurance sector – and unlike the latter, ICT has recorded exclusively positive growth since 2010 (OECD 2021). The market valuations of the major US tech companies, first and foremost the GAFAM group, have grown even faster than their contribution to GDP, in recent years far exceeding the figures of the dotcom boom of the late 1990s (Randewich 2017): in 2018, for the first time since 2000, the IT sector again accounted for more than one-quarter of the market capitalisation of the companies listed in the Standard & Poor's 500 (Kawa 2018). As of 2022, it is the sector with by far the largest market capitalisation, by almost 15 percentage points (Lemke 2022).

The herd instinct of private venture capital also casts an instructive light on the growth expectations that are bound up with the digital sector (Figure 3.1). In the United States about 70 per cent of all venture capital flows into information and communications technologies. Today much more potent private equity and sovereign wealth funds are active in this field alongside the classical venture capital firms (more on this below).

The advance of digitalisation is demonstrated very clearly by the growth in investment and the explosion of internet traffic (in particular for services) (Table 3.2).

The rise of venture capital

A specific form of capital plays a central role in this flow of resources from the financial to the tech sector. This is private venture capital, which today increasingly also originates from private equity and sovereign wealth funds. Venture capital was already the powerhouse driving the rapid expansion of the digital economy during the dotcom boom of the 1990s and – as Stefan Kühl (2002, 2003) demonstrates – shaped the specific business models of the bubble.

The global significance of private venture capital has only grown further since the 2008 financial crisis. There are several reasons for this. Despite the extremely expansive policies of the US and eurozone central banks,

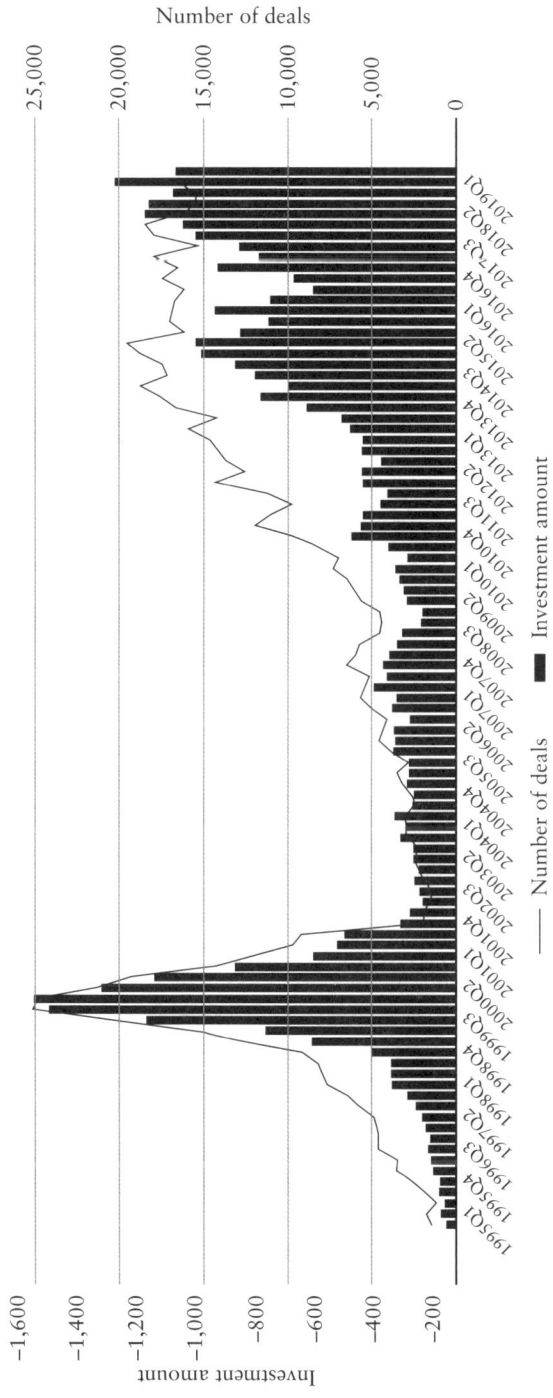

Figure 3.1 Venture capital investment in ICT, United States

Source: PwC and CBInsights 2019.

Table 3.2 Indicators of digitalisation

Indicator	1990	2000	2005	2010	2015	2020
Venture capital investment in ICT, United States (billion US$)	7.30 (1995)	119.2	20.1	26.1	78.3	130.0
Global internet traffic (PB/month)	0.001	75.25	1,802.75	13,751	72,521	254,000
Proportion of global population using internet (%)	0.05	6.73	15.70	28.93	40.46	59.94
Proportion of population making online purchase in previous year, EU (28)* (%)			22	40	53	65
Online advertising turnover, United States (billion US$)		8.09	12.50	26.00	59.60	139.80

* For age group 16 to 74. Data for 2005 is EU 25. Data for 2020 is EU 27 without United Kingdom.

Sources: Sumits 2015; Cisco 2016, 2019; PwC 2022; PwC and IAB 2021; International Telecommunication Union 2022; Eurostat 2022a, 2022b.

bank lending has failed (especially in Europe) to achieve the desired quantitative effects, in the sense that the money – in the form of loans – has not arrived in the real economy (Schildbach and Wenzel 2013). This quantitative easing has, on the other hand, led to an immense increase in the global money supply:[3] in the OECD it increased ninefold between 2008 and 2022, from US$51.1 trillion to US$478.4 trillion (OECD 2022). While the stock markets were patently incapable of absorbing the growing supply of money, the start-up economy (alongside the property sector) magically attracted investment with its promise of disruptive (Christensen 1997) and highly scalable (C. Shapiro and Varian 1999) innovations and new markets.

Here there was (and still is) enormous structural demand: young enterprises seeking finance but lacking the securities required for traditional bank loans. They produce no machines, possess no land, build no factories and run no vehicle fleets:

> Tangible capital can serve as collateral, providing lenders with some pro-
> tection against default … As a result, firms with an abundance of physical
> assets can finance themselves readily by issuing debt. In contrast, a company
> that focuses on software development, employee training, or improving
> the efficiency of its organisation will find it more difficult and costly to
> borrow, because the resulting assets cannot easily be re-sold. (Cecchetti and
> Schoenholtz 2018: n.p.)

The ability of start-ups to acquire investment from venture capitalists
depends on expectations of growth. One empirical indication of this is
the rapid growth of the number of so-called *unicorns*, defined as start-
ups whose market value exceeds US$1 billion. The number of unicorns
increased more than twelvefold globally between 2014 and 2021, from 83
(A. Stern 2017) to 1,070 (CBInsights 2022).[4] As well as private capital, the
sovereign wealth funds, for example from Norway, Singapore and Saudi
Arabia, were also drawn to the generous promised returns. Private venture
capital is still regarded as considerably more 'patient' than capital raised on
the stock markets (Deeg, Hardie and Maxfield 2016), making it ideal for
funding protracted growth phases without profits.

A third reason for the growing relevance of private venture capital is
a phenomenon one could describe as the 'Piketty effect': the fundamental redistribution of growth gains from income to wealth, especially in
the context of the expanding importance of the financial sector in highly
developed economies (Goda and Lysandrou 2014; Piketty 2014). Growing
wealth means more capital seeking investment opportunities – for example,
in the absence of lucrative alternatives, through venture capital.

It is therefore no surprise that the volume of venture capital invested in
the United States hit a record of about US$311 billion in 2021; that rep-
resented an increase of 106 per cent in comparison to 2020 (CBInsights
2021), by a factor of 5.1 in comparison to 2014 and by a factor of 6.0 in
comparison to 2001 (PwC and CBInsights 2021). Gigafunds are increasingly
involved. The best-known is the Vision Fund 1, run by Japan's SoftBank
and largely funded by Saudi Arabia, which started with the incredible sum
of US$100 billion. SoftBank launched its Vision Fund 2 in 2019 after losing
US$18 billion on its investments in Uber and WeWork.[5]

Financialisation and digitalisation: two sides of the coin

Steady growth in ICT investment by banks, investment companies and
venture capital funds from the 1970s onwards was driven by three motives:
to create their own technical networks; to realise mathematically complex
product innovations such as high-frequency trading; and to seek investment
opportunities in growth markets.

By the 1980s American banks' spending on digital equipment and software was growing at an annual rate of 19 per cent (D. Schiller 2014: 50). And until recently 'financial services companies' still made up 'the second largest sectoral source of demand for ICTs, following the communications industry' (D. Schiller 2011: 925). There is thus a co-evolutionary relationship between financialisation and digitalisation, where the material practice of the financial system is decisively influenced by 'electronic and digital technologies, by the comprehensive integration of data processing and telecommunications' (translated from Vogl 2011: 105).

Financialisation has also played a decisive and reciprocal role in the creation and expansion of the material infrastructure of the internet. For example in 2010 the US infrastructure provider Hibernia Networks laid the first submarine communication cable since the dotcom crisis of 2000. The purpose of the new cable was to speed up data transfer by five milliseconds. While this minute gain in speed offered no special benefit to ordinary users, it was decisive for banks involved in high-frequency trading (D. Schiller 2014: 55). Acknowledging the foundational importance of financialisation for the rise of the digital economy, Schiller concludes: 'Networks, and the software-driven products and practices that permeated them, became neither more nor less than the infrastructure of this globe-encircling high-tech financial system' (D. Schiller 2014: 47).

Strictly speaking this reciprocity, which persists to this day, proves only that investors believed (as they still do) that profits can be made with digital technologies. That does not yet say anything about the processes and practices on which this confidence – which has remained relatively stable across multiple decades and through several economic crises – is based. A comparison between the profit logics in the financial sector and the digital economy is revealing. On closer examination it transpires that we are dealing in both spheres with practices exhibiting structural similarities, and thus with filiations that are structural as well as historical.

In 2018 a newcomer from the digital economy seized first place in the Forbes list of the world's wealthiest billionaires. This was Jeff Bezos, the founder of Amazon, which failed to make a profit in its core e-commerce business for twenty years but whose market valuation puts Bezos at the top of the global rich list. Bezos, who still holds about 10 per cent of the company, is not just a colourful character whose fixation on growth, expansion and radical rationalisation verges on the manic (Nachtwey and Staab 2015). The example of Bezos and Amazon illustrates very well the emergence of the structural filiations between the financial system and the internet economy.

Before Bezos founded Amazon he worked at the Wall Street hedge fund D. E. Shaw, which was one of the places where high-frequency trading was invented and numerous sophisticated algorithms were developed (Stone 2013). In other words, Bezos brought explicit financial know-how into his new business. His career is thus paradigmatic for the migration of economic expertise from the financial system to the internet economy. There are also clear indications that online advertising, as the second central business model in the commercial internet alongside e-commerce, also learned from and was modelled on the financial markets. There is an interesting personal connection here too. It is reported that the online advertising businesses of Google and Facebook, as the two companies that dominate the field, were established under the supervision of one and the same person, who was previously a quant[6] at Goldman Sachs (García Martínez 2016).

Business strategies: growth and closure

The first structural parallel between the financial system and the internet economy is found in the relevance of growth and closure processes for the underlying business strategies: following the example of the financial sector, the leading companies of the commercial internet have always pursued radical growth while tolerating long periods of consistent losses. The point of such strategies is to secure control over specific markets in order to activate lock-in mechanisms that permit them to control market prices (Staab and Nachtwey 2016). In other words, this is a strategy designed to address the problem of the fundamental superabundance of digital goods. The point of this is to prevent the falling prices predicted by the theorists of post-capitalism by making the leading companies into gatekeepers controlling access to specific products and services (Dolata 2015). This goes some way to explaining how digital companies were able to acquire the capital required for their radical but loss-making growth plans on the financial markets. Financial institutions themselves have historically responded to superabundance of their goods with growth and closure, with enormous success in terms of profits.

Like the internet giants, banks deal in products that are fundamentally superabundant and non-rival, and consequently with partially isomorphic supply structures (on which more in the next chapter) (Postberg 2013). They derive their profits from the creation of money and other payables. Fundamentally, all the banks in a specific currency area offer the same range of products. A euro-denominated loan is equally functional for the borrower whether it was created by Deutsche Bank or any other financial institution. And technically speaking, any financial institution can sell options long and short. With no special knowledge required to market financial products, the field is in theory open to all. And in practice tight limits are placed on interest rates – the price of the product money – by mechanisms operating outside the framework of supply and demand. Under these conditions all the banks can do is 'compete to maximise sales of a product that is both identical and inexhaustible'. They must 'attempt, without heed to price stability, to maximise their "production" of money while minimising the costs (of risk)' (translated from Postberg 2013: 152). The entire financial sector depends on consistent growth to increase its profits (Crotty 2007).

At the same time, the financial sector has been characterised by concentration. In the 1990s and 2000s the developed economies experienced both expansion and concentration, leading to a concentration of their financial systems. Ever more wealth is held by an ever smaller number of ever-growing banking conglomerates (Sahr 2017a). Although the average returns on traditional long-term loans have fallen since the 1980s, major banks have still been able to increase their profit margins (Crotty 2007: 9). There are two reasons for this. Firstly, the growth and increasing concentration of the major US and European banks created an effect that has been described as 'implicit subsidy' and discussed in the aftermath of the financial 2008 crisis as the 'too big to fail' problem (Noss and Sowerbutts 2012). The great concentration of assets and liabilities in a handful of institutions made them 'systemically relevant'. In other words they and their investors expected that the relevant government would rescue them from any threat of insolvency. This lowered their refinancing costs, with the expectation of state rescue functioning as an implicit subsidy. The cost saving for banks in the European Union in 2012 alone has been estimated at €234 billion (Kloeck 2014). Secondly, the growing banks have been able to expand their influence on pricing through a mixture of competitive and cooperative strategies that Crotty (2007: 9) terms 'oligopolistic market power'. Together with the implicit subsidy, this made switching to smaller competitors increasingly costly for customers – the 'switching costs' rose. It is a very similar mechanism that makes the digital companies, which also trade in superabundant goods and are increasingly partially isomorphic, so attractive to investors. Today's commercial internet is a highly centralised space, structured by power (Dolata 2015), far from the anti-hierarchical decentralisation championed by the theorists of post-capitalism. Decisive sub-markets are monopolistic or oligopolistic: operating systems (Apple, Microsoft, Google), search (Google), professional (LinkedIn as part of Microsoft, Xing), social networks (Facebook) and e-commerce (Amazon, Alibaba, plus Google and Apple via their app stores).

The roots of the market concentration that characterises the commercial internet are, as described above, intimately bound up with the (im)material character of digital goods and the logic of networking processes. For one thing, practically infinite scalability permits easy distribution and non-rivalry of digital goods (Brynjolfsson and McAfee 2014) (very similar to financial products) and rapid growth of companies offering popular goods (because the relatively simple distribution infrastructure means that supply problems are rare). These advantages have been amplified by the rapid rise of cloud computing where server capacity is increasingly frictionless and can be bought in as required. For another, the network effects made possible by the internet (C. Shapiro and Varian 1999) mean that the inherent logic of particular markets systematically encourages the formation of monopolies (Staab and Nachtwey 2016). Because the utility of many digital goods – including operating systems and most services in the Google universe and on Facebook – increases with the size of the user base, the number of providers that succeed is usually small, often enough just one. While the post-capitalists still hope for decentralisation, influential Silicon Valley ideologists like investor and PayPal co-founder Peter Thiel (2014) have long been working to lend a social aura to the quasi-monopolies of the commercial internet. As Thiel argued in his 2012 Stanford lectures (published in book form in 2014), the leading companies of the internet are 'creative monopolies'. Only they can ensure efficient distribution of digital goods. They are socially desirable, he argues, because their systematic integration of products and services drives efficiency and innovation in ways that a decentralised internet cannot. He certainly does not deny that this enables monopoly profits, but portrays this aspect as a benefit for the public and the economy.

This genre of Silicon Valley manifesto always underlines the supposedly volatile nature of digital markets. Infinite scalability, simple distribution and non-rivalry of goods as well as the network effects associated with ordering processes in the corresponding markets mean – at least in theory – that new companies can grow rapidly and potentially threaten established rivals. In the 1990s a succession of businesses experienced phases of great market power that turned out to be relatively short. Just remember the speed with which Google's superior search algorithm eclipsed market leader Yahoo. The decisive concept behind that expectation is 'disruptive innovation' (Christensen 1997): the idea that those who rest on their laurels can be swept from the market in an instant. The concept of disruption has highly problematic ideological implications (Lepore 2014) and serves in practice above all to legitimise the spending of enormous amounts of venture capital in the start-up world (Staab 2016). At the same time this ideology of radical transformation has very real effects in terms of protecting the monopolies and oligopolies that emerged in the expansion phase from the mid-1990s.

Today's internet giants respond to the vulnerability of digital monopolies by relying increasingly on closed socio-technical ecosystems. High transaction costs are incurred where users wish to convert data between systems, for example between Apple and Google. An iPhone or iPad gives its owner strong incentives to source other products (such as music) from Apple too. The same applies to Google's smartphone operating system Android, where the ability to network with other Google services offers many benefits to users. Both Google and Apple are also investing in smart home technologies, various forms of robotics, networked road vehicles, artificial intelligence (AI) technologies and expanding their own cloud infrastructure.

However, the companies that have to date dominated their respective core markets (Google in internet search, Amazon in e-commerce etc.) are increasingly coming into competition with one another as they develop expansive socio-technical ecosystems (for example in the areas of hardware, cloud computing or operating systems). Here we are dealing with oligopolistic market structures that, as elsewhere, enable exorbitant profits to be made. The beating heart of the commercial internet is not the decentralisation expected by the theorists of post-capitalism, but power and control (Dolata 2015). It is structured not by the collaborative paradigm of the digital commons (Rifkin 2014; Mason 2016), but by the concentration of power in the financial sector, which had already had to learn to reconcile economic superabundance with profit-making.

Hermeneutics of business models

A further structural filiation appears in the generation of profits through secondary use of the data gathered through the respective services. This is most prominent in online advertising, where global market volume exceeded US$705 billion in 2021 (Zenith 2021) and revenues in the same year in the United States alone totalled US$153.1 billion (IAB and PwC 2021). Internet advertising has exhibited double-figure growth rates every year since 2010 (IAB and PwC 2022). One indication of the systemic importance of online advertising for the profits of the big internet companies is that only twelve of the world's hundred most visited websites in 2013 generated their income primarily through sources other than online advertising (Wikipedia representing a prominent example) (Jin 2013). The internet platforms offer speculative revenue-making opportunities in the form of advertising space. Facebook's advertising revenues in 2022 amounted to more than US$113 billion (Meta Platforms 2023), while Google recorded revenues of US$209.4 billion (Google 2022).

The major internet companies' strategy of generating profits through secondary use is based on a model that was probably not 'invented' by the financial sector but has certainly become a central feature there. Derivatives have been central to the enormous growth of financialisation (LiPuma and

Lee 2004). 'Derivative' is an umbrella term for a wide range of contracts that derive their value from the performance of an underlying asset or index. They include options and futures. While such instruments have been around a long time and are often economically useful, they remained very marginal until the 1990s. Yet by the 2000s they were the most 'valuable' part of the global economy (Arnoldi 2009).

Secondary use and capitalising on time

While the value of conventional loans depends ultimately on the expectation of repayment of principal and interest, certain derivatives allow profit to be derived from gambling on third parties' repayments. In other words, structurally analogous to online advertising, the good generated and traded is users' data; here, the borrowers' data. The example of options illustrates the range of applications. Options play an important role in the real economy. Traditionally, for example, farmers insure against price fluctuations in the global markets using put options: when they sow their seed they buy the option to sell their grain at a fixed price. However, in a further step, investors can also buy and sell options that allow them to bet on rising or falling grain prices. Especially in the form of so-called swaps (the infamous credit default swaps, or CDS) this secondary utilisation (from the perspective of buyer and seller) can even be applied recursively to the financial system itself (Arnoldi 2009). One can for example make money by betting on third parties' debt repayments. Certainly the great interest in this instrument cannot be explained by an elevated need for its original function as a form of insurance.

The macroscopic parallels are by no means merely superficial. The described practices of internet and finance companies are essentially about betting on the homogeneity of time (Vogl 2011). Google's exorbitant advertising profits are the outcome of a never-ending auction process where interested parties compete to place their links on the results pages of frequently used search terms. A taxi operator in Hamburg, for example, will want to appear at the top of the results list for searches containing the terms 'taxi' and 'Hamburg'. In Google's AdWords auction 'search engine marketers' bid for options on lists of search terms. The price of a place is determined by Google's assessment of the usefulness of the link to the search user, the frequency of the search term and other factors. The value of the placing to the customer results in turn from the expected difference between the ad's cost and the revenue attributable to it (by way of page views). So we are dealing with speculation based on calculable odds. Ultimately Google receives revenue where customers believe that past internet search patterns can be projected relatively reliably into the future.

As we know, the derivatives business is essentially based on the same methodology (LiPuma and Lee 2004; Esposito 2010; Vogl 2011). Options, futures and so on can only be priced at all under the assumption that patterns of behaviour are predictable (Sahr 2017a). This is an essential – not incidental – property of these value-extraction processes. In fact derivatives only became a viable source of profit after the so-called Black-Scholes model became the accepted standard in the 1980s and 1990s. This pricing formula assumes that past risk patterns will continue into the future. In this way uncertain forecasts become blueprints for money-making (Martin 2009: 119; see also Vogl 2011: 104).

High-frequency gambling

Closer examination of the practices of the internet giants in the field of online advertising reveals another parallel. Google's advertising auctions occur in real time. In other words, while each user search is being processed an auction mechanism is running in the background. This too was modelled on the financial markets. The stock market has seen steady growth in the importance of automated trading. By 2012 algorithmic trading accounted for about half of US stock market transactions (Gerig 2015). Here computer algorithms automatically monitor market trends and buy or sell shares or currency according to predefined criteria. Automated transactions can also be used for longer-term investment projects ('systematic trading'), but mostly they operate in a timeframe of a fraction of a second (high-frequency trading, 'flash trading').

The prevalence of computerised transactions has a huge influence on pricing and trends in the financial markets. Flash trading also offers a source of profit outside the 'actual' product, because all it does is to commodify temporal differences in share prices. Money is earned by being faster than others, in other words by shrinking time. This systematic acceleration of economic transactions finds its structurally analogous counterpart in the real-time markets for online advertising. 'It is fair to say', Ann-Christina Lange, Marc Lenglet and Robert Seyfert write, 'that algorithms are now the primary interacting agents operating in the financial markets' (Lange, Lenglet and Seyfert 2016: 149). The same can be said of the digital economy.

With its commodification of time and its orientation on providing an architecture for 'the rest' of the economy, the digital economy is thus operating – and attracting investment – in a very similar way to the financial sector. It is true that the combination of market competition and very low marginal costs makes it practically impossible to derive a profit directly from many primary products. However that certainly does not mean – though the theorists of post-capitalism wish otherwise – that there are no profits to be made in the digital economy.

Market developments: risk distribution, exit logics and the arithmetic of crisis

The final parallel consists in the practice of generating profits through speculation in the context of particular investment strategies and financing structures. An entirely new source of profit for the banks emerged in the financial system in the late twentieth and early twenty-first century (Sahr 2017b). While the business of the traditional banking system was essentially to finance long-term investment from local customer deposits, since the 1990s and 2000s more and more money has been earned through structures that are generally referred to as 'shadow banking'.

The distinction refers less to specific types of institution (investment versus retail banking for example) than to a strategy of risk fragmentation by means of complex derivatives. This essentially means the securitisation practices that gained notoriety through the 2008/09 subprime crisis. When debt is securitised, pools of smaller loans with different risks are combined and transformed into structured debt obligations. 'Structured' means that 'tranches' are graded from low risk (and low expected yield) to high risk (and high yield). The holders of the expensive tranches are first in line to receive interest payments; if defaults occur, the purchasers of cheaper but more risky tranches are first to lose out. Before the financial crisis, especially high-risk tranches were often pooled yet again, securitised a second (or third) time and sold across the world. These deals were extremely lucrative for the banks (especially US banks), which were able to sell supposedly low-risk tranches to big global investors (such as pension funds) that would not have been interested in financing the original debts (American mortgages and consumer loans). They paid a great deal more for the securities than the banks had had to spend on the original loans because the risk associated with the 'final product' of securitisation was assessed to be smaller than that of the 'raw material'. In this way the banks developed from lenders (originate to hold) to vendors (originate to distribute) and were motivated to generate ever more loans to satisfy the growing demand. The logic of this profit-generating process thus consists in profiting from risks one has created oneself by persuading others that they are good investments – and then getting out quick. In this new iteration the source of profit is no longer successful loan repayment but a timely exit.

Structurally similar practices of risk fragmentation through investment cascades and the associated exit orientations (Kühl 2002) are also found in technology start-up funding. Here venture capitalists hope to reap huge profits by investing in new businesses that are expected to grow extremely rapidly (a so-called 'hockey stick').[7] That is exactly what the leading companies of the commercial internet have achieved. Here again, this involves

constructing complex risk cascades whose benefits and pitfalls for the participating investors depend on future developments. Opportunity and risk are
distributed in funding rounds. The initial founding of the start-up is usually
financed with a relatively small stake from the founder(s) plus so-called 'seed
money', supplied as a rule by 'angel investors' who choose to participate at
this very early stage. In successive rounds the start-up seeks to acquire successively more capital, above all from private venture capitalists. The sums
involved in this process are gigantic. The most active investors include established funds – most famously the many headquartered on Sand Hill Road in
Menlo Park – as well as the major internet companies themselves, gigafunds
like SoftBank's Vision Funds and various private equity funds.

Just as the price of securities is predicated not on the volume and risk of
the original loans, but on the expected (re)sale value, the value of the stakes
secured in successive funding rounds is orientated on the speculative profit
to be achieved by a well-timed sale. The expectation of an initial public
offering (IPO) (Kühl 2002) or other form of exit is often already priced in
when a company is founded; investors make their engagement conditional
on explicit exit plans laying out timing and return, profit and risk. So from
the firms' perspective exponential growth in valuation is not just advan-
tageous but – as the propagated objective – preconditional for acquiring
investment capital. On the one hand, turning a profit means monetising
your stake in good time. On the other, the mechanism is subject to a logic
of systematic acceleration because the timeframe within which the investment is expected to generate the expected return becomes shorter with each
funding round (Klingler-Vidra 2016: 694). While seed capital usually has
an exit perspective of seven to ten years, the intended investment period for
growth capital invested in later rounds is just one to three years (Klingler-
Vidra 2016). Venture capitalists are always thinking of the end when they
begin their engagement. As I will lay out in the next chapter, this drives
structural speculation dynamics that can trigger and exacerbate economic
crises. What we see in the start-up world is a systematic acceleration of capitalist accumulation processes on the model of the financial markets.

The legacy of the crisis and the crisis as legacy

The consequences of the historical and structural filiations between the
financial sector and the internet economy are social as well as economic.
The structuring effect of private venture capital in particular has made the
commercial internet an important source of economic risk. It is all too easy
to forget that this market was the epicentre of the last global economic
crash but one. Today, too, the financialisation of the internet economy

generates systemic risks that, via various mechanisms, become drivers of social inequality.

Exit capitalism revisited: a whiff of the nineties

So the commercial internet not only learned its money-making from the financial markets but plainly also inherited the latter's propensity for risk-taking and crisis. One could say a whiff of the late 1990s is in the air, in the same sector that just twenty years ago gave us one of the biggest speculative bubbles in world economic history (Blomert 2005: 190). Today we observe similar symptoms of crisis in various areas, and again they are systematically bound up with the financialisation of the economy. The venture capital operating in the start-up world is only the tip of a much bigger iceberg, an environment where companies themselves become speculatively traded goods. One sign of this is the ability of investors to make large profits on unprofitable firms: 78 per cent of tech companies that went public in 2021 in the United States did so without investors ever having seen an operating profit (Ritter 2022). The last time that indicator was higher (81 per cent) was in 2000 at the height of the dotcom boom. The actual business model here is simply to time the exit correctly. So flotations of loss-making firms are just one symptom of a market built on speculative expectations, where venture capitalists derive enormous profits from businesses that cannot even demonstrate a functioning business model.

Speculation as business model

In order to gain a deeper understanding of this dynamic we need to take a closer look at the role of venture capital in the start-up world. As in the 1990s, the importance of venture capital in today's start-up economy derives from the fact that 'companies in growth markets ... generally lack access to bank loans' (translated from Kühl 2002: 197), and must therefore turn to other sources of finance. Venture capitalists fill that gap, insisting in return on arrangements granting them great influence over the companies' development – where they do not actually found companies themselves. The business of venture capitalists is not to produce and distribute specific products and services, however. As Kühl (2002: 201) writes, the decisive question for success or failure of a venture capital investment is solely whether the stake can be sold at a profit. The more optimistic the new investors' estimates of a firm's growth prospects, the greater the potential profit. And growth prospects are assessed on the basis of past developments, so start-ups – in contrast to traditional new businesses – require rapid investment-driven growth.[8]

Kühl notes that the 'exit logic' of venture capital, established by investors in the course of the dotcom boom, has percolated into all areas of the start-up economy and also affects founders and sections of their staff. Founders, he says, are only able to acquire venture capital if they can plausibly promise rapid returns. One indication of the exit logic among founders of venture capital-funded start-ups is that they are expected to include their own exit in their planning (Kühl 2002: 202).

Employees, as Kühl notes, may share the exit orientation where it offers them a financial interest. Because start-ups generally pay lower salaries than established firms, highly qualified staff such as programmers are often granted options on a share of expected exit profits. This means that long-term market success is less decisive for their earnings than whether the company can persuade investors that it is on course for spectacular future growth and profits to match. This means, Kühl observes, that founders and staff often stay on board exactly until their share options can be realised (or for as long as they are prevented from cashing in by their employment terms or options contracts). This is not a career disadvantage for the founders as long as the investment climate remains positive. Quite the opposite: successful exits generate a success narrative that in turn improves the prospects of acquiring venture capital for the next start-up. Kühl (2002: 203) draws together these strands to identify a new type of 'serial entrepreneur'. In the start-up world that label signifies strategic and economic competence.

The profit logic of venture capital is intimately bound up with faith in specific growth markets. Like today, this role was assumed in the 1990s principally by the commercial internet. As Kühl writes, the dotcom boom was only the latest phase in an approximately ten-year cycle of venture capital. It was preceded for example by boom/bust cycles for hard drives in the early 1980s and PCs in the late 1980s (Kühl 2002: 204). The latest cycle of exit capitalism began in the digital economy after the financial crisis of 2008.

In the boom phase shares in a company can be sold successfully exactly as long as the belief in growth lasts. If the belief is lost, capital generally withdraws extremely quickly: 'Selling becomes successively harder for those who remain in the market; everyone tries to sell their shares as best they can' (translated from Kühl 2002: 218). This is the moment when the bubble bursts. The last to get out are the losers. Those who reach the exit in time have won their bet. Kühl (2002: 218) concludes: 'If one dares to mention the word "speculative bubble", well venture capital is nothing other than trading in the "speculative bubbles" that form in growth markets'.

Even the COVID-19 pandemic could not stop the cycle. Instead, global venture capital investments doubled between 2019 (US$309.1 billion) and 2021 (US$671 billion) (KPMG 2022a). The global centres of this dynamic are located largely in the United States (US$329.7 billion; around 49 per cent) and China (US$106.4 billion; around 16 per cent), as well as various Asian countries. Europe has also seen an increase in spectacular investment rounds and a tripling of venture capital investment between 2019 (US$43.2 billion) and 2021 (US$122.6 billion) (KPMG 2022b).

From IPOs to acquisitions

In retrospect, the bursting of the dotcom bubble was a necessary market correction. The profitable segments of the commercial internet (in particular online advertising and e-commerce) were uncharted territory in the 1990s. The bubble ultimately burst after investors began realising that few of the listed companies had any viable business model. The precondition for the market correction was a specific exit strategy: during that period the initial public offering (IPO) was the preferred option for cashing in.

Friends and colleagues of the brokers were especially likely to benefit from the difference between issue price and listing price. Arthur Levitt, at the time Chairman of the US Securities and Exchange Commission, wanted the general public to profit too (Blomert 2003). One factor prolonging the bubble was the neo-conservative reforms instituted by the Reagan administration, which hindered transparency in the American share markets (Blomert 2005) and thus delayed market corrections involving bankruptcy of failing companies. In particular the oligopoly of the big auditing firms developed 'an internal codex of so-called cooperative auditing', from which they profited systematically through their exorbitant fees (translated from Blomert 2005: 189). Nevertheless the air drained from the bubble when investors began examining the books more closely after IPOs.

For all the parallels to the situation in the 1990s, there are also important differences. Today, stock market flotations are less often the tool of choice for a profitable exit. Between 1990 and 2000 there were almost 4,500 IPOs on US exchanges, more than twice as many as in the following twenty years (Ritter 2022: 3). In 1996 alone, well over 600 firms went public in the United States; in 2020 it was just 165, rising to 309 in 2021 (Ritter 2022). The figures for other countries are similarly striking. In Germany, for example, at the height of the dotcom boom in 1997–2000 there were more than 400 IPOs; between 2014 and 2021 just 72 (Kirchhoff 2021).

What differentiates mergers and acquisitions from IPOs is their comparative lack of transparency. Even more importantly, there is absolutely no requirement to publish the accounts of acquired start-ups. It is fair to assume that the buyers have little interest in harming their reputation by identifying mistakes. As long as one can assume that most exit acquisitions have functioning business models or more or less realistic valuations, no structural problem arises. However, if we consider the calculations of venture capital, essentially seeking to capitalise directly on rising markets, and the strategic opacity that characterises start-ups, there are certainly ample grounds to doubt that assumption. Assuming that the speculative and risk-taking calculations of typical investment structures are associated with systemic dangers of the kind that resulted in the dotcom bubble and crash, we could conclude that we are looking today at similar problems, although possibly with different effects. The risks of a start-up world characterised by venture capital are no longer corrected by events generating more realistic market valuations but transferred into the balance sheets of large, acquisition-hungry companies. The risks now affect the labour market more than the financial markets. The losers under these conditions are not investors acquiring shares in start-ups through IPOs but companies and their employees. The counter-thesis would be that acquisitions enhance the innovative potential of the acquiring companies and open up new growth and employment opportunities. While the latter assumption predominates in economics, the current functioning of private venture capital would tend to confirm that the new form of exit capitalism is associated with new types of risk. The socio-economic logic that unfolds here suggests, as I discuss in greater detail in Chapter 6, a redistribution from income to wealth. Those who profit from exit capitalism are certainly on the same side of the equation as the venture capital firms.

Workers in the exit cycle

The risks of this exit strategy are borne not only by workers in the acquiring companies, but also those in the start-ups themselves. The most obvious systematic source of individual risk here is the partial substitution of immediate income by shares in the company, which is typical for the start-up world. In the technology sector highly qualified staff are only available at salaries that many start-ups cannot afford. They are instead attracted using share options, which do not represent current income but promise big rewards in the event of a lucrative exit. Stories about simple coders becoming multimillionaires by earning an early stake in a company that later became extremely successful are two-a-penny in the start-up world. That might sound too good to be true, and indeed staff are rarely given equal treatment with investors. Although both groups typically receive preference shares that can be converted into ordinary shares on a stipulated date (exit), investors are entitled to a share of the exit profits that staff (and generally also founders) do not receive. For example, their preferential shares may guarantee a specific return in any flotation, liquidation preferences or seniority. The longer a company exists before an exit – in other words, the more funding rounds it has behind it – the less clarity staff are likely to have about the value of their own shares, as the economists Will Gornall and Ilya Strebulaev demonstrate for the 'unicorns' (2017).[9] What all this means, to put it very simply, is that powerful investors will be served first, and may even have their profits defined in advance. Often enough these guaranteed profits come at the expense of other shareholders.

For workers whose income has been partly substituted by a promise of future capital gains, this has several important implications. Firstly, the value of their share falls systematically with every funding round in which investors receive new privileges. Secondly, it is they who shoulder the greatest risk of losses. In the event of liquidation – which is the fate of most start-ups in the medium term – they are also last in line (and can expect to receive nothing). Thirdly, staff generally assess the value of their options on the basis of the listed price for the ordinary shares. This means that they systematically overestimate their value, with all the associated risks for personal financial planning and lifestyle choices.

Aside from these economic risks, which are inherent to the sector's risk cascades, the work itself is not immune to effects of investors' exit strategies. Debates over the quality of work in start-up firms revolve primarily around specific ways of organising work. Concretely, this generally alludes to 'agile software development', an organisational paradigm based on teamwork and iterative processes – where certain observers see both possibilities and risks for 'good work' (Pfeiffer 2014; Boes et al. 2018). As Kühl (2002) points out, the repercussions on the working atmosphere of practical organisational aspects such as the loss of 'face-to-face-interaction' in rapidly growing organisations were already apparent in the 1990s.

Whether specific forms of organisation are employed more to benefit workers' autonomy or to increase the pressure of work obviously depends in part on the company's growth and associated restructuring. But the calculations of venture capital also play a significant role, and research suggests that the exit goals of investors and entrepreneurs can have a considerable influence on organisational restructuring. The inherent flexibility of the agile organisations that dominate the sector means they are predestined to undergo regular adjustment to new requirements, if need be against the interests of the workers. An empirical example from my own research illustrates the point. The software company in question acquired serious venture capital in its second funding round, which it invested in improving its product and acquiring customers. But things began to fall apart as the planned exit date approached. The software simply failed to function. The development department informed management, which insisted on sticking to the timeframe agreed with the investors. Instead management stepped up pressure on the development department. The customer complaints that flooded marketing were dealt with only superficially, because management's concern was to expand or at least hold the customer base. The frustrated programmers soon quit en masse. From this point on, the start-up was to all intents and purposes nothing more than a call centre. All effort was channelled into preserving the customer base, which the founders and investors hoped would secure a lucrative exit price. Chaos ensued, and the remaining staff worked ever longer hours. One former employee reported:

> The problems just ballooned, but management were concentrating entirely on developing the new customer area. Nothing but stress. They promised customers that duplicates would be deleted immediately, and that's how our sales people sold it, as they didn't know any better. ... So sometimes I'd be sat there for three or four hours, clicking through directories to collect up the duplicates. Then they were sent to operations and deleted. All manually! (translated from Staab 2018: 226)

While everything else was subordinated to the scheduled exit date, the quality of work suffered. The company's existence now revolved exclusively around the figures that would decide its exit value: in this case the size of its customer base. Work on the more or less useless product was practically suspended.

In the world of venture capital that was simply logical. The real product was never the software, but the company itself, whose value resulted from the expectations generated by specific indicators. In the described case the bet paid off. The exit was a success, and the firm was sold for an eight-figure sum. The buyer liquidated it about a year later. The comment of an experienced founder suggests that this may have been an extreme case, but by no means implausible:

> You often hear that about exits, when things didn't turn out like they expected. Or the technology wasn't so great. Until the customer realises that the technology is basically junk, you can still string them along for a while. ... That's pretty dodgy of course, it's about maximising the benefit to the seller. ... If strategists are involved in the pitch ... then it's going to be sold, and you can really pimp it up. ... They want a sick exit and then fuck it. (translated from Staab 2018: 226)

Mega-IPOs and the geopolitics of digital markets

Let us return to the topic of market developments in the financialised digital economy. One reason why investors and founders tend to be reticent about flotations is the currently good climate for acquisitions, which has led to something of a rethinking. Especially in the United States, start-ups and investors frequently orientate their activity on the objective of acquisition by a leading digital firm or other major company. At the same time the enormous sums streaming into the sector since the 2008 financial crisis have led to the emergence of the unicorns, whose global number increased twelvefold between 2014 and 2021 alone. This 'herd' of unicorns represents a group of companies whose chances of exit through acquisition logically shrink as their valuation grows. The higher the valuation (and purchase price), the smaller the circle of potential buyers. Theoretically one can still imagine that firms like Netflix or Spotify might be bought by Google or Apple; whether such an acquisition would make economic sense is a different matter. Apart from this select group of potential purchasers, the only alternative exit option at the end of the day is a flotation. A number of very highly valued start-ups have chosen to go down that road in recent years – for example Snap, Dropbox, Spotify, Lyft and not least the biggest unicorn of them all, the ride-hailing company Uber.

The example of this start-up on steroids and its lead investor Vision Fund illustrates very well the market dynamics involved. For a long time Uber's market valuation knew only one direction: up, and steeply. The first time it fell was at the end of 2017 after the firm encountered regulatory problems and growing local competition in a number of important markets. While previous rounds had valued Uber at about US$70 billion, SoftBank came in on a valuation of 'just' US$50 billion. For a long time a market valuation of US$100–120 billion was discussed for Uber's much-postponed flotation. Observers of the digital economy awaited this IPO with a good deal of nervousness. Since its founding in 2009 Uber had always made gigantic losses: US$7 billion in the seven quarters leading up to its IPO (Richter 2020), and another US$7 billion in 2020. The following year, 2021, saw a sharp decline in losses to 'only' US$469 million (Uber Investor 2022), which can probably be attributed mostly to Uber selling its autonomous driving unit (valued at US$10 billion) and massive layoffs during the pandemic.

Its business model is also comparatively easy to copy; worse still, its economic viability is by no means proven (Sherman 2017). In view of the difficulties mentioned above, Uber and its competitors rely on the typical method employed by internet companies to capture markets: subsidising consumption. Customers are attracted with low prices, drivers' remuneration remains relatively high or is supplemented by recruitment bonuses. As long as the competition consists of other ride-hailing firms and traditional taxi operators Uber can neither significantly reduce pay nor increase its prices. If it did, its drivers and users would simply migrate to the competition. Political interventions also prevent Uber cutting 'wages' at will in certain national markets, which is why the company has increasingly tried to adapt to regional regulations (Valdez 2022).

Uber thus has no road to long-term economic success other than market control (which would potentially provoke anti-trust intervention, as Western anti-trust law slowly responds to the power of the digital platforms). The strategy of ruinous competition is extraordinarily expensive for Uber, however. When the flotation did finally occur in May 2019 the rather disappointing valuation came in at about US$80 billion.

This was exactly the point where SoftBank with its gigantic Vision Fund became essential to the market sorting process. At first glance SoftBank's investments in the mobility sector appear incompatible. Around 2018 it held interests in rivals Grab, Ola and Brazil's 99, in addition to its large stake in Uber. At that point, more than 90 per cent of all rides booked on any given day (about 45 million) were provided by companies belonging to the SoftBank empire (*Economist* 2018a). In March 2018, shortly after the SoftBank investment, Uber unexpectedly withdrew from the Southeast Asian market. Like previous similar moves in China and Russia, the deal gave Uber a minority stake in the local market leader. In this case, one could observe the digital geopolitics of capital first hand: the economic experiment – whose outcome is still anything but certain – consisted in carving up global growth markets, not by companies competing but through the integrated strategies of extremely wealthy investors.

Can Uber turn a profit?

To get a grasp of the social implications of this development we will need to dig a little deeper. Even where investors create local monopolies, Uber's success depends on multiple factors. First of all, if Uber is to survive in the long term these markets must be profitable enough to secure the valuation achieved in the flotation. In fact Uber's share price fell by almost 20 per cent in the first two days of trading and by April 2022 was still only 80 per cent of its 2019 IPO price, with a market valuation of US$61 billion.

Second, even if we assume that Uber is able to achieve a monopoly in important markets, the underlying calculation is more than risky: consumers use Uber because it is cheap. Uber is cheap because it subsidises its services using capital from investors. If it ceases subsidising, it must increase its prices and/or reduce its labour costs. Uber cannot raise prices significantly, however, because users would switch to alternative means of transport. They ride Uber because Uber is cheap. Reducing pay requires certain conditions to be in place, including a relative surplus of labour. This was the case in the United States for a time after 2008, and is a structural feature in many emerging economies and developing countries. Let us assume that labour costs can be reduced, in line with the investors' economic interests. Then, once again, the exit capitalism of the 2010s would be exposed as a constellation systematically designed to redistribute from income to wealth – from Uber drivers to SoftBank's shareholders.

Thus, where markets function as monopolies and ride-hailing platforms successfully reduce drivers' remuneration, we observe a radicalisation of social inequality that is associated with great potential for social unrest. Capital sometimes encounters pushback even before regulatory authorities intervene. In India, for example, by 2018 there were already strong signs that SoftBank portfolio companies and competitors Ola and Uber were coordinating their prices. This led to a protracted strike in Delhi and Mumbai that was so successful that Uber had to fulfil most of the drivers' demands. Aside from the minor concrete victory, this illustration of the dynamics of capital in the digital economy shows above all that the effect of exit capitalism has been to encourage an asymmetrical polarisation of income and wealth. The logics inherent to digital capitalism make it a source of radicalisation of social inequality.

The practicalities of speculation

So do the described parallels between financial markets and internet economy, and between the dotcom boom and the present phase since 2008, suggest that the commercial internet was built by capitalist cynics to knowingly steer the global economy into its next crisis? That would probably be an overstatement. What we see reproduced in practice here is a specific underlying understanding of economic innovation – and acceptance of massive risk – shared by the trinity of consulting firms, investors and entrepreneurs. Here there is certainly a sharp awareness of the risks inherent to the second dotcom boom since 2008. For example, 91 per cent of 900 venture capitalists surveyed in 2016 believed that the unicorns were structurally overvalued (Gompers et al. 2016).

Yet these risks are accepted, probably primarily because the investors are driven above all by short-term considerations of personal gain, where their profits depend absolutely on overvaluations. The ideology of digital capitalism plays down the inevitable failures as necessary stumbling blocks on a general trend towards economic growth and prosperity. The background to this 'justification system' (Boltanski and Chiapello 2003) is a specific ideological constellation that is by no means without an empirical basis. The 'spirit of digital capitalism' (Nachtwey and Seidl 2017) venerates 'disruption' and cares little for stability or social responsibility. The idea of 'disruption' originates from Clayton Christensen's management bible *The Innovator's Dilemma* (1997) and has become the battle-cry of the self-appointed revolutionaries of capital: destroy the old to make way for the new. The objective is eruptive growth, with no place for slow, incremental improvements.

Of course the proponents of this logic do not believe that they are promoting a downward spiral, still less preparing the ground for anti-capitalist counter-movements. Slumps are mere blips in an inexorable upward trend, the cycle of boom and bust. Not that investors or entrepreneurs can express such views openly while simultaneously investing in a growth market. But they all know it, and in retrospect hype, bust and recovery can certainly be reconciled. This attitude comes over very clearly in an interview I conducted in 2017 with a veteran of the dotcom boom. Jeff studied engineering at Stanford in the mid-1980s, followed by a business major at Harvard. We met for a gluten-free lunch in Palo Alto. After graduating, Jeff worked for several decades in the semiconductor and computer industry, including for the famous firm Silicon Graphics, whose former headquarters now houses Google's corporate campus. In our discussion he lauded today's commercial internet, the Silicon Valley business culture and his own career in euphoric tones: 'I think we're living in a golden age for technology, innovation and growth. That's a very rare thing, and I feel privileged to experience it.'

But the dotcom crash of 2000 was a calamity, especially because Jeff was emotionally and financially invested in the firm he worked for:

> Our business shrank by two-thirds and we had to shed 40 percent of the staff. We were an intellectual property provider so we didn't manufacture anything. We enabled our customers to produce personalised microprocessors. When the bubble burst we were hit hard, man! My firm was almost dead. ... It's funny when you're living in a bubble. You know it's somehow crazy, but you don't realize quite how crazy. You are literally inside the bubble! But as long as the music is playing, you've got to get up and dance.

When I pointed out the contradiction between his praise for today's developments and criticism of the 1990s, he did not initially understand what I meant. When I asked straight out whether we were not in the middle of another bubble, he was incredulous:

> Of course it's a bubble! I expect valuations to fall. Investors follow trends, they want returns. If interest rates are historically low you can't turn a profit with stuff like bonds. So should capital flow into riskier investments, boom regions like Silicon Valley? Sure, I think so. Will a lot get wasted in the long run? Of course! But in the end we'll be a lot better off than if we never tried.

That's just how growth works. Markets overheat. In the process new products are developed, staff trained and infrastructure created. When the market collapses the capital is gone but the three other elements remain.

There is a pause and then the products, skills and infrastructure become the basis for the next round of expansion, which can again only be to the good of the workers, consumers and investors.

Here the advocates and critics of digital capitalism find themselves in agreement. Nick Srnicek, author of the ground-breaking *Platform Capitalism*, writes for example that 'the 1990s tech boom was a bubble that laid the groundwork for the digital economy to come' (Srnicek 2017: 23). Like Jeff, Srnicek describes a situation where the infrastructure created during the bubble enabled the rise of the GAFA complex.

Jeff applies the same motto to economic cycles and to his own life: 'Growth creates opportunity.' You have to grasp your chances with both hands, failure is always a possibility, contingency is priced in. Today Jeff lives in Provence for three months a year. The dotcom crash spared him. The firm he worked for survived and was sold some years later. He invested his exit profits in a second house in Menlo Park. Its rapidly appreciating value gives Jeff and his wife a good standard of living, and they rent it out when they are in France. The monthly rent has doubled in the past eight years.

Financial capitalism online

Despite the crisis-prone nature of growth markets one should not simply assume that the protagonists do not believe they are delivering the benefits that politics and society expect from them. The paradigm of a restructuring of capitalism aligned with the interests of financial capital shimmers through in Jeff's comments. Digital capitalism, whose beating heart is the commercial internet, did not just spring from nowhere. The rise of the GAFA group and the dynamism of the markets are systematically connected with the growing demand for information and communications technologies since the 1970s. These are the technologies behind the progressive automation of production and administration, the globalisation and networking of value chains. Another factor was the investing, risk-taking Keynesian state, which also watched over the neutrality of that era's growth markets and thus laid the regulatory groundwork for the initial burst of innovation.

But above all, digital capitalism is a child of financialisation. The connections between the financial sector and the internet economy are particularly close and systematic. On the one hand, historical filiations created a growth tandem: investment and demand from the financial sector funded the expansion of the ICT sector. The financial sector, in turn, employed the new technologies to transform its own business models, products and operations – that in turn often shaped the commercialisation of the internet. This represents a structural filiation between the financial sector and internet companies, where central economic structures of the commercial internet are borrowed from the financial markets. The internet giants learned from finance how to operate successfully in an economy of superabundance. Concentration and closure are two of the decisive strategies used to essentially make superabundant resources scarce, which we will examine in greater detail in the following chapter. High-frequency gambling, algorithmic market control and capitalising on time, as described for online advertising, also emulate models that first emerged in the financial markets.

Finally, the central importance of private venture capital for the growth, structures, profit logics and market risks in the start-up economy must be mentioned. Without this aspect it is simply impossible to understand the development of digital capitalism. Private venture capital remains the central force financing the market expansions of the internet giants. To this day, this form of capital determines the calculations of the start-up planets orbiting the GAFA suns. Private venture capital is also a central factor behind today's less labour-based and more wealth-based capitalism, and exacerbates its inequality-deepening dynamic. The question today is no longer how to expand demand, but how to secure returns. After decades of slowing economic growth this is an increasingly pressing challenge for capital. Today private venture capital seeks its salvation in the only markets offering rapid growth, where the risk cascades it creates are typical of the kind of speculative markets that also preceded the dotcom crisis and ultimately encourage redistribution from employment income to wealth. In other words, digital capitalism has not only learned from the financial markets how to earn money, but also assumed their susceptibility to economic and social crises.

The centrality of private venture capital is associated with specific effects. Firstly the current situation strongly resembles the 1990s, when enormous sums of private venture capital flowed into technology start-ups. The typical exit orientations of that period still characterise important parts of the start-up world. Again investors are securing great influence over entrepreneurial decisions by using particular legal vehicles to generate opacity, and offering profit-sharing options to founders and selected staff. The logic of growth markets today is as follows: under the conditions of exit capitalism the traded good is not the products of the young enterprises but shares in their ownership.

Nevertheless, systematic shifts in the structure of the exit process can be observed. While in the 1990s IPOs were the conventional route to capitalisation, today acquisitions are also very important. One effect of this is that more time elapses before risks are corrected by the market. Time will tell whether the falling proportion of IPOs amidst free-flowing investment merely indicates that the market in question is still liquid enough to draw investors away from the risk of a flotation, or whether the shift in typical exit paths presages a new logic of risk distribution. A handful of spectacular mega-IPOs can systematically destabilise the market just as much as a flood of smaller flotations (as in the 1990s). This applies especially to the unicorns that might seek to go public in the coming years, with critical analyses suggesting that typical examples of the genre are worth only two-thirds their apparent market valuation (Gornall and Strebulaev 2017). These overvaluations are also (and above all) symptoms of a market structured by the calculations of private venture capital, where each new funding round prices in new expectations of future profits, creating systemic risks.

The shift from IPOs to acquisitions does nothing to eliminate the risks that flotations materialise relatively suddenly in the form of collapsing prices and the cascade effects that tend to follow. According to Kühl's cyclical theory of exit capitalism, in the early 2020s we are coming to the end of an extended, decade-long boom. Without the transparency provided by flotations it is not necessarily obvious where the initial trigger will occur that could bring the entire house of cards tumbling down. As long as old innovations can be marketed in new guises and momentum can be maintained, the market for tech firm acquisitions cannot be expected dry up.

From the perspective of an analysis of digital capitalism, this raises the question whether we might be dealing with a systematic change in the length of the typical exit cycle. That would imply new risk groups and crisis manifestations. If exits are generally realised through acquisitions, it is no longer investors who are principally affected. Instead the risks seep into the balance sheets of established companies, with potential knock-on effects on their employees. In particular with start-ups, the exit orientation impacts directly on the quality of work regardless of the chosen method.

In a broader sense, the question of the susceptibility of the current exit cycle to crisis must remain open for the time being. Whether the risks systematically generated by venture capital are resolved comparatively quickly in IPOs or left to seep slowly but steadily into the rest of the economy to suppress margins, wages and growth, only time will tell. What the observable dynamics of capital all share in common is that they mitigate systematically towards sharpening of social inequality. Whether dodgy acquisitions, risky mega-IPOs or the geostrategic reorganisation of the digital markets, the described dynamics are more suggestive of growth in wealth to the detriment of labour than of a development ultimately benefitting the broader masses. From this perspective the commercial internet is no harbinger of a post-capitalist future but a risk-laden profit-making machine – not an economy of the digital commons, but *financial capitalism online*.

Notes

1 In addition to the cited literature, Chapters 3, 4 and 5 are based on empirical data collected by myself and my team in various research projects. The macro-economic market data is derived from various sources, which are identified in the text (mainly company reports, but also blogs and the business press). For additional detail see the tables in the appendix. The cited interviews and case studies mostly originate from research projects I have conducted, alone or with colleagues, in recent years.

2 Measured in *chained dollars*. The US government uses chained dollars to adjust statistics for inflation, making it possible to compare values from different years in real terms. This improves the measurement of growth rates.

3 The US Federal Reserve was the first to reduce interest rates to zero after the financial crisis. The European Central Bank has been pursuing the same policy since about 2009.

4 Most of them based in the United States (148), followed by China (69) and Europe (26, of which five in Germany) (figures for 2017).

5 Focussing on AI start-ups, Vision Fund 2 originally set a target of US$108 billion but started with just US$2 billion. The amount contributed by SoftBank itself has grown gradually to US$40 billion.

6 Quants write the software for trading and other purposes in the financial sector.

7 Because the curve looks like an ice-hockey stick: after a short phase of slow growth (the blade) the curve shoots up (the handle).

8 Normally in terms of growth in the number of customers or users, or revenue – but not profit.

9 The biggest unicorn of all, ride-hailing platform Uber, is an extreme but instructive example: by 2016 it already had twelve different classes of capital.

4

A system of proprietary markets

The best way of getting a vivid and realistic idea of industrial strategy is indeed to visualize the behavior of new concerns or industries that introduce new commodities or processes ... or else reorganize a part or the whole of an industry.

Schumpeter 2003 [1942]

The dynamics that unfolded in the digital economy after the dotcom bubble burst around the year 2000, and especially after the 2008 global financial crisis, mark the transition from a digitalising to a genuinely digital capitalism that has established its own economic base in the commercial internet. Unlike the industrial monopoly capitalism of Schumpeter's time, the commercial internet is in principle an economy of superabundance.

Problems in such economies of superabundance arise above all on the supply side. Goods that are readily available must be made artificially scarce to transform them into capitalist commodities. If successful, this opens up unimaginable possibilities for making profits. Selling things whose production is practically free is certainly the dream of every capitalist. But superabundance is only one aspect of a constellation that has allowed the leading companies to successively expand their global influence.

For the other side of the equation we must look to the political economy of post-Fordism. The problem here is not so much the underproduction of industrial monopoly capitalism, but relative saturation and consequently underconsumption. Long before digitalisation brought the problem of superabundance to the fore, systematic manifestations of crisis were appearing on the demand side in the major capitalist economies.

The heart of the economic programme embodied by the leading companies of digital capitalism can be understood as a response to the twin problems of modern capitalism: market saturation and superabundance. Both can be understood, as I will show in this chapter, using a model I refer to as 'proprietary markets'. This is the basis for the implicit promise of growth that has turned the digital economy into a magnet for investment and for the rise of its leading companies to become the world's most valuable companies. But before we spell out in detail how proprietary markets function, we need to understand the political economy within which the commercial internet was able to become the saviour of a capitalism suffering secular stagnation.

Born of crisis

The developed welfare state, democratisation of the workplace, and the expansion of political and social rights (Dahrendorf 2007) all originated in a historically unique period of growth, which lasted barely twenty years (Streeck 2011) and is widely described as 'Fordism'. Leaving to one side for the moment the (absolutely relevant) asynchronicities between individual states, the developed OECD economies profited broadly speaking from high growth rates between the early 1950s and the mid-1970s. This growth rested on a combination of specific factors that played out differently in different national contexts.

An insight from regulation theory (Boyer and Durand 1993; Aglietta 2015) is helpful for understanding this development. Even if the national contexts may vary, stable phases of capitalist development are always characterised by three elements. The first of these is an *accumulation regime*, in the sense of a specific form of circulation of capital (in Fordism the combination of mass production and mass consumption). The second significant component is the underlying *production model*, representing a specific relationship between the organisation of production, competition and labour relations (Boyer and Durand 1993; Boyer and Freyssenet 2003; Dörre and Brinkmann 2005; Brinkmann 2011). This boils down to the dominant mode of production (in Fordism the characteristic Taylorist method); the manner in which companies relate to their markets and the innovation and competition strategies they pursue (in Fordism standardised mass-produced goods and competition between large enterprises); and the respective iteration of the social contract between capital and labour (in Fordism the successive expansion of workplace rights) (Dahrendorf 1965; Müller-Jentsch 2009). Thirdly, the production- and accumulation-related aspects are accompanied by a *mode of regulation*, which essentially means the structuring of the socio-economic by the state, as well its ideological legitimations. The welfare state and the corporatist containment of the trade unions were decisive aspects of the Fordist mode of regulation. The engine of Fordism began to stutter towards the end of the 1960s, soon followed by a collapse in growth rates (Figures 4.1 and 4.2).

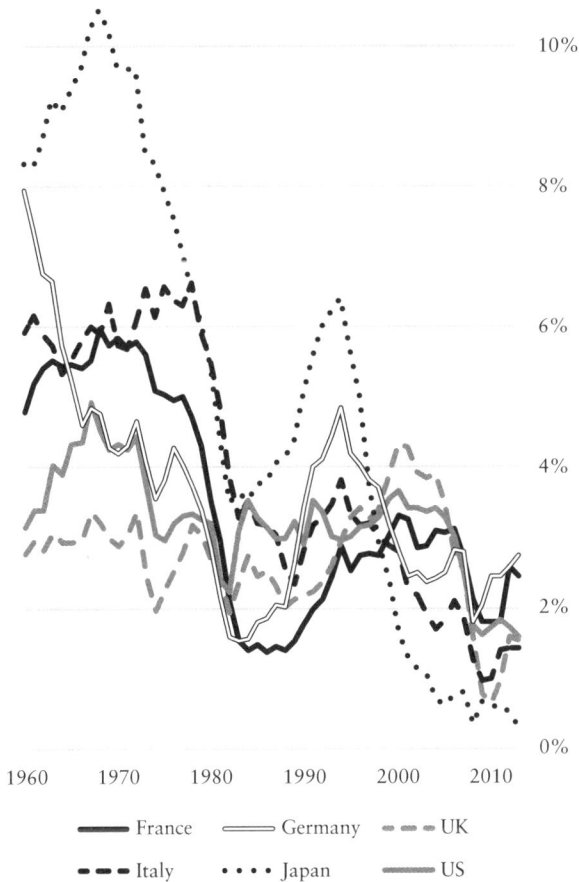

Figure 4.1 Real GDP in major industrialised countries, annual growth rate in per cent, moving ten-year average

Source: Author's calculations using data from Penn World Tables (output-side real GDP, chained PPP).

These fell throughout the OECD world, from 3–10 per cent to today's level of 0–2 per cent. The central factor in the initial crisis of Fordism was that the dynamic coupling of mass production and mass consumption no longer functioned properly. The productivity gains arising from the transition to Taylorism and standardised mass products had been exhausted. 'Basic needs had by and large been covered' (Streeck 2012: 30).

According to Wolfgang Streeck it was the high growth rates of the golden years of Fordism that enabled the creation of the institutions that temporarily quelled the conflict between the profit motive of capitalism and the legitimacy demands of democracy. Strong trade unions ensured

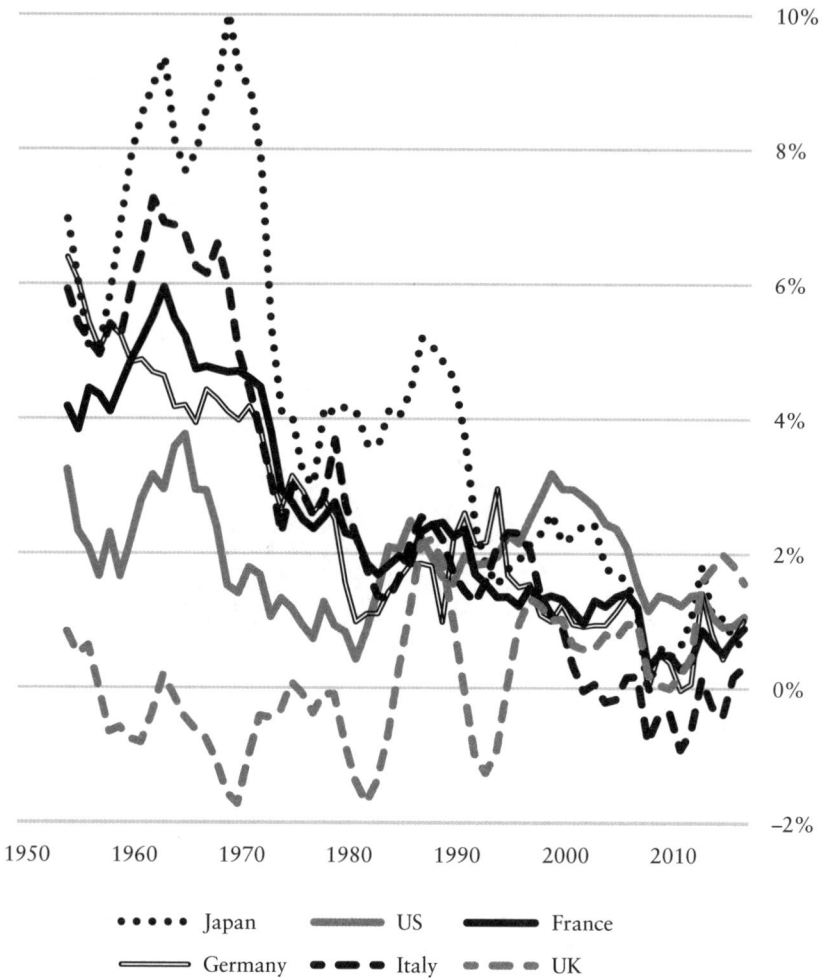

Figure 4.2 Labour productivity in major industrialised countries, annual growth
rate in per cent, five-year moving average

Source: Author's calculations using data from The Conference Board (Output, Labor,
and Labor Productivity, 1950–2018: Growth of Labor Productivity per person
employed, percent change) (The Conference Board 2018).

rising wages, while expanding welfare states invested in social infrastructure. In return the trade unions and social democratic parties set aside any
further-reaching ambitions, such as socialising the means of production or
overcoming capitalism.

At the heart of this development lies the question of social inequality,
which capitalism systematically produces but cannot resolve. But because

inequality undermines the legitimacy of the democratic order, there is, Streeck argues, a systematic tension between capitalism and democracy. Fordism only temporarily suspended that conflict.

Saving democracy from capitalism

The collapse of economic growth placed growing pressure on the historical compromise between democracy and capitalism. Should social entitlements and public services be cut to ensure that profits continue to rise? Or would this – in the Cold War environment of rival systems – strengthen anti-capitalist forces that could potentially pose a threat to liberal democracy? Pay cuts were not yet on the table; the trade unions remained strong and their members had learned to expect steadily rising wages. Nor, given the memory of depression, fascism and world war, was higher unemployment yet regarded as a plausible way forward.

Instead a whole series of political measures were introduced to prevent or compensate for declining private demand. Initially monetary policy was relaxed, to pursue a strategy of encouraging moderate inflation. Increasing the money supply encouraged the trade unions to continue to demand large pay rises, which temporarily checked the fall in mass consumption (Streeck 2014).

After ten years the tide turned against loose money. The wealthy and large parts of the middle classes came to regard 'printing money' as highly problematic in the longer term, as inflation devalued much of their savings and assets. This drew them into a highly unlikely coalition of interests with the ordinary consumer. Amidst rising consumer prices, inflationary policies gradually became unpopular among the groups that had previously profited from rising wages.

As inflationary policies were phased out at the end of the 1970s, the spectre of unemployment returned to many of the heartlands of late Fordism. As well as causing legitimacy problems, unemployment also had direct negative effects. Rising unemployment not only led to higher social spending, but also caused a decline in private spending, threatening a vicious circle of falling demand, shrinking profits, redundancies and finally higher social transfers.

The national paths varied, but in the end all led to the same outcome: public debt. In Italy and France the state used its broad ownership of key industries to support wage levels and demand. The United Kingdom, Austria, the Scandinavian countries and to a lesser extent also the United States chose more classical Keynesian methods, investing heavily to stabilise mass consumption, avert rising unemployment and stimulate demand. In all these countries this led to an expansion of state borrowing, especially as social and welfare costs rose. The same dynamic came into play rather later in Germany and Japan, both of which had pursued strategies of export-driven growth in response to weak internal demand following the Second World War. They were accordingly less affected by declining domestic consumption.

Towards the end of the 1970s this policy slowly but surely encountered its limits. The trade unions remained strong and unexpectedly militant, still often securing generous pay increases. Their power was broken in a series of set-piece conflicts in the early 1980s, in particular the defeats of the US air traffic controllers in 1981 and the British miners' strike in 1984–85. At the same time, resurgent neoliberal economic theories treated growing state debt as a systemic problem. Tax cuts, initially in the United States and the United Kingdom, and later in other OECD economies, meant even larger budget deficits, reductions in social spending, cuts in the welfare state, a weakening of the trade unions and generally growing social inequality (Crouch 2008).

One response to the legitimacy risks inherent to such policies was a restructuring of the Fordist production and accumulation model. This transformation has frequently been described as tertiarisation, in the sense of a shift of the focus of employment from the secondary sector (manufacturing) to the tertiary (services) (Fourastié 1954; Bell 1973; Häußermann and Siebel 1995). The move received support from unexpected coalitions. States were interested in expanding new labour markets to absorb the losers of industrial modernisation (and thus also counteract the problem of falling demand). But the Fordist regime had also come under internal pressure from its labour force (Boltanski and Chiapello 2003). The issues here were much broader than levels of pay and stagnating demand for mass-produced industrial goods. By the 1960s and 1970s workers were kicking against Taylorist production methods and labour control (Edwards 1979). Employment in services promised greater autonomy and independence (Bell 1973).

The accumulation model of tertiarising capitalism was also changing. The prime source of growth was now the deregulated financial sector. Tertiarisation also set in motion a new mechanism of social polarisation. Alongside the rise of the increasingly academic 'service classes' (Erikson and Goldthorpe 1993), a new service proletariat emerged at the other end of the hierarchy (Blossfeld and Mayer 1991; Staab 2014; Bahl and Staab 2015). Comparatively slow productivity growth (Baumol 2013) and low unionisation rates gave rise to a new low-wage sector with a specific class fraction.

In the United States, Colin Crouch (2009) argues, a regime of growing private debt helped to shore up purchasing power and bridged the divide between the new 'underclasses' and the winners of socio-structural transformation. The hour of the private consumer loan struck in the 1990s when the Clinton administration committed to budget consolidation and cutting public spending – while growth was still far from the zenith of Fordism. Consumers became increasingly responsible for stabilising demand in the 'privatised Keynesianism' (Crouch 2009) of the late 1990s and early 2000s. Political measures expedited the trend by relaxing lending rules and deregulating the financial sector.

As a result, 'the ratio of debt to GDP in advanced economies [rose] from 167% in 1980 to 314%' in 2011 (Cecchetti, Mohanty and Zampolli 2011: 1). Most of this 147 percentage point increase was attributable to private households (56 percentage points), whose debt grew faster than corporate (42 percentage points) or government debt (49 percentage points) (Cecchetti, Mohanty and Zampolli 2011). In the United States (and in other countries including Spain) most private consumer borrowing went into the property sector. Property buyers took on unsustainable debt in the expectation that rising house prices and stable interest payments would function as a sustainable source of income. But the subprime bubble burst in summer 2007, and the crisis quickly spread to the banking sector and indirectly to the eurozone. As governments sought to boost demand by consuming future growth (which is what debt actually is), privatised Keynesianism turned out to be another dead end – after inflation and state debt. It is certainly no coincidence that this was precisely the moment when the commercial internet and its leading companies stepped into the limelight of capitalist reorganisation. But before we seek the essence of digital capitalism we must explore and understand the transition from Fordism to post-Fordism.

From Fordism to post-Fordism

Since the recessions of the early 1970s the principal concern of the political part of the political economy had been to buy time with inflation and borrowing (Streeck 2014). The strictly economic responses to changes in productivity gains and demand naturally occurred within the sphere of business, where there was historical precedent for crisis leading to transformation of the predominant model of production. If we think less in terms of the structural transformation of accumulation patterns (tertiarisation, financialisation) and more about changes in the model of production, for example in the car industry, we find ambitious renewal initiatives here too (Jürgens and Krzywdzinski 2016). Probably the most important development was lean production or 'Toyotism' (Dohse, Jürgens and Malsch 1984), which sought to boost efficiency principally through closer integration of supply chains ('just in time') in manufacturing and closer IT networking in administration and management. Even before the advent of lean production, greater individualisation of products had become a priority of industrial restructuring. The progressive and still ongoing turn away from standardised mass products was also an attempt to interest consumers in new goods for which they had no pressing utilitarian need.

These developments – individualisation, lean production, financialisation and tertiarisation – embody the transition to a new type of capitalism widely discussed as post-Fordism (Hirsch and Roth 1986; Dörre and Brinkmann 2005). Again regulation theory provides illumination. Specific differences are found at the level of the model of production. In broad-brush terms, Fordism was an era of hierarchical models where management's modus operandi was to issue direct instructions within large, vertically integrated enterprises. This relatively rigid model offered little freedom to the individual worker, but promised dependable career paths. The labour rights established during Fordism (secure contracts, expanding co-determination and company pensions) emerged in this context of relatively solid connections (Kirchner and Beyer 2016) between individual and company.

In post-Fordism companies were more strongly orientated on the financial markets. Shareholder value became a central principle of management (Höpner 2003). In practice that frequently meant less profitable (non-core) divisions being hived off as independent units, with a network of external suppliers supplanting the integrated, hierarchical structures of Fordism. While workers in the core industrial enterprises were often able to defend or even expand their rights and standard of living, the probability of enjoying such benefits declined successively with distance from the core. Precarity proliferated in the form of temporary contracts and agency work, with workers with different rights and status sometimes working side by side (Nachtwey 2016a).

The privileged status of the core workforce was a product of a specific relationship between companies and their markets in the Fordist constellation. Klaus Dörre and Ulrich Brinkmann (2005: 88) speak in this connection of a 'primacy of production over the market'. This refers to the aforementioned aspect where the major manufacturers were operating in largely unsaturated consumer markets at a time of growing consumer purchasing power. This unique combination permitted them to sell highly standardised products in volume. They had considerable latitude to control prices because the oligopoly markets typical of Fordism were still relatively protected from real global competition and prevented price dumping (Sweezy and Baran 1966). The major producers, not the anonymous mechanisms of a neutral market, set the prices and secured generous returns.

Primacy over the market also enabled core industries to shield their workers from market risks and offer them lifetime careers. Workers and their trade unions became accustomed to rising wages, and ended up insisting on settlements beyond the threshold of unsustainability.

The relationship between companies and markets shifted in post-Fordism. Globalisation and trade liberalisation intensified competition in many markets; prices came under pressure, and with them the profits of established companies. The paradigm – the primacy of production over the market – was reversed. Market mechanisms now structured the economic processes. This applied not only to competition between core enterprises, for example between German and Japanese car makers. The market became an increasingly important control mechanism on two other levels too: within the increasingly decentralised networks of post-Fordist companies and for labour control within enterprises (Marrs 2008; Brinkmann 2011).

The Taylorist labour process is generally regarded as the Fordist control paradigm, with emphasis on subdivision of tasks (typically on production lines) and separation of manual and mental work (Braverman 1975). Administrative tasks were often extensively standardised too. The new control mode (Dörre and Röttger 2003; Sauer 2011) of post-Fordism often grants much more freedom to individual workers, but also exposes them to greater market risks, for example where a department can decide how to achieve its targets but its workers' pay is tied directly to its performance. Targets and internal competition (for example between permanent staff and agency workers) are the decisive instruments of this mode of control.

Dramatic as these changes were, the expected benefits for individuals, companies and national economies failed to materialise. Although moderate productivity gains were secured and profits stabilised to an extent, this occurred largely at the expense of workers. Between 1995 and 2014 the share of productivity gains accruing to labour fell in two-thirds of OECD countries (Schwellnus, Kappeler and Pionnier 2017). This stagnation of real wages was another factor making it necessary to support demand by increasing debt.

A new accumulation regime in the making[1]

The distinctions I have described between the Fordist and post-Fordist models of production are naturally strongly heuristic and obscure real existing differences in path dependencies and in the inertia of particular elements. What I am interested in here is not to produce the most detailed description of Fordism and post-Fordism, but to extract ideal-typical constellations that cast a sharper light on the contrasts with digital capitalism.

In order to grasp the dimensions, one must understand the historical arithmetic of production, accumulation and regulation. A specific mode of regulation emerges largely as the adjustment of politics and society to social problems created by the dynamics of a specific form of economy – or to use Streeck's terms, to make capitalism provisionally 'compatible with democracy'. The expansion of the welfare state and the importance of the trade unions, for example, should be understood as responses to the social unrest associated with the Taylorist production regime and the potentially highly unequal accumulation of profits. Production models and accumulation regimes are always in a race with the efforts of other social forces to rein them in. In relation to digital capitalism this means that we can describe modes of production and strategies of accumulation, but it cannot yet be assumed that there is any significantly elaborated mode of regulation for the specific problems of the digital economy – even if many such initiatives in direction can be observed.

Digital technology is almost everywhere today. But the commercial internet in the strict sense is an economic field of its own, to whose mechanisms our technology-permeated societies have only begun to adjust. The accumulation regime of digital capitalism is not yet hegemonic, and it is by no means certain it will become so (even if the ambitions and enormous power of its leading companies certainly point in that direction). What we can do is to sketch out the implications of the structures of production and accumulation in digital capitalism. Methodologically I hew to Schumpeter's analysis of industrial capitalism. He described his own method as follows:

> The best way of getting a vivid and realistic idea of industrial strategy is indeed to visualize the behavior of new concerns or industries that introduce new commodities or processes ... or else reorganize a part or the whole of an industry. (Schumpeter 2003 [1942]: 89)

Proprietary markets lie at the heart of digital capitalism. My descriptions of Fordism and post-Fordism underline the centrality of the nexus of business and regulation for analysing models of production. This applies especially to the 'digital model of production' (Nachtwey and Staab 2020); after all, the special thing about the leading companies of the commercial internet is that they are not primarily producers operating in markets, but markets in which producers operate. The concept of the 'digital platform' has emerged to describe this state of affairs. 'Platforms are digital infrastructures that enable two or more groups to interact' (Srnicek 2017: 43; see also Rochet and Tirole 2003). On platforms producers, providers, customers, advertisers etc. enter into communication processes with one another. As quasi-markets, platforms bring supply and demand together. This fact is overlooked in many typologies of the platform economy, or not treated as a theoretically relevant factor. Srnicek (2017: 49), for example, distinguishes five types of digital platform: '*advertising platforms* (e.g. Google, Facebook), ... *cloud platforms* (e.g. AWS, Salesforce), ... *industrial platforms* (e.g. GE, Siemens), ... *product platforms* (e.g. Rolls Royce, Spotify), ... [and] *lean platforms* (e.g. Uber, Airbnb)'.[2] The obvious distinction here is the profit model: advertising platforms earn money with advertising, cloud platforms by leasing digital infrastructure, industrial and product platforms by increasing productivity and transforming goods into services,[3] lean platforms by minimising fixed costs.[4] Srnicek identifies the data-driven business model as their fundamental commonality. The decisive inputs from which value is extracted are not the labour and natural resources of the industrial model, but users' data that enables the platforms to sell personalised advertising, supply appropriate infrastructure services and so on. That may be true, but it is not a statement of real analytical precision about the accumulation logic of digital platforms. Instead it risks confusing euphoric expectations of economic democratisation – which dominated early intellectual reflections on a 'cognitive capitalism' of free-flowing information (Boutang 2011) and the rise of 'social production' (Benkler 2006) – with the reality of the contemporary internet.

Another concern is much more important than trivial criticism of the vagueness of a term. Sorting the world of the digital platforms by business sector or product category paints a picture where unequal actors appear equal and ignores the power structures of the commercial internet (Schwarz 2017). Google and Apple are clearly not on the same level of the hierarchy as companies in the 'second tier' (Dolata 2018) (Netflix, Spotify or Uber for example) – still less with some medium-sized IT company in the provinces or freelance programmers in Manila. In fact, none of the companies in the second, third or fourth tiers can operate without relying on the technical ecosystem of one of the meta-platforms. What we need to understand is not so much the variety of different types of platform but the logic under which the individual elements are brought together by just a handful of companies.

If we wish to understand the structure of the commercial internet – of digital capitalism – through its key enterprises, we must first understand their logic of operation and expansion. This involves four forms of social control: information control, access control, price control and performance control.

Hierarchising the internet

The aforementioned socio-technical ecosystems, which can also be characterised as proprietary markets, form the heart of digital capitalism.[5] Socio-technical ecosystems are complexes of technical elements (hardware, software, server infrastructure), integrated into a coherent system in order to provide 'attractive all-round offers' (Dolata 2015: 515).

> Such ecosystems are not simply overarching technical infrastructures. With all their offers and services they also create social spaces in which users

shape their routines; establish specific patterns of search, communication and consumption; and develop reproducible routines of behaviour and utilisation that tie them to the offerings of a specific corporation. Switching systems remains possible, but only at the price of extensive reorganisation or even reconstitution of personal channels of expression and activity in the web. (translated from Dolata 2015: 511 f.)

These ecosystems are proprietary because they are owned or controlled by a company. They are markets because of their function of connecting supply and demand. The way leading companies of the commercial internet have become meta-platforms (Nachtwey and Staab 2020), in the sense of entities that themselves systematically integrate smaller proprietary market-places, generates dependencies: no Uber, no Spotify, no Instagram without Android or iOS. In effect the commercial internet is structured as a system of hierarchical markets where the proprietary meta-markets tower over the smaller marketplaces.

This hierarchy of markets raises interesting questions. For example one can justifiably object that there is a systematic difference between individual marketplaces, which have historically frequently been privately owned, and the overarching category that we tend to speak of as '*the market*' and is assumed to possess a certain neutrality. *The market* cannot fulfil the functions ascribed to it by neoclassical economics (match-making, pricing) if it discriminates between market participants.

From this perspective proprietary markets are always problematic in theory – but rarely in practice. A privately owned marketplace can demand fees from participants: from customers who must pay to enter, or from vendors who have to pay for a stall. The profits that accrue to the market owner are attributable more to privilege than performance (Sahr 2016). The proprietor can also create barriers that exclude consumers or producers. The market is then unable to function neutrally, potentially distorting the pricing mechanism. In especially invidious cases, proprietors may erect barriers to competition, for example by excluding particular vendors who sell products they want to sell themselves, or making rivals hard to find.

It is scale effects that turn these theoretical issues into real problems. If my son's school holds a fete and charges for stalls or asserts a monopoly on cake sales, one can discuss the moral issues involved, but nobody would treat that as a real problem. The reason is simple: because nobody really depends on that market. Customers can easily buy the same products else-where, and vendors can move to another marketplace if they object to the conditions. This also heavily constrains the possibilities for making profits from market ownership.

Four forms of control

It is a very different matter where the alternatives are heavily restricted or non-existent. Then market owners can in principle increase the margins they extract as rents from vendors, producers and customers as they wish, and decide who is permitted to access the market and on what terms. If a few market owners also control most of the supply relatively exclusively, their power to derive rents from their status is even greater. For that to happen, two conditions must be fulfilled. Firstly, something approaching the entire range of relevant goods and services must be available through the respective proprietary market. In practical terms this means that as many producers as possible – ideally all of them – must be represented in the proprietary marketplace. Whenever new products appear, they must be incorporated by the proprietary market to prevent the emergence of alternative marketplaces that would reduce the rents. It is this dynamic that generates the logic of expansion inherent to proprietary markets. Secondly, consumers must be made directly dependent on the marketplace, because it is only attractive to producers and vendors if it successfully addresses the matching problem. The logical conclusion is closure (lock-in).

Expansion and closure require a coherent set of control strategies: (1) data control seeks exclusive appropriation of market information to accumulate exclusive knowledge about supply and demand trends: this involves sophisticated systems for gathering data on prices, transactions and stocks through constant monitoring of producers and consumers. This surveillance is often what is meant in practice by the wonderful 'new business models' created by the availability of huge data sets. The 'data extractivism' of the 'surveillance capitalists' (Zuboff 2019) serves in this context primarily to ensure the functioning of their proprietary markets. Data power enables (2) effective control of access to the marketplace. On the producer side, the platforms can decide which competition they wish to admit or exclude. On the consumer side they can control who sees which offers at which prices. As well as opening up a business of its own – algorithmic pricing – this also enables the platforms to pursue the lucrative strategy of (3) price control: their power over supply allows them to manipulate competition between market participants to serve their own profit interests. For example, platform operators can decide to strategically expand supply in order to optimise consumer prices (and thus sales). But they can – and do – also exploit their market data and access to launch and systematically promote their own offers. Finally, this bundling of control power enables a fourth strategy: (4) performance control, as the ability of market operators to dictate in detail the producers' terms and conditions. One particularly visible tool is the customer reviews systematically employed by platforms to measure the quality of services and thus to enforce the platform operator's own standards of discipline on the producers.

So have the leading companies of the commercial internet already established functioning and absolutely closed proprietary markets? No, because a proprietary market is not perfect until it possesses an effective monopoly. And that is not yet entirely the case in the commercial internet. One prominent archetype of proprietary market is the app stores of the mobile internet. Here we see a global duopoly of Google (Android) and Apple (iOS). But even a duopoly can be effective. For most app developers it is irrelevant whether there are one or two app stores. Given the requirement of interoperability, they cannot afford to play one system against the other, and must offer their apps on both markets.[6] To that extent producers (app developers) in this part of the commercial internet are subject to the logic of the proprietary market despite theoretical competition between two companies.

In very general terms, the digital capitalism of the leading companies falls under the proprietary market paradigm. In the following I will deepen my analysis of the dynamics of expansion and closure, and elaborate the associated effects on the accumulation regime of digital capitalism. I will refer to examples from the five companies where the logic of proprietary markets is most prominent: Google, Apple, Amazon, Alibaba and Tencent. These illustrate the dynamism of distribution – and inequality – generated by the proprietary markets model, especially for the factor labour. They also reveal what distinguishes this emerging accumulation model from its historical predecessors.

Expansion and closure

The leading companies of the commercial internet are highly expansive business enterprises that have built extensive technical/economic networks and are highly valued, in some cases extremely profitable, and above all liquid (Table 4.1).

In 2017 Google held an astonishing US$98 billion in liquid funds; Amazon (US$74 billion) and Apple (US$144 billion) also have plenty of cash in hand. These companies can fund acquisitions from their small change. Their Chinese counterparts have caught up in terms of market valuation, but still lag behind on liquidity. Yet in comparison to many traditional manufacturers, the Chinese platforms are still awash with cash. Alibaba and Tencent have each also created a complex web of firms in China and abroad. As well as cash reserves, both firms rely on a myriad of investment vehicles such as in-house banks MyBank (Alibaba) and WeBank (Tencent).

Table 4.1 Liquid funds and market capitalisation of selected internet companies

	Liquid funds* (billion US$)	Market capitalisation (billion US$)
Google	97.585 (31 March 2020)	1,722
Facebook	61.95 (31 December 2020)	583
Amazon	73.933 (31 December 2020)	1,582
Apple	143.713 (26 September 2020)	2,954
Alibaba	69.933 (31 December 2020)	269
Tencent	33.385 (31 December 2022)	444

* Cash, cash equivalents, short-time investments.

Sources: Respective annual reports for 2020, market capitalisation as reported by *Wall Street Journal* as of 22 April 2022.

Alibaba also controls at least twelve funds,[7] through which it invests in various areas such as smart health, film and video projects, bike-sharing and much more. Here again, they have expanded their own ecosystems through investments and acquisitions (see Table A1 in the appendix).

All the named firms generate enormous turnover in their core business, which in some cases forms the only relevant source of profit. Google (80 per cent) and Facebook (98 per cent) remain extremely dependent on online advertising, a market they divide between them in large parts of the world. Amazon derives 82 per cent of its turnover from its e-commerce

Table 4.2 Internet companies: core business data 2020

Company	Google	Apple	Amazon	Alibaba	Tencent
Year ending	2020	2020	2020	2020	2020
Revenue (billion US$)	181.6	274.5	386.1	73.16	54.61
Core business	Advertising	Hardware*	E-commerce	E-commerce	Services
Turnover (billion US$)	148.7	233	317.37	62.92	29.33
Proportion (%)	80.0	84.9	82.2	86.0	53.7
R&D spending (billion US$)	22.4	15.2	42.7	7.1	4.8
Proportion of turnover (%)	15.1	6.8	11.1	8.0	8.1
Employees	135,301	147,000	1,468,000	251,462	85,858

* only iPhone, iPad, Mac.

Sources: Respective annual reports for 2020, financial data from EU Industrial R&D Investment Scoreboard 2020; US Securities and Exchange Commission 2020.

platforms – although its cloud business Amazon Web Services is considerably more profitable. Apple remains essentially a hardware manufacturer, and highly dependent on a single product (the iPhone). Alibaba's turnover comes from its core e-commerce business, and Tencent, which entered the online gaming market in 2003, still earns most of its revenue from digital services in that field. All of them achieve their economic success with a relatively small number of employees: Google has just 131,301 globally, with which it achieved a turnover of US$181 billion in 2020. By comparison Volkswagen employed 662,575 in 2020 for a turnover of about €223 billion (Volkswagen 2020).

Despite their strong focus on dominating their respective core sectors, the tech giants have come successively closer to fulfilling the first criterion of the proprietary market: availability of practically all relevant goods. Most readers of this volume can probably still remember a time when Google was just a search engine and Amazon only sold books. Today all the leading companies possess sophisticated and differentiated portfolios of products and services. The logic of expansion is reflected in their investments and acquisitions. Google alone lists more than two hundred acquisitions, from small firms bought principally for their staff and expertise to major hardware manufacturers like HTC (above all for its patents) and numerous companies purchased for important technology components (see also Table A2 in the appendix).

To understand the developments, the fact that the leading companies have become increasingly similar to one another through their acquisition strategies is more important than an exhaustive list (Dolata 2015). Google has entered the e-commerce sector with Google Shopping and invested €550 million in the second-largest Chinese platform JD.com, thus poaching in Amazon's territory (Wired Staff 2018). Google has also (like Amazon) produced its own hardware lines,[8] attempted to establish its own social network, knocked Microsoft off the top spot for browsers, and with Android developed an operating system to rival Apple's iOS. In terms of internet searches Amazon is the second most widely used search engine after Google (Pasquale 2015), and a direct competitor of YouTube via its Prime video platform. With its smart speakers (actually smart microphones) Amazon currently leads a market over which Google, Apple, Facebook and Microsoft are all also fighting. Amazon's rather successful attempts to secure a growing slice of the online advertising cake are tantamount to a declaration of war (Hirsch and Castillo 2018; Soper and Bergen 2018).

China offers a similar picture. In recent years, the three leading companies of the Chinese-style commercial internet have invested heavily in autonomous driving and artificial intelligence (AI), where they stand in direct global competition with their American rivals. Expansion and competition between the Chinese internet giants has apparently become too much even for the Communist Party, which has blocked certain economic activities, like the IPO of Alibaba's Ant Financial (Zhong 2020), and forced Tencent to limit screen time in video games for minors (Huang 2021). It has, moreover, assigned the platform giants specific sectors under the banner of maximising efficiency: Baidu for autonomous driving, Alibaba for Smart City and Tencent for health digitalisation. In light of the Party's agnostic attitude to market competition, it apparently sees more mileage in differentiating between its national champions than in going even further down the road of isomorphism.

Portfolio expansion serves first and foremost to round off and stabilise the respective ecosystem.[9] The closer a meta-platform can get to representing the totality of the market, the less likely it is to lose its customers. Dolata refers to 'lock-in strategies', achieved by reducing 'switching necessities' and increasing 'switching costs' (Haucap and Heimeshoff 2014; Dolata 2015).

We can divide the expansion of the leading companies roughly into three phases. In the first phase they created local monopolies or at least established strong market positions. Google dominated internet search, Apple secured an important slice of the hardware market, Amazon dominated Western e-commerce, Alibaba did the same (in a different organisational form) in China, Tencent established dominance in the gaming market.

The second development phase involved establishing and securing socio-technical ecosystems. Expanding on Dolata's observations, technical hierarchisation mechanisms that enable platforms to subordinate other providers are key to successful control of such ecosystems. In the current cycle combining hardware and operating system is the decisive mode, which is why the operators of operating systems (in other words Google and Apple) have been able to build true meta-platforms. Amazon has long been aware of this problem, while Google's lack of hardware is a weakness. Both have made efforts to gain a foothold in the smartphone and tablet markets. It is also important to systematically expand the material base, the gateways into the respective ecosystem: from PCs to smartphones and tablets to smart home devices like speaker/microphones and soon cars. Occasional cross-subsidies between GAFA companies stand in the same context: it has been reported that Google paid Apple US$15 billion in 2021 to remain the default search engine on Apple's devices (up from US$3 billion in 2017) (Moreno 2021). Google has already secured a place for Android in fully networked cars made by several traditional manufacturers (Plass-Fleßenkämper 2017).

Cloud, AI, fintech – infrastructures of proprietary markets

When building their socio-technical ecosystems, the meta-platforms also attempt to incorporate as much as possible of the product portfolio of the commercial internet. The effect of this strategy has been to make the leading companies increasingly similar, as they launch competing products and services rather than concentrating on their core business. Expanding their in-house offer is just one step towards becoming equivalent to the market. In recent years the acquisitions of all the leading companies have concentrated principally on cloud capacity, virtual assistants and fintech (financial technologies, in particular proprietary payment systems).

The key to understanding the current third wave of expansion lies in these strategies. Once one has understood that the leading companies are essentially platforms, and that platforms are structured as markets in a deeply fundamental sense, it becomes clear that these three fields of expansion are more than simply additional product categories. Cloud, AI and fintech are not equivalent to video services, music streaming or e-mail accounts. These are not simply new goods or services to be added to the ecosystem. They are crucial *infrastructure* for proprietary markets.

Fintech applications, in particular proprietary payment systems, complete the profile of the individual platforms at the consumer interface. They make it possible to control payments and to use the accumulated data to develop secondary products such as credit ratings and consumer loans: to generate new sources of revenue and expand their own product portfolio. The models are Alibaba and Tencent, each of which possesses an army of fintech subsidiaries. The most prominent aspect of their respective proprietary finance complexes are the payment systems Alipay and WeChat Pay. In 2020 the former reported an incredible 1.2 billion registered users, while the latter was not far behind with 1.0 billion (Statista 2021). The Alipay/ WeChat Pay duopoly has the Chinese mobile payments market almost completely under its control (T. Chen 2017; Shao 2018).

Controlling payments through proprietary systems offers platforms two crucial benefits. Firstly, they collect transaction fees that increase their revenues. Given the enormous transaction volumes, this is certainly economically relevant: around US\$9 trillion in China in 2016 (T. Chen 2017), rising to about US\$13 trillion in 2017 (A. Shen 2018) and projected to reach US\$97 trillion by 2023 (Rolfe 2019). Secondly, payment systems integrate consumers, and even more so vendors and producers, directly into the proprietary markets.

Cloud applications are another central infrastructure element. They permit successive integration of product and service portfolios by securing and expanding information control. The leading companies' data centres become the locus where they store and process all their market-relevant user data. No ecosystem today functions without this infrastructure operating in the background. To draw an analogy to industrial society, this is the equivalent of a system where a handful of companies each construct their own – only slightly overlapping – road networks complete with service stations, which they claim connect the whole of society. Many other companies cannot do business without access to these systems, which they must pay to use. Returning to the real (online) world, the platforms expand their power by connecting their digital systems with the analogue infrastructure. Rounding off the analogy, in a world of fully networked cars the digital companies may soon also control the data of the masses of autonomous vehicles that we are told will soon be rolling the roads.

The analogy is by no means far-fetched, if we realise that the leading companies have successively appropriated parts of the high-speed data networks that are required to make effective use of the cloud. Google led the way in 2010 with a trans-Pacific cable linking the United States with Japan (Weise 2016), and since 2016 the platforms have stepped up their construction and purchases of fibre optic cable. By September 2018 almost 16 per cent of the global total of 1.2 million kilometres of submarine cable were at least partly owned by one or more of the leading companies. Google alone controls 8.5 per cent of global undersea cables, and the GAFA companies have purchased capacity accounting for at least another 2 per cent.[10] And these figures cover only publicly reported investments. According to Alan Mauldin, director of the market research institute TeleGeography, it must be assumed that they already control more, or plan to do so (Weise 2016). Occasionally the rival tech firms also cooperate (*coopetition*). For example, in 2016 Google and Facebook jointly funded a cable between Hong Kong and Los Angeles (Wired Staff 2016), and Facebook and Microsoft laid a trans-Atlantic cable in 2017 (Weise 2016; Ong 2017).

Infrastructure is even more important now that the consensus on net neutrality has crumbled.[11] Owning it makes the leading companies independent of network operators whose data transfer charges would otherwise eat into their profits. And by building their own proprietary infrastructure the GAFA companies can successively squeeze out the network operators.

As well as increasing numbers of businesses, states and other institutions have come to depend on this infrastructure. This development is exemplified by the staggering growth of the leading cloud provider Amazon Web Services (AWS), which as of 2022 held 33 per cent of the global cloud market (followed by Microsoft, Google and Alibaba) (Canalysis and Statista 2022). The long list of businesses and organisations using AWS underlines its centrality to the global digital infrastructure. By its own account, Amazon has had more than one million customers ranging from prominent 'old economy' corporations like Kellogg's, Unilever and BMW to NASA, the United Nations and the US Department of Defense.

Today AWS is vital for other digital companies. Its customers in this field include German business software powerhouse SAP, the lodging platform Airbnb and the video streaming service Netflix, which routes its entire traffic through AWS. But its significance is even broader: Americans learned on 8 February 2017 just how important Amazon's private infrastructure has become for the entire commercial internet, when services like Netflix, Spotify, Tinder, Dropbox and thousands of others were blacked out for four hours. What had happened? Someone at AWS had 'mistyped', accidentally taking more servers offline than planned. This went down as the day 'half the internet went offline'; one could just as well say that most of the market disappeared for four hours.

The buzzword of artificial intelligence also becomes a little more tangible if we examine how it is employed by the leading companies of digital capitalism. The term AI is used in two different senses: as a metaphor for the successive networking of objects and processes by algorithms, where it encompasses almost anything done by a programmer; but also in a narrower sense, where we use AI to refer to processes of machine learning.

In machine learning, algorithms relatively independently search large data sets (big data) for patterns (correlations) and draw conclusions from the results. Big data is the basis (input) for this technology, and it is the leading companies that control the big data sets. Correspondingly, public concern about AI is closely associated with the possibility that the leading internet companies at the technological cutting edge might bring this new 'general purpose technology' (Brynjolfsson and McAfee 2014) under their exclusive control.

The leading companies are indeed investing heavily in AI-capable infrastructure for their research departments and data centres, leveraging the systematic relationship between computing power and AI (Hwang 2018). As well as expanding their server capacity, they are also investing in developing their own AI chips (Gurman and Frier 2018). The objective of this infrastructure expansion is not just to introduce a new product category or component (even if this is naturally still an important aspect). The real point is to successively lock in their proprietary markets by occupying yet another consumer interface. Ever larger parts of the rest of the economy become dependent on the meta-platforms.

On the consumer side this development is most visible in the most concrete uses of AI: voice assistants and chatbots that round off and expand the leading companies' market profiles. The point of these tools is to make it even easier for consumers to operate in the proprietary markets, to eliminate one of the last advantages of bricks-and-mortar retail: spoken interaction. In the form of smart microphones like Amazon's Echo, the Apple

HomePod and the Google Home devices, the leading companies are advancing ever further into their customers' private lives. The market for these devices has absolutely exploded, especially in the United States where smart speaker sales tripled between 2016 and 2017 alone (Associated Press 2017); by spring 2018 every fifth US household already owned one (Perez 2018). In 2021 global sales of smart speakers grew to 39 million units compared to 9 million in 2018 (Canalys 2018; Strategy Analytics 2021).

Google and Amazon still dominate the market, with a combined market share of just under 50 per cent. But the competition from Apple and the Chinese companies Baidu and Alibaba, with about 10 per cent each, has increased strongly (Strategy Analytics 2021).

No *alternative*

In the mobile sector of the commercial internet the lock-in is already well advanced. By occupying central infrastructure functions, the app store operators Google and Apple in particular have succeeded in creating proprietary markets where suppliers and consumers have no alternative in practical terms. This is reflected in the rapid growth of supply. Almost all the 2.6 million applications in Google Play come from third-party developers. The number of apps offered has increased seventyfold since 2010 (Figure 4.3). Apple's App Store has grown even more strongly.

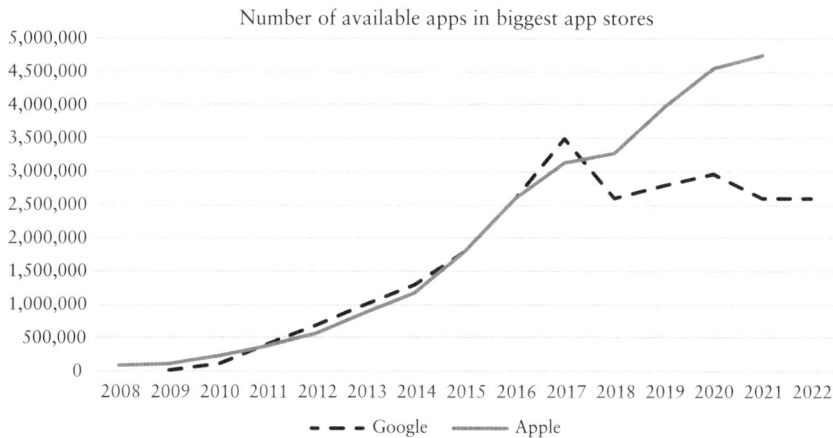

Number of available apps in biggest app stores

Figure 4.3 Google Play vs. Apple App Store I
Source: Pocket Gamer 2022; AppBrain 2022.

Note: The dip in the line for Google reflects massive deletions conducted in summer 2018 to remove clones and malware. That also represents an example of the company's almost unlimited power to control what is sold in its app store.

Revenue in billion US$ **Revenue of the largest app stores**   Percentage share of total
sales

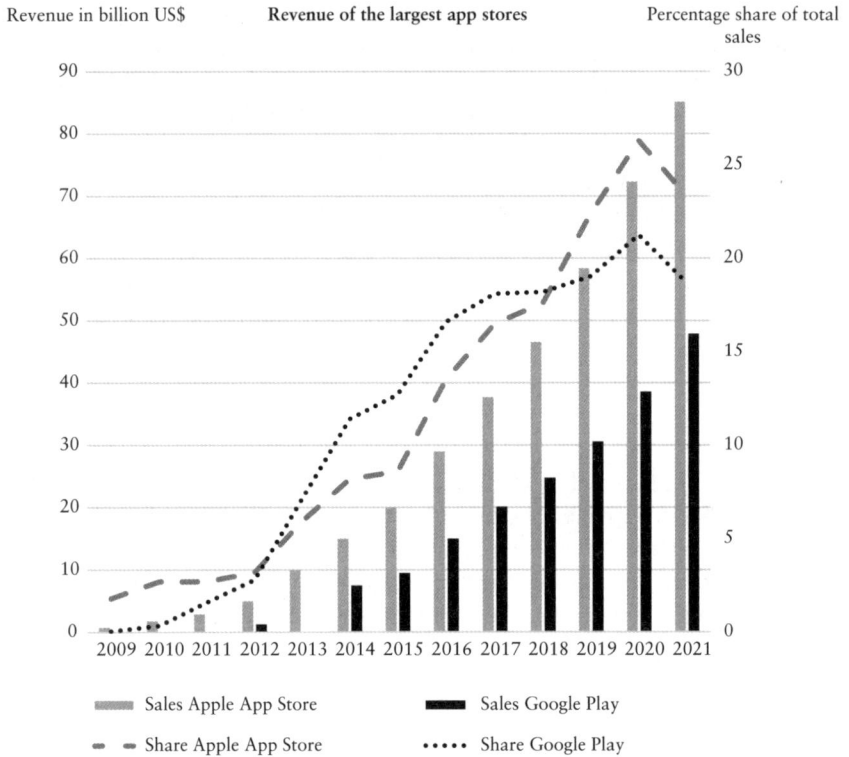

Figure 4.4 Google Play vs. Apple App Store II
Source: Iqbal 2023.

Although Apple in particular gained a reputation for removing third-party apps for business reasons, the real trend points in the other direction: unbroken growth. And increasing sales in their app stores meant market ownership rents for Google and Apple (Figure 4.4).

Google's Play accounted for 18.6 per cent of the company's total turnover in 2021. It is much the same with Apple. The analysts' fixation on Apple's hardware, which still accounts for the lion's share of its profits, tends to obscure the real capitalist innovation.

App stores could be said to be the archetype of the proprietary market in the commercial internet, where the logic of economic rents through market ownership is most clearly observed. Apple for example keeps 30 per cent of every financial transaction that passes through its proprietary system – as market ownership rent. But this development is by no means restricted to the operating system owners Google and Apple, where it is materialised particularly clearly in the respective app stores. A successive integration of third-party vendors is also under way in Amazon's Marketplace. The first Marketplace, where other traders offer their wares, was created in the United States in 2000. Today there are twenty national Amazon Marketplaces.[12] Amazon's fees for third-party vendors using its proprietary market vary depending on which tasks Amazon fulfils for them. The Amazon Marketplace has been growing uninterruptedly for years. In 2021, as in prior years, it attracted more than one million new third-party vendors globally, about 3,000 per day (O'Connor 2022). Through Amazon they sold goods worth US$390 billion, a year on year increase of 30 per cent (Kaziukènas 2021). Vendors from China and Hong Kong have joined Amazon's market in droves, underlining the extent to which the meta-platforms have become global markets. Amazon offers Asian sellers a relatively unique means of accessing many Western consumer markets (Dunne 2019). Practically speaking, they have no alternative, even if Alibaba also has a foot in the door (for example via its consumer platform AliExpress). Between 2019 and 2022 third-party vendors accounted for about 50–60 per cent of all units sold via the Marketplace (Marketplace Pulse 2022).

This expansion is also reflected in the number of available products and categories. While Amazon began in 1995 as a platform selling only books, it is today probably easier to list the consumer goods that are not sold through Amazon. The charges for their market presence are not the only aspect where producers feel the power of this empire. It is an open secret that, especially in lucrative sectors, Amazon evaluates the performance of particular products with an eye to copying them and removing the third-party vendor from its own ecosystem (Tilley and Anand 2018). The same practice is also documented for China's second largest e-commerce company, JD.com (C. Chen 2018). Amazon pursues a similar tactic with its web services, frequently promoting third-party products before eventually launching its own (Tilley and Anand 2018).

The impact of the platforms' financial firepower is especially strong in the area where economic theory would expect new competitors to be emerging: the start-ups. Amazon's Alexa Fund, for example, invested in new firms developing applications for Amazon's voice-controlled speaker. The fund was designed to allow Amazon, as the primary investor, to secure control over firms operating on the periphery of its socio-technical ecosystem (performance control and information control); for example investment can be tied to purchase options. If a valuable company ultimately decides not to sell to Amazon, Amazon wins twice over: it cashes in on its stake and can still exploit the acquired expertise to copy the product (Tilley and Anand 2018).

Amazon's most important global rival, Alibaba, operates exclusively through third-party vendors and offers no products of its own. Instead it makes its e-commerce profits exclusively through fees and advertising.

This is another gigantic expansion story, where Alibaba's multi-platform e-commerce network is not only active in retail, but also operates a kind of wholesale platform and much more.[13] Alibaba's e-commerce business is gigantic, recording US$84.54 billion in sales on 'Singles Day' alone in 2021 (Kharpal 2021). Founder Jack Ma's ambitions peaked in his pet project, the 'electronic World Trade Platform' (eWTP). Before announcing his retirement from Alibaba in 2018, Ma propagated the idea of a global e-commerce platform for 'small' businesses (annual turnover under US$1 million) that would exempt them from duties and taxes and ensure that their consignments pass quickly through customs.

By integrating small and medium-sized traders into a global infrastructure Ma was seeking to make his own company into a global market. One could hardly formulate the claim to ownership of the market more baldly. The project also plays a key role in the state-led Belt and Road Initiative, the global infrastructure project to expand China's global trade routes and in the long term reduce its chronic economic overcapacity (H. Shen 2018: 2693). According to Hong Shen (2018) the 'Digital Silk Road' and the company Alibaba are virtually identical.

The second leading Chinese company, Tencent, is also a complex network of firms, platforms and services. Like all the leading companies, Tencent's rise was based on a specific corner of the commercial internet, in this case a messenger. Today Tencent is the world's largest gaming business in terms of turnover, with steadily growing electronic commerce and online advertising operations.

From its economic base in online gaming, Tencent has integrated ever larger parts of China's commercial internet into its proprietary system through countless strategic investments and acquisitions.[14] In the process it has expanded its activities into social networks, ride-hailing, cloud services and digital banking. Recent years have seen open investment rivalry between Tencent and Alibaba, concentrating above all on China and Southeast Asia. In 2016 alone Tencent spent US$6.3 billion on this race, while Alibaba invested US$5.6 billion (Cendrowski 2015). That is more than the total venture capital investment in the whole of Europe in the same period (OECD 2017a: 125). In the process Tencent's priorities have shifted from its traditional domain of online gaming to commerce and business services for the participants in its proprietary market (T. Chen 2018) – a sign of the company's growing integration around its central platforms.

The heart of Tencent is the 'super app' WeChat. WeChat is at first glance only a messenger like Facebook's WhatsApp. In fact it is a proprietary marketplace with infrastructure functions (Plantin and de Seta 2019), encompassing practically all the products and services of the commercial internet. Its developer claims it has 'no competitor but itself' (Deng 2019: n.p.).

By 2022 WeChat had more than 1.3 billion users, almost all of them in China (Tencent 2022). Numerous providers operate integrated mobile stores within the application, in effect sub-platforms to which Tencent controls access. In 2017 more than 10 million businesses, as well as 'entrepreneurial individuals' (Bude 2001) like celebrities and journalists, had such official accounts (Mittal 2017). And, in a clear indication of the centrality of financial applications, the number of third-party vendors in the Tencent ecosystem more than quintupled after the introduction of the proprietary payment system WePay. This has led to a rapid growth of financial transactions on WeChat. In 2016 the number of users shopping on WeChat doubled, more than 300,000 'offline' shops used WeChat Pay, and more than 200 million users had registered their bank details on WeChat. Like other leading companies, Tencent pulls no punches when dealing with competition in its own ecosystem. Rivals are unceremoniously banned from its social media app WeChat, especially where they challenge Tencent's information control by promising stricter data privacy standards (Deng 2019).[15]

The WeChat model represents a structural challenge to the other leading companies. Transactions conducted in sub-applications within the WeChat app are beyond the reach of the app store revenue systems, as implemented by Google and Apple. But the operating system operators cannot afford to simply exclude such a popular application from their stores.

Why proprietary markets?

Let us return for a moment to the question from the beginning of the chapter: why do proprietary markets exist? And why have they appeared now? The simplest answer is that it is merely a matter of technical and economic feasibility, emerging through the nexus of financial firepower and the historical contingencies of path-dependent politico-economic, technological and market developments. All these are indeed enabling factors, as laid out in this and the preceding chapters. From a historical perspective the two intrinsic problems of contemporary capitalism outlined at the beginning of this chapter stand out: the problem of superabundance (supply side), which only grows as the digital transformation progresses, and the systematic problems of market saturation (demand side) experienced by the advanced OECD economies since the 1970s.

Proprietary markets and the problem of superabundance

As far as economic sociology is concerned, markets are concerned with 'exchange of scarce things' (Sahr 2017a: 148). Indeed, scarcity or restricted availability is a necessary condition for market exchange processes to emerge at all (Sahr 2017a: 148). The point about proprietary markets is that they are the cause of scarcity, not its effect. They solve the problem of superabundance by restricting access to goods.

To recap briefly, the prophets of post-capitalism see digitalisation of the economy as the beginning of the end of capitalism. The marginal costs of most products fall as digitalisation progresses. Rifkin for example assumes that digital technologies will revolutionise energy and manufacturing: solar panels on every roof, feeding electricity to fully automated factories. The marginal costs of producing goods in these factories will fall successively towards zero. The products consist of superabundant components, and are increasingly difficult to sell profitably. These superabundant goods have real existing precursors in many of the commodities of today's commercial internet: music and video files, e-books and other documents, software, video games, information and so on. In fact we are already dealing with a logic of relative superabundance today, resulting simply from the scale effects of an almost global distribution structure, the internet. If a digital product can be accessed globally and reproduced for marginal costs of practically zero, the (potentially large) initial costs incurred in its development pale with every additional free copy.

One can argue that this theoretical perspective skates over the complexities of digitalisation. Of course any attempt to develop a theory will be open to accusations of oversimplification. I do believe, however, that the conceptualisation of the commercial internet as an economy of superabundance is largely correct and begs the question of how exactly its leading companies have been able to become the growth engine of a capitalism plagued by stagnation. The answer is that proprietary markets are based not on scarcity but on strategies to solve the problem of superabundance: they are instruments for creating an artificial shortage of potentially superabundant goods.

One effect of the socio-technical ecosystems is to generate systematic lock-in strategies on the demand side (the consumers) (Dolata 2015). Such efforts to tie users more tightly into a proprietary system go hand in hand with an ever-expanding offering to reduce 'switching necessities'. If one can use all the products of the commercial internet through a single locus, for example in the Android universe, there is simply no need to leave it. The strategy of subsidisation, as described in Chapter 3, is used to promote the expansion of proprietary markets and also boosts this dynamic. Not only do consumers have no need to leave a proprietary system; the goods themselves are frequently highly subsidised or even supplied for free (on the basis of secondary use), especially in the expansion phase.

On the demand side, this has made the meta-platforms in particular increasingly equivalent to the market itself. Because they tend to have exclusive access to specific consumer segments, they can dictate – on the supply side – terms to producers. In other words, producers are denied relevant access to consumers unless they agree to the conditions of the respective proprietary market.

Before we move on to the opportunities for market-owning businesses to accrue economic profit, it is central to understand that this construction of market relationships represents an attempt to solve the problem of super-abundance. By assuming the market function for their users (or 'becoming the market'), the meta-platforms in particular gain leverage to control the supply side. It no longer matters that particular products are potentially available in abundance, because their price and thus profit results not from scarcity of supply but from a logic of access control: the power to decide whether goods are made available at all. For example it is irrelevant that an app can be copied at zero cost if consumers can only access it through a specific system. By controlling the distribution channels (the market function), proprietary markets are in principle able to restrict supply as they please.

The underlying lock-in strategies are systematically connected with the four forms of control that are fundamentally characteristic of proprietary markets: *data control* secures exclusivity of market information by quantifying and analysing stocks, prices and transactions. Automated surveillance of users of specific ecosystems makes it possible to precisely calculate demand trends and attract producers with the promise of especially efficient market access (and thus to sweeten their structural subordination to the dictates of the market owners). *Access control* enables the meta-platforms to adjust supply and/or demand. They decide which offers consumers get to see. They also possess the power to restrict or even sever access to consumers if a supplier refuses to accept the relevant conditions. Thus, as well as making superabundant goods artificially scarce, proprietary markets also make it possible to dictate 'market prices' to producers (*price control*). The platforms can also set and enforce standards for the traded goods (*performance control*).

All in all, the platforms ensure that they are the biggest beneficiaries of this system. The ability to control supply makes the digital capitalism of the platforms more hypercapitalism than post-capitalism. The ability to derive profit from goods that are actually superabundant opens up the possibility of generating unearned revenue – which is the definition of economic rent (for more on this see Chapter 6).

Proprietary markets and the rationalisation of consumption

Returning to the political economy of post-Fordism, the problem of super-abundance only covers one of the two dynamics to which digital capitalism offers answers in the form of the proprietary market model. The structural weakness of demand that has plagued capitalism since the end of the Fordist expansion – its 'consumption problem' (Staab 2016) – remains at first glance untouched by the strategies described above.

In fact the digital capitalism of the commercial internet offers only a rather dubious 'solution' to the problems of market saturation. Nevertheless the economic promise explains part of the hype that has emerged in the past ten years around the leading companies. The functionality of these technologically optimised markets makes these companies into machines of *rationalisation of consumption*.

The economic crisis of Fordism is intimately bound up with initial saturation effects that appeared in the early 1970s in the highly developed economies. To put it in a nutshell, by some point the new middle classes of the post-war era had acquired all the relevant durable goods they needed, and sales suffered. The answers developed within the system failed to provide any long-term relief. Wage suppression reduced demand just when it was most needed. Globalisation of production brought growing competition with new rivals in emerging economies and developing countries, and slashed the prices of many products (and thus also the profits of established manufacturers). This juncture marked the transition from the producer markets of Fordism to the consumer markets of post-Fordism (Nachtwey and Staab 2020). The mechanism still operates today, where the smartphone markets supply ever cheaper products at ever higher quality, while few hardware manufacturers – Apple excepted – manage to make any relevant profits.

That was the situation into which the meta-platforms of the commercial internet emerged, with a very different economic programme. The economic significance of new technologies is generally held to be increasing productivity. In this understanding, manufacturers increase their profits by rationalising production, by employing increasingly efficient methods. Paul Krugman speaks for most economists when he asserts: 'Productivity isn't everything, but in the long run it is almost everything. A country's ability to improve its standard of living over time depends almost entirely on its ability to raise its output per worker' (Krugman 1999: 11). Yet it still remains contested whether the implementation of digital technologies since the 1970s actually made any meaningful contribution at all to labour productivity and economic growth (Gordon 2012, 2016).

Proprietary markets, on the other hand, are, in a very deep sense, consumer-oriented rather than production-led. Their function is to bring producers and consumers together. The ace up their sleeve is more or less exclusive access to the consumers, who they tie ever more tightly into their proprietary systems through lock-in strategies. The growth of the leading companies of the commercial internet is, in other words, based not on productivity gains but on their implicit promise of generating surplus profits in the sphere of consumption. Online advertising (Google, Facebook, Amazon), e-commerce (Amazon) and new distribution channels (platforms, app stores) – until recently the absolutely decisive sources of the leading companies' profits – are all driven by an expectation of generating consumption that would not otherwise be realised. Three methodological strategies stand out: universalisation/ acceleration, recursivity and individualisation of consumption.

Firstly, the digital technologies of the leading companies have facilitated an enormous acceleration of consumption processes: on the underground, on the toilet, in the lunch break – with a smartphone, shopping is never more than a click away. The goods are delivered to the door the same day. This lends market-equivalent internet companies competitive advantages over traditional retail. For example, consumers can use e-commerce websites anywhere, any time. No inconvenient opening hours, no time-consuming trips to crowded shopping centres. Stationary retail thus becomes a comparably 'inefficient' locus of consumption. One of its last advantages is its immediacy, where customers take their purchases straight home with no need to wait. That explains the e-commerce companies' obsession with same-day delivery.

Of course no stationary retailer can keep up with the centralisation of supply afforded by the e-commerce giants. Amazon for example provides not just a sheer endless range of material products on its website, but also various streaming services, digital products like e-books and even flexible labour through crowdworking platforms like Amazon Mechanical Turk and Amazon Home Services.

The point of universalising access and supply and accelerating consumption is to reduce the inefficiencies of older distribution systems, which the new options offered by the proprietary markets suddenly leave looking highly inconvenient. The overarching economic goal of this practice can be framed as a programme of intensification of consumption, whose implicit promise is to sell more products through more efficient distribution processes – which would be tantamount to solving the consumption problem.

The same applies, secondly, to the increasingly radical individualisation of the sphere of consumption, in particular in the context of online advertising. The rationalisation strategies pursued here reflect a dynamic trialled in manufacturing since the early 1980s. As the Fordist expansion faded and the markets for standardised mass products began to exhibit signs of saturation, manufacturers responded by individualising their products. The idea was that people might be quicker to replace their shoes, cars or whatever if the respective replacements were felt to be more personal. Manufacturers sought to apply the sociological insight that, as well as simply satisfying needs, consumption serves above all to distinguish through differentiation (Bourdieu 1982; Veblen 1986 [1899]). By the 1980s this process was already so advanced in parts of the car industry that, for example, no two identical cars left the production line at Volkswagen's Wolfsburg plant on any given day (Streeck 2012: 32).

The promise of proprietary markets – to identify ever more specific preferences (potential acts of consumption) through their proprietary technologies of data control – therefore fell on the fertile ground of an economy whose problems were located precisely in the transition from product development to real consumption. The leading companies of the commercial internet now promised to follow up the individualisation of production with a corresponding individualisation of consumption; to sell products to customers who would not otherwise have felt they needed them. The implicit promise was the generation of additional consumption that would not have existed without the infrastructure of the proprietary markets.

Thirdly, the data gathered through advertising, purchasing processes and virtually any interaction in the internet (data control) generates a recursive process that strengthens customer loyalty. The vendor and the potential customer remain in permanent contact, mostly without the customer even noticing. This enables the vendor to immediately identify and capitalise on trends in taste and fashion. The digital 'prosumer' (Ritzer and Jurgenson 2010; O'Neil andFrayssé 2015) is also part and parcel of the successive integration of consumers into the production process, whether by using their feedback to modify products already in the development phase or websites where consumers configure their own fashion.

When consumers spend hours designing an Ikea kitchen or a Nike or Adidas trainer, the companies in question are not only gathering useful data. They are also building customer loyalty, for example where a personalised shoe makes it into the online store. Ultimately such practices create social relations between companies and their customers – and promise to secure consumers' future purchases. Media theorists even speak in this connection of a 'new political economy of subjectivation', whose principal purpose is 'to sell commodities, manipulate moods, inject ideologies, and influence behaviors' (Langlois and Elmer 2019: 236).

Privatised Keynesianism reloaded

In this respect digital capitalism stands in the tradition of post-Keynesian demand stimulation, described by Colin Crouch as 'privatised Keynesianism': private consumer debt in particular has risen since the 1980s to sustain demand and fill the gap left by the stagnation of wages. The privatised Keynesianism 2.0 of the leading digital companies and their ilk has emulated certain aspects of credit-driven demand stimulus, for example when their subsidiaries act as consumer lenders. To date, it must be said, the demand stimulation has consisted above all in the subsidisation of consumption by venture capital, cross-subsidisation using profits generated elsewhere (for example when advertising revenues fund Google's free services) and the cannibalisation of 'analogue' competitors (for example when e-commerce with its much smaller margins bleeds stationary retail dry). Nevertheless the longer objective of the rationalisation of consumption – as in the credit-driven model – is naturally to maximise private consumption. The outlined strategies can therefore be understood in macroeconomic terms as another attempt to expand private demand.

Of course these strategies can only drive economic growth if they actually activate reservoirs of untapped demand – if people spend money that would not otherwise enter the circulation of goods. In relation to private demand the prime candidates are savings and wealth. But great wealth – unlike low and middle incomes, which generally flow directly into consumption – usually ends up elsewhere. Nothing in the strategies of the leading companies of digital capitalism suggests that is going to change any time soon:

> When wages are stagnant or even falling in real terms, with obvious negative effects on private demand, the digital strategies of rationalisation of consumption are rather akin to fishing in increasingly overfished waters. Employing the most advanced electric nets in conjunction with stupendously detailed knowledge about fish populations permits the leading companies of the commercial internet to secure an ever greater share of the catch. But this contributes exactly nothing to increasing fish stocks. One fisher's gain is the others' loss. (translated from Staab 2017: 50 f.)

Market control and rent extraction

The rationalisation of mechanisms of consumption is not conceived in the first place as an instrument for promoting general prosperity, but above all as a vehicle for acquiring competitive advantages: for the platforms over their traditional competitors, such as stationary retail; and for the involved producers over those who have stuck too long with outmoded distribution channels. So it is unsurprising that the strategies of rationalisation of consumption coincided with the expansion of the proprietary ecosystems. The real profit calculation in this model comes to the fore with the successive consolidation of the power of the leading companies. It is driven not by reciprocal benefits for producers and market owners, but by the market control of the meta-platforms.

Rationalisation of consumption is only one of the strategies the leading companies pursue in response to market saturation and the associated 'secular stagnation' (Summers 2013) of advanced capitalism. Proprietary markets are essentially structures for extracting economic rents. As markets themselves, secured by the aforementioned control technologies, they are able to siphon off profits from the producer side in the form of fees and secondary use. Market saturation and the growing problems of underconsumption in the economy as a whole also play into their hands. The more saturated markets are, the greater the incentive for producers to heed the leading companies' promises of efficient distribution and the development of hitherto untapped sources of demand. The more complete the proprietary markets become through expansion and closure, the greater their power over the producers. Ultimately this dynamic points to a situation where the interplay of the driving forces of the political economy and the strategies of the leading companies makes the latter so powerful that very few producers can even afford to ask to negotiate their terms of participation. It follows that in a system of proprietary markets the leading companies can basically set their own margins at will. What is there to prevent Google or Apple keeping 40 rather than 30 per cent of app store revenues? Any entity with the power to set its own margins can enjoy bountiful profits and exorbitant growth even under conditions of stagnation – as long as political regulation does not interfere.

I will examine the effects of this logic in greater detail in Chapter 6. For the moment we note that this characteristic is also the starting point for distinguishing between digital capitalism and (post-)Fordism, following regulation theory, as the dominant accumulation pattern has also shifted with the rise of the proprietary markets. Its functional logic differs fundamentally both from the producer-structured marketplaces of Fordism and from the markets of post-Fordism, which were characterised by an expansion of real competition between firms (Nachtwey and Staab 2020). Whereas Fordist producers determined supply, prices, and thus their own margins, post-Fordism was more consumer-driven (Crouch 2009; de Grazia 2016). Supplier and buyer were able to choose between alternative marketplaces, which tended to strengthen the market mechanism (Nachtwey and Staab 2020). A system of proprietary markets, on the other hand, is based on the logic of trader markets, where the meta-platforms themselves define the rules of the competition they host, and thus structure the market mechanism to their own advantage. As already laid out above, what we are dealing with at present is at most an accumulation regime *in the making*, although it is already making significant inroads.

Understanding proprietary markets

As different as the various leading companies of the commercial internet might appear at first glance, they all share a structural similarity. They all follow a development model that can be characterised as a proprietary market. After establishing monopoly dominance in a particular subfield of the commercial internet, each leading company has pursued a radical expansion strategy. Firstly, they systematically expanded their offering through acquisitions and investment until they controlled access to all products and services traded in the internet, and to the data gathered in the process. Secondly, they acquired ever more consumers for their ecosystems, making the platforms increasingly attractive to third-party vendors. Additionally they have invested massively in securing their market functions by creating their own infrastructures to protect their control over the relevant data and strengthen their ability to control access, prices and performance.

The leading companies of the commercial internet are less producers operating in markets than markets operating on producers. This is the source of most of their power. As market owners they oversee – in growing sections of the economy – who is admitted to the market and under what conditions (access control). Their profit model lies in exploiting this privilege to extract economic rents. The combination of proprietary infrastructure with scalable digital goods enables the market function to be expanded – theoretically infinitely – at minimal marginal cost. Profits from market ownership thus tend to be unearned income. The latest fields of investment – cloud, AI and fintech – expand and complete the market function.

The logic of proprietary markets applies in one way or another to all the companies of the GAFA complex, although none of them can be reduced entirely to this. Google still dominates online search, but it has always fulfilled a market function as a mediator between information producers (such as newspapers), information consumers and advertisers. With its Play Store, Google also possesses one of the most highly developed proprietary markets in the mobile internet. Apple appears at first glance to be the company most like a conventional manufacturer, deriving as it does the bulk of its profits from the sale of digital devices. But Apple was also a pioneer of the new profit model with its iPod and the attached iTunes store; its App Store is not only the quintessence of a comprehensive proprietary market, but also a rapidly growing and increasingly important source of profit. Facebook is a social network, but has also become the decisive purveyor of news and information to its users (Grieco 2017) – which has upturned power relations in the media (Caplan and boyd 2018; Nechushtai 2018). Amazon's primary source of profit is its cloud services, while its original base, the e-commerce platform, represents a proprietary market par excellence.

The point is not to reduce the leading companies of the commercial internet to their role as proprietary markets. The crucial point about the model is that it describes an empirically incomplete but historically significant motion within the inexorable process of capitalist transformation. Like the dynamics of capital that shape the digital economy, the proprietary markets model represents a programme for radicalising social inequality, systematically shifting gains from income to wealth, from producers and their employees to platforms and their owners.

Notes

1 The following contextualisation of the commercial internet within the frame of regulation theory is based on a paper co-authored with Oliver Nachtwey (Nachtwey and Staab 2020).
2 Essentially Rolls-Royce now leases jet engines rather than selling them.
3 Industrial platforms use data extracted from their production and products to generate and sell new services (for example remote servicing packages for machines with predictive maintenance capability) or to convert their entire business model from sale to leasing (for example where a car manufacturer operates a car-sharing fleet accessed through a proprietary platform).
4 For example Airbnb has no hotels, Uber and other ride-sharing platforms own no vehicles.
5 The evidence underlying the discussion in this section is drawn largely from the work of Ulrich Dolata, in particular his paper 'Volatile Monopole: Konzentration, Konkurrenz und Innovationsstrategien der Internetkonzerne' (2015). My own contributions relate to: the temporal dimension (updating post-2014); the selection of cases (adding data from leading Chinese companies); the interpretative level (where there are significant differences between Dolata's original findings and mine); and integrating Dolata's ideas into my own theory.
6 The apps have to function on both Android and Apple devices.
7 Alibaba publishes very little information on its investment funds. My team worked to aggregate publicly accessible data. Table A1 in the appendix provides a brief overview of Alibaba's known investment funds.
8 Google Pixel (smartphones, tablets and laptops) and Amazon Fire and Kindle (smartphones, tablets and e-readers).
9 Table A2 in the appendix provides a summary of the fields where Google, Apple, Amazon, Alibaba and Tencent are expanding their product portfolios.
10 Author's calculations from 2019 using data from TeleGeography (online: www.submarinecablemap.com) as well as Mauldin 2017 and Zimmer 2018.
11 'Net neutrality' means that network providers are prohibited from discriminating between users. Data from the blogger in the basement moves just as fast as traffic from Google, Amazon and Netflix.
12 Australia, Brazil, Canada, China, France, Germany, India, Italy, Japan, Mexico, Netherlands, Poland, Saudia Arabia, Singapore, Spain, Sweden, Turkey, United Arab Emirates, United Kingdom, United States.
13 The network comprises: Alibaba.com (international B2B platform), 1688.com (Chinese B2B platform), AliExpress (international B2C platform; Chinese

traders sell to international customers), Taobao (Chinese C2C platform), Tmall (Chinese B2C platform), Tmall Global (international B2C platform; international traders sell to Chinese customers), Juhuasuan (B2C platform for flash sales), Lazada (B2C platform in Southeast Asia).

14 A total of 265 investments since the company was founded, of which 123 were as lead investor (Dowling 2018).

15 In response to the growing power of Alibaba and Tencent, the Chinese Communist Party has introduced a whole range of regulations since 2021. New competition rules for tech companies specifically target Alibaba and Tencent, while China also passed its first comprehensive data protection legislation. At the beginning of 2022, it was announced that government regulator CAC would impose far-reaching transparency requirements, including rules concerning the algorithms that form the heart of the platform economy (Kharpal 2022).

5

Work in digital capitalism

Proprietary markets act in two directions: on the producers and on the consumers. For all the justified criticisms of 'surveillance capitalism' (Zuboff 2019), consumers are the big economic winners of the current expansion. As the leading companies concentrate on growing their user base, consumers profit from free or cross-subsidised goods and services. As long as there is still a certain degree of choice between different proprietary markets, there will be limits to the platforms' market power vis-à-vis consumers. That certainly cannot be said of the producer side. Here the meta-platforms dictate prices and conditions to vendors who rely on appearing on their proprietary markets.

What is at stake here is more than just a few per cent of profits. In the relationship between platform operators, investors and producers lies the key to understanding power and inequality in digital capitalism, the apparent paradox that will concern us in this chapter: if digital capitalism is by nature a system of proprietary markets functioning via the extraction of economic rents, why does the factor of human labour nevertheless become increasingly important? Why does the discussion about 'digitalisation' revolve around phenomena of intensification of labour control and the increasing automation of production (Spencer 2018)?

The first explanation is arithmetical in nature. In the commercial internet we are dealing with platform operators that retain about 30 per cent of producers' profits while employing their market power to keep prices in their market as low as possible. The leading companies are still in a – perhaps never-ending – process of expansion. Ever more users (consumers) have to be integrated into their ecosystems and kept there. On the producer side these processes generate systematic downward price pressure – which must feel like a disagreeable materialisation of the 'total competition' of which classical liberal economics always dreamed. As every business economics student knows, economic pressure drives cost reductions, for which the first candidate is labour: through technical substitution, reducing pay and/or increasing the pace and intensity of exploitation. The means to achieve this is a radicalisation of labour control which, in an ironic turn, itself builds on the platform model.

Proprietary markets as the model for restructuring work

Aside from the expansionary dynamic of the meta-platforms, there is a second systematic connection between the internet economy and the rationalisation of work. Following Schumpeter, *imitation* is central to understanding the diffusion and implementation of innovations. In various areas of the economy today leading internet companies serve as the model for rationalisation measures. This is not restricted to the restructuring of entire sectors, such as agriculture, on the platform model (Schössler 2018), but also includes the penetration of particular control strategies based on the platform model – such as peripheralisation of labour by technical infrastructures, control of information in the labour process and targeted deployment of innovative rating and scoring systems.

The ramifications of this development are naturally hard to predict because companies are in a process of permanent efficiency maximisation, all the more so when cost pressure is elevated. The history of labour control certainly did not begin with the internet, and path-dependent developments in individual sectors, branches and companies mingle with new control models borrowed from the internet. The aura of the platform economy as the avant-garde of the digital transformation has, however, undoubtedly eased the adoption of particular control instruments from proprietary markets.

Data control and performance control – one-way transparency

The owners' ability to control information is the basis for the functioning of proprietary markets. This control is based first of all on acquiring the largest possible amount of data. To do so the internet companies have created all-encompassing socio-technical structures that permit effective 'surveillance' of market participants, generally in association with the objective of predicting their behaviour (Zuboff 2019). Various technology components serve the structured acquisition of data. *Interfaces*, for example, are designed to influence user behaviour. The very fact that the commercial internet can only be accessed via prestructured spaces illustrates the essentially trivial observation that the interfaces and the actors controlling them effectively constrain and control the users. *Tracking technologies* frequently run in the background, enabling the extraction of producers' and consumers' data as well as personal targeting for secondary uses, in particular online advertising. One use of *ratings* is to generate trust between consumers and vendors in anonymous markets. From eBay traders and Uber drivers to Airbnb hosts and guests, every actor in the commercial internet gets a rating-based score. But ratings are also an instrument for generating and appropriating new sources of data produced by the parties participating in the rating process.

Closing the gap

The permanent observation and collection of data enables platforms to follow users in real time and to respond directly to their actions. For example, searching online for a particular product seamlessly activates a specific advert. One could say, with Anthony Giddens (1984), that control is asserted through technically automated recursivity. In order to understand the logical implications of this development it will be helpful to review the history of the idea of recursivity in sociology and its normative implications. It was popularised in the late 1980s, especially by Giddens, as a critique of unidirectional, deterministic theories of power. Rejecting simplistic Marxist constructions, Giddens argued that power was never monodirectional. 'Strategies of control' and 'technologies of power', he argued, have always been historically incomplete, and always leave space for actors to 'discursively reflect upon the nature of the activities in which they engage' (Giddens 1987: 11). In this logic, consistent and continuous coordination is what makes organisations truly social formations: power is not simply imposed from above, but adapts continuously to the reflexive acts of various actors – whereby the incompleteness of control creates openings and a certain degree of autonomy for the subjects (Staab 2014).

One can interpret this circumstance functionalistically as a humanisation of power by giving its subjects a practical say, or critically as the absorption of practical criticism and the creative potential of reflexive action into more efficient exploitation.[1] But whether functionalistic or critical, all such perspectives concur on the broader context: power is not a one-way street but unfolds in the interaction between control instances and subjects. Any freedoms enjoyed by the subjects are ultimately created by the time lag before the control system responds to their (from the perspective of the control instance undesirable) behaviour. For example, if a worker employs a tool in a manner that requires less energy but damages the tool, it may be some time before this is noticed. For that duration, the worker enjoys the liberty to preserve their strength.

If we consider the commercial internet from this perspective, it is quickly clear that information control in proprietary markets is deployed systematically to automate recursion – indeed that this represents an absolutely central aspect of the expansion of proprietary markets.

Let us return to the example of online advertising. Selling online advertising requires real-time observation of consumers' wishes and predictive analysis to reveal desires that the individual in question has not even expressed. Here real-time analysis integrates individual behaviour recursively into a control context. The advert appears without any noticeable delay, immediately after the relevant behavioural stimulus, on the basis of an auction running unnoticed in the background. Action and reaction are fully automated, with the advert adapting in real time to the behavioural data gathered by the system.

The automation of recursion also shrinks the time a control system requires to adjust to unintended, reflexive behaviour. In the commercial internet it is the monopolisation of consumers' and producers' data that conditions the specific form of information control behind this process. Recursion is transformed from a source of freedom to a tool of power. This is increasingly also the case in the world of work. And to a great extent the data used to automate recursion is gathered through direct observation of workers.

Algorithmic management: from the market participants to the workers

Interfaces, tracking and ratings are elements of a new framework of labour control, or 'algorithmic management' (Beverungen 2017). The control technologies used in the digital labour process are strongly reminiscent of their precursors in the platform economy. Modern business software, for example, imitates many elements of proprietary markets, repurposing them to manage labour.[2] The software used for administrative tasks also gathers data within the workplace (data mining) and employs it to monitor performance.

For example, as Eva-Maria Nyckel demonstrates, Salesforce's cloud-based customer relationship management (CRM) software fully automates data gathering:

> Automated data gathering and processing in Salesforce makes all relevant workplace activities visualisable and controllable. The process management software automatically registers things a human supervisor might easily miss, creating a system of almost seamless surveillance where every click is recorded. Automated data collection in Salesforce also includes continuous updating of workers' key performance indicators (KPIs), tracking of all user activities and automatic integration of external information such as online marketing data on current and prospective clients (whether an e-mail sent

by the company has been opened or a link has been clicked). The process management software transposes the practice of data gathering to the level of registration by algorithm and thus enables a new form of quantification and surveillance. Everything the workers do on their computers is tracked, recorded and analysed. Automated data gathering and graphic representation in Salesforce creates a largely self-regulating feedback loop. (translated from Raffetseder, Schaupp and Staab 2017: 236–7)

This feedback loop is not restricted to monitoring and data collection. The system also processes the data for management and control purposes. For example, workflow monitoring makes it possible to assign tasks to precisely those workers who are currently 'underemployed'. Here quantification of labour leads directly to performance pressure because no to-do list is ever finished: the system automatically generates new instructions, ceaselessly driving workers to increase their output (Raffetseder, Schaupp and Staab 2017). Monitoring is also directly tied to sanctions. Input masks leave workers no choice but to operate within the heuristics of the respective 'algocratic' (Aneesh 2010) system, which is always looking over the worker's shoulder, detecting incorrect entries and flagging them for immediate correction.

With the advent of the internet of things, this immediate feedback, which one could describe as a filiation of the logic of proprietary online markets,[3] now metastasises out of the disembodied world of software into the physical world of hardware. Today, tracking and algorithmic management affect sectors as disparate as retail (L. Evans and Kitchin 2018), creative and office work (Moore and Piwek 2017; Moore 2018a, 2018b) and industrial manufacturing (Raffetseder, Schaupp and Staab 2017; Schaupp and Staab 2018; Schaupp and Diab 2020). Simon Schaupp elaborates on the phenomenon in his studies on industrial applications. The developer of a smart glove relates how wearables

seek to give the worker immediate feedback on his actions, on his work sequences, alerting him directly and physically when an event or error occurs. I believe that is the best aspect of wearables. If it is attached to his body he does not have to concentrate on an external screen at his work station. He gets immediate feedback whether he chose the right or wrong part. We confirm correct parts and scan them into the system with a green light. And we have a buzzer, a sound, when something went wrong. (translated from Raffetseder, Schaupp and Staab 2017: 240)

'Digital Taylorism' (Nachtwey and Staab 2015; Staab and Nachtwey 2016) introduces a new quality of performance measurement and control, where technical means now permit direct monitoring of remote and distributed work processes. The methods of Germany's Industrie 4.0 – as the acknowledged pioneer of digital control in analogue contexts (Schaupp and Diab 2020) – are not a jot more humane than comparable technologies employed for example by Amazon. As such examples show, data control becomes labour control.

Control gaps and subversion

Employers see good reasons to utilise data in this way. As experimental work (Lee and Baykal 2017) and field studies (A. Shapiro 2018) show, workers take an extremely dim view of algorithmic management systems. And where they cannot rely on the kind of voluntary cooperation that functions in the commercial internet, such systems have to be designed to be all-encompassing. As Min Kyung Lee shows, decisions made by algorithms tend to be perceived as less fair (Lee and Baykal 2017), so the dissemination of algorithmic management spurs an urge to disobey.

As numerous other studies confirm, workers develop manifold strategies to deceive the algorithms and escape the grip of technological management (Lee et al. 2015; Schor and Attwood-Charles 2017; Schor et al. 2020; Attwood-Charles 2019). When confronted with rigid algocratic management software, workers find their own solutions, for example filling input fields with meaningless characters in order to proceed to the next step ('dummy entries'; Raffetseder, Schaupp and Staab 2017).

Another well-documented example is the work of ride-hailing drivers in the United States. The app used to dispatch Uber drivers has three core features (Lee et al. 2015): automatic assignment of ride requests to drivers, prioritising geographical proximity; the notorious surge pricing, where prices increase when an area is underserved; and customer reviews using the five-star system that has become ubiquitous in the commercial internet.

In practice many drivers apparently avoid taking on certain rides. This is not without risk, and can eventually lead to exclusion from the platform (and loss of income). However, that applies only when the driver is logged on. So many drivers turn the app off when driving through areas where they prefer not to take rides. In response Uber introduced a small bonus for every unbroken hour the driver remains available. 'When drivers desired a break' without losing the benefit 'they parked in between the other ride-sharing cars' (Lee et al. 2015: 6). Min Kyung Lee and colleagues found that about half the drivers ignored surge pricing incentives because their unpredictability interfered with workday planning. The rating system, on the other hand, was relevant to many, with drivers feeling pride in high ratings and shame about poor reviews. But many of the interviewees felt the reviews were capricious and 'not reflective of their driving performance and services'.

Similar practices of subtle resistance have been documented across the on-demand and gig economy (Schor et al. 2020; Attwood-Charles 2019;

Wood et al. 2019), including for digital remote working organised through platforms. One gig worker in Kenya described how he dealt with monitoring by screenshot: 'It comes once every 10 minutes. Once it has shown up in a 10-minute block you leave ... you have nine minutes to do everything that is totally non-related to work.' A translator in the Philippines employed a different strategy: 'Since I'm technical I connect my laptop to my TV ... so I have two screens, I'm watching YouTube while I'm working on the platform ... because the screenshot is only for the main [monitor]' (cited from Wood et al. 2019: 64).

Automated wage repression

However such anecdotes from the world of algorithmic management should not create the impression that the control strategies employed there are ineffective. Ratings supply a good example. They are, as described above, a core technology of proprietary markets. But today they are also widely employed as instruments of labour control. E-commerce companies, which were quick to introduce customer reviews, are pioneers here too. In August 2015 an article describing Amazon's 'Anytime Feedback Tool' caused waves. The *New York Times* piece by Jodi Kantor and David Streitfeld (2015) described how the software used at Amazon's Seattle headquarters enabled staff to evaluate their colleagues and convey the assessments to management. The report suggested that the gathered information often appeared verbatim (but anonymised) in performance reviews. This form of denunciation introduces direct personal control into the work environments of software engineers, middle management, marketing, human resources (HR) and advertising departments. Power is horizontalised in a peer-to-peer system (Staab 2016).

Rating tools bring digital labour control into core HR activities. A case from Germany illustrates how this functions. In 2017 a leading e-commerce company implemented an especially comprehensive rating system named Radar. At the time of our research Radar was employed in the company's Berlin offices. Staff were expected to use the software in a set rhythm, and not just for situation-specific praise or criticism as in the case of Amazon. The system receives information gathered by various means. High-frequency, real-time evaluations allow information about colleagues to be reported immediately after interactions, a procedure very similar to the high-frequency ratings used in the commercial internet, for example where Uber customers rate their driver. Radar also includes deep biannual worker/co-worker assessments employing the same type of questionnaire used by line managers for employees' annual performance reviews. At the time of the research staff had to give and receive at least five reviews per half year, managers at least ten. The longer reviews comprised a qualitative description (text) and a quantitative rating (scale). This form of evaluation by colleagues generated paranoia. One related:

> At some point I began feeling extremely under pressure, well that was just when we started with the new feedback rounds. That was already rather a lot of psychological pressure, for me with my negative feedback, and I wasn't allowed to delete it. I handed in my notice a week later, after that discussion, because it's just too harsh for me.

The employees felt they were under permanent surveillance: 'We don't know who gave us feedback or on what basis. ... If you asked what happened with the data you got no answer. ... You got the impression it could be used against you.'

That was indeed the case. An algorithm calculates a score for each worker, using criteria that remain opaque. The score forms the link between labour control and the responsibilities of the human resources department, which uses it to categorise staff as low, good and top performers – and to distribute the associated sanctions and rewards. One employee reported:

> If you fall in the middle range you get lost in the crowd. But if you are in the top or bottom group, on the basis of all the feedback statistics, you have to go to a kind of committee, where there's another lot of people. No idea how they were selected. And they discuss it all again, you, your position, your performance. Your team leader is allowed to be there, but not to speak. They can only listen, not say anything. ... And then they discuss. Nobody knows what exactly. So there's a certain pressure not to fall into this bottom group. And of course it's crazy. Because anyone can give feedback to anyone else. So you can really knife someone in the back.

While top performers receive pay rises above inflation and enjoy decent prospects of promotion, good performers are told to pull their socks up, and receive pay rises in line with inflation. Wherever possible, low performers' contracts are simply not renewed; where it is too late for that, they receive no pay rise (and a de facto loss of purchasing power).

In other words, the system is employed as an instrument of automated wage repression. As suppliers of data, the workers are subject to the same socio-economic logic that producers experience in proprietary markets. The completely opaque criteria on which the rating process is based serve to reinforce power and control.

The possibilities of algorithmic control

In order to understand the context and broader objectives of applications designed to extract and analyse work process data it is worth returning to

Amazon once again. As a machine for generating, absorbing and exploiting data, Amazon demonstrates the possibilities opened up by data mining and modelling in the field of business administration. If we recall, as a proprietary market Amazon sells its own products and products bought in from manufacturers (retail); but third-party vendors can also sell their goods through Amazon's Marketplace, which has grown increasingly important.

Until 2018 these two divisions were run by different teams. The retail team was responsible for buying from and negotiating with suppliers, and played a crucial role in the early years. In order to persuade producers to offer their products on a largely unknown website, Amazon recruited highly paid sales veterans, with good contacts for example to publishers (Soper 2018). For years the company systematically tracked the performance of these retail experts and compared their results with the market trends. When had the retail team forecast demand developments correctly? Where had they got it wrong? When had the number of units ordered fallen short of actual demand?

In the Marketplace, on the other hand, transactions were much more strongly automated from the outset. Any third-party vendor could simply register and sell their products on the website, setting their own prices. Amazon observed the sales data very closely and gained ever deeper insights into the demand dynamics in individual product categories.

A few years ago Amazon launched an initiative titled 'Hands off the wheel', based in part on the data gathered in the Marketplace. The objective was to shift 'tasks like forecasting demand, ordering inventory and negotiating prices to algorithms' (Soper 2018: n.p.). Initially the retail team was able to cancel or amend algorithmic decisions. But the algorithms turned out to be so reliable that they were applied to ever more activities. And human staff no longer had a veto.

Since 2016 negotiations between Amazon and producers have normally been conducted via automated proprietary interfaces. Instead of calling the purchasing manager, firms log onto a portal to learn what products Amazon would like to buy from them, in what quantity, at what price and when. The fusion of the Marketplace and retail teams marked the completion of the latter's data-driven automation.

Similar strategies are conceivable wherever comprehensive data extraction meets information control. The market leaders in business software have taken exactly that route, for example acquiring start-ups with expertise in automating administrative tasks (Staab and Nyckel 2019).

The cited examples illustrate an important trend: automation strategies developed in the commercial internet are increasingly affecting white-collar jobs and the lower rungs of management (Staab 2016), where calculative, predictive, administrative and social tasks can apparently be fulfilled better – or at least more cheaply – by algorithms. In the medium term this can bring about a radicalisation of power. In the long term those who control the data will leverage their automation successes into ever greater market power – and they will be able to sell these capabilities back to their economic and social peripheries. The basis and foreseeable outcome of these processes is a highly unequal situation where data control is realised through one-way transparency.

Access control and price control: one-way rights

One-sided data control is not the only form of control metastasising from the commercial internet into other parts of the economy. The same applies to the access and price controls that are so central to profits from market ownership. As laid out in detail in Chapter 4, market owners can effectively shape economic competition by exercising access control. This gives platform operators the power to control prices.

Here again, these enormously successful strategies are emulated in the world of work. Of course employers have always been able to choose who they employ, which is also a form of 'access control'. But their growing information control gives them relatively new and automatable options. Returning again to the example of Radar, the fusion of performance evaluation and HR development in such systems illustrates very clearly how, for workers, information control transforms into access and price control (in this case the price of labour, or the pay). Furthermore, the scores generated by Radar serve to divide the workforce into groups. The most important factor here is the implementation of an effective system of algorithmic pay control in which only the small group of high performers has any prospect of real pay increases.

This produces a 'collective of unequals' (Mau 2017) where privileges and sanctions are still allocated largely on a group basis. But tendencies towards increasing personalisation are already visible. For example, low performers do not automatically lose their jobs; their specific contractual status is included as an individual factor. The power of the data creates a metric 'justification' (Boltanski and Chiapello 2003), whose function is to legitimise inclusion and exclusion in the workplace.

Dilemmas of quantification

As tracking technologies become increasingly sophisticated, the logical destination is increasingly personalised quantification of entitlements. The first insurers have already begun experimenting with fitness trackers that measure not only the wearer's objective output but also the effort involved. Whether a person exercises to their limits or avoids breaking sweat could be relevant when calculating insurance risks, and insurers hope to personalise premiums using such methods. These technologies can naturally also be applied to workers. Pulse and perspiration reveal how much effort a worker has to exert to complete a particular task. Would it not be fair to include this 'objective' effort factor when calculating pay and bonuses? Or to demand more of the fittest and strongest workers?

The effects of such developments on social inequality are illustrated very well in pioneering fields of performance quantification, in particular in professional sport. One very good example is found close to Silicon Valley, although in this case not in any of the tech firms. I am talking about a major league baseball team, the Oakland A's. In his book *Moneyball: The Art of Winning an Unfair Game* (2003; film with Brad Pitt, 2011), Michael Lewis describes how the team achieved great success on a modest budget after manager Billy Beane applied the new technologies. Beane developed a sophisticated method for measuring the performance of baseball players. Because baseball is a highly formalised sport where players relatively frequently complete actions alone, advanced data analysis allowed the manager to determine each team member's individual contribution to the overall result. It turned out that players who had been regarded as average often made very important contributions.

After this system was adopted throughout the league, an unintended effect on income distribution became apparent. Since 1985 the major league baseball teams have been required to reveal what they pay their players. The political scientist Willie Gin (2018) was able to demonstrate that the moneyball revolution led to a kind of market failure – or one could say, the factor labour got squeezed. Although average players became more important – in economic terms more productive – because their true value was recognised and they were selected more frequently, their pay fell in relation to their contribution. The economic logic operating here is not hard to unpick: increasingly granular performance measurement increased the number of players assigned to the middle group on the basis of their productivity. Information control expanded the pool of available 'workers' in the middle of the talent hierarchy, leading to sharper competition and ultimately to downward pressure on salaries (Gin 2018). In other words, the ability of team managers to control prices was improved.

Symbioses of market control and labour control

Similar dynamics also appear at the other end of the income spectrum. Gig economy and crowdworking platforms supplying cycle couriers, coders and copywriters are an established feature of the modern service world (Benner 2015; Huws et al. 2017; Pongratz and Bormann 2017). Because they need no 'physical assets' of their own, Nick Srnicek (2017) speaks of these as 'lean' platforms: a ride-hailing business has no vehicle fleet to maintain, an agency supplying cleaners has no need to stock cleaning materials. In analytical terms these entities can be conceived of as hybrid. The people who actually do the work are 'customers' of the platforms through which they find their jobs. But firms like Uber and Deliveroo also do things for their 'customers' that employers would be expected to do for their employees. For example ride-hailing firms process payments for their drivers. At the same time the platforms definitely exercise control over the labour process. In this respect the workers are not 'customers', and this aspect of the relationship is much more similar to regular employment.

While traditional producers also assume non-market obligations towards their employees and cannot simply dismiss them when sales dip, the crowd-working platforms treat labour as an external factor to be controlled and managed using the strategies of the commercial internet. If someone has time to work as a courier, they log onto the corresponding app and indicate their readiness to work. If the market is currently saturated they receive no jobs and no pay. Ratings are also employed to control access. Anyone who falls below a defined threshold is sieved out. If the algorithms observe a specific pattern of inactivity (in terms that may be completely opaque: information control), a firm like Uber will automatically block the user. Thus control over information and access also enables the platforms to exercise far-reaching control over the cost of labour. Market control becomes pay control.

This also occurs in platforms that at first glance appear to have little in common with the gig economy, such as the video portal YouTube. YouTube's advertising revenues depend heavily on the extremely popular channels of prominent YouTubers. The latter account for an important share of this market, generating the attention that YouTube's owner Google turns into profit. The most influential YouTubers can earn thousands of dollars a month. But here again it is the platforms that ultimately control the price of labour: alterations to the algorithm that calculates the share of advertising revenue can have rapid and dramatic consequences. In another example of the connection between market control and pay control, many YouTubers lost up to three-quarters of their revenues when YouTube changed its advertising strategy in spring 2018 without informing them in advance (*Economist* 2018b).

The platforms' pricing algorithms represent the holy grail of cost control, and are heavily protected company secrets. Investors regard the quality of the algorithms as decisive for a company's value (Solomon 2015, cited from

A. Shapiro 2018: 2961). The platforms modify them as they please, rarely if ever consulting those who do the work. Certain delivery platforms dictate the terms for tips through their apps (for example 10, 15 or 20 per cent). Others simply exclude the possibility of tipping; Uber only introduced this option under public pressure, seven years after its launch. This is enormously important for such workers (A. Shapiro 2018: 2960), for whom tips may represent up to one-third of their income. The calculation process itself is another important factor. In the food delivery sector, for example, models based on distance rather than time required create systematic disadvantages in areas of high-rise housing, because the long distances within the buildings are not taken into account (A. Shapiro 2018: 2961).

The reserve army mechanism in the digital economy

Algorithms controlling access and prices are merely the technical substrate of a complex social process. To function successfully they require specific conditions in the labour market. In the same way as proprietary markets rely on large numbers of producers competing with one another, crowd-working platforms systematically exploit the 'reserve army' mechanism (Butollo 2016). A market situation of ruinous competition between workers presupposes a relative surplus of labour. The success of such strategies also depends on the unemployment rate and on political factors such as the existence of a minimum wage and the level of the welfare state safety net. Expanding the supply of labour is, however, certainly crucial to the long-term success of such platforms (Srnicek 2017).

The platforms have plainly been very successful in creating competition between workers. Various strategies are applied in the gig economy. Most delivery services require their couriers to accept jobs without knowing the delivery address, in order to minimise rejections (A. Shapiro 2018: 2962) and optimise their labour supply. Dynamic – or surge – pricing represents another means to the same end, where higher pay is offered ostensibly to cope with elevated demand. The real object of the exercise, however, is to create an oversupply of labour (A. Shapiro 2018: 2963): the pay for a specific order may be higher, but with more competition for jobs the real hourly rate falls (A. Shapiro 2018). One is inevitably reminded of the way proprietary markets control the supply side.

While there are geographical bounds to the potential labour pool for delivery riders, other tasks can be performed anywhere in the world. This brings the Global South into the digital outsourcing economy. It is estimated that 70 million people worked in the global remote gig economy in 2017 (Heeks 2017), with annual growth of 26 per cent (Kässi and Lehdonvirta 2016). A study by researchers at the University of Oxford found '54% of respondents reporting that there was not enough work available and just 20% disagreeing' (Wood et al. 2019: 68). This undersupply of work naturally enables the platforms to control the prices. The workers are certainly aware of the situation: 44 per cent said 'they felt easily replaceable' (Wood et al. 2019: 68). The truth of that is vividly illustrated by the example of the rapidly growing market for data labelling for the car industry. Training the image recognition algorithms that are central to the objective of autonomous driving requires the categorisation of enormous libraries of traffic images, most of which is done by crowdworkers. The work is distributed across the globe, with the top earners making one or two dollars an hour (Schmidt 2019: 40). In 2018 large numbers of Venezuelan crowdworkers started appearing on the major platforms. When Florian Schmidt conducted his study they represented about 75 per cent of users (Schmidt 2019: 42). At the time Venezuela was suffering hyperinflation and food shortages – creating good preconditions for low labour costs.

Notes

1 The latter position is prominently argued by Michael Burawoy (1979), whose classic work on the factory regime of Fordism describes how the workers themselves played a part in making Taylorism hegemonic.
2 I would like to thank Eva-Maria Nyckel for these insights from her research on Salesforce and its CRM software.
3 Echoing the knowledge transfers between the financial sector and the digital economy (see Chapter 3), it is no surprise that companies like Salesforce orientate on the leading platforms. The Salesforce headquarters (San Francisco) is geographically close to Google (Mountain View), Facebook (Menlo Park) and Apple (Cupertino); it also cooperates on technology (for example with Amazon Web Services), pursues strategic partnerships (with Google) and shares personnel (Salesforce chief product officer Bret Taylor previously worked for Google and Facebook) (Aytay 2017).

6

Privatised mercantilism, inequality and conflict

We have examined the role of the state in the emergence of the digital economy, the dynamics of capital involved, digital capitalism's characteristic accumulation paradigm, its filiations in the sphere of labour. It is now time to draw these strands together.

Again we can tap Schumpeter for a clearer picture of the contours of digital capitalism, by contrasting our findings with his observations on industrial monopoly capitalism. Both are capitalist constellations exhibiting great concentration of power in their leading companies. In fact, one could be forgiven for jumping to the conclusion that digital capitalism is merely the revenant of the industrial monopolies that Schumpeter describes in *Capitalism, Socialism and Democracy*. Of course we are dealing with new processes of economic concentration that demand a new analysis of capitalism. But from Schumpeter we can borrow a specific perspective that joins up the problems, agents, logics and effects.

Yet we come to very different conclusions than Schumpeter. We have to tackle digital capitalism not as a *problem* of scarcity (as Schumpeter rightly did with industrial capitalism), but in terms of superabundance. Its *leading companies* are not rational producer monopolies, but proprietary markets whose *raison d'être* consists in extracting economic rents. Its *dynamics* are driven much more by rent-seeking than by entrepreneurial motivations. The *objective* is not to maximise production, but to capitalise on what are actually superabundant goods. The *effect* of this constellation is not the death of capitalism, as Schumpeter expected, but a radicalisation of its underlying traits, in particular social inequality.

There are two takeaways from his brief summary. Firstly, digital capitalism is not a completely new form of capitalism[1] – this is not previously unknown technologies creating an entirely new economy. Instead, we are witnessing the return of a rather primitive form of capitalist accumulation, in the novel guise of highly modern technologies. The term I propose to describe this is *privatised mercantilism*. Secondly, this perspective enables us to describe the social *effects* a great deal more precisely. We can now concretise the growing social inequality inherent to digital capitalism as a logical consequence of rent extraction.

Privatised mercantilism

In contemporary political economics the concept of mercantilism is most frequently applied to describe the economic policies of countries like Germany and China, specifically the combination of export-driven industrial policy with domestic pay restraint (Höpner 2016). The analogy I draw here refers much more to the original meaning, the phenomenon of early merchant capitalism, and to the business – rather than state – practices of the contemporary era.

Historically 'mercantilism' is associated with two things. Firstly, the mercantilism of the sixteenth to eighteenth centuries is understood as a result of the first more or less complete economic *theory*, even if it was composed of many strands that shared only certain basic features in common. The most important of these is its function of expanding the wealth of absolute monarchs. In this respect, in line with Adam Smith's influential critique (Smith 2013 [1776]), contemporary mainstream economics regards mercantilism as a thoroughly defective theory – but also as the forerunner of the 'true' liberal economic theory that followed.

Secondly, 'mercantilism' is used as a simple descriptor of the early capitalist economic *practice* that characterised the political economy of pre-liberal European states (P. J. Stern and Wennerlind 2013; Magnusson 2015) and in the seventeenth century shaped economic policy in England and France in particular (Arrighi 1994: 145; Horrocks 2017 [1925]). The ideological core of that practice was an understanding of the world economy as a zero-sum game. One state's prosperity had to be extracted from another. The central means for accomplishing this was trade, the decisive objective a favourable balance of trade. Concretely, this meant exports of manufactured goods had to exceed the cost of imports, in particular of raw materials.

Why was trade the decisive mechanism of accumulation and why as a zero-sum game? The answer lies in the economic structures of the epoch. It was only with the emergence of more complex manufacturing during this period that Europe gradually experienced meaningful improvements in efficiency (Kocka 2016). The productivity gains were admittedly still rather marginal. The dominant economy was pre-industrial, characterised by 'the coexistence of the rigidity, inertia and lethargy of a still elementary economy and the first limited and sporadic – but also vital and even powerful – signs of modern growth' (translated from Braudel 2016 [1976]: 15). The fuel that drove these first 'powerful movements' and shook the largely stagnant

feudal economies was merchant capital (Kocka 2016). In a world characterised by slow growth, it is no surprise that this flowed primarily into trade.
In such a constellation, unequal exchange is the only way to make profits
above the moderate rates of existing economic growth.

The historical roots of the great capitalist enterprises are also found in
this sixteenth-century constellation (Arrighi 1994), in particular in the form
of the major trade monopolies, which were generally private enterprises
possessing privileges granted by the state (P. J. Stern 2013). The home
states of trading companies like the British East India Company granted
them trading monopolies for particular regions and/or products (P. J. Stern
2013), and frequently also the right to raise troops to enforce and protect
their interests overseas (Wallerstein 1998 [1980]).

In other words, the leading companies of classical mercantilism were an
expression of a *mixed economy* supported by state interests. They were also
one of the two central elements of the markets of the age. The states built
their external trade relations on trade monopolies – in other words enterprises that were historically especially similar to what Braudel described
as the anti-market (*contre-marché*) and understood as the true nature of
capitalism (Braudel 1986 [1979]).[2] Domestically, on the other hand, free
markets were widely encouraged, in particular in manufacturing where
market forces were supposed to increase efficiency and keep consumer
prices low. Essentially the political economy of mercantilism meant dominating trade in order to control production and consumption.

As children of industrial modernity we are so accustomed to understanding both prosperity and social inequality in terms of the effects of technological change that we can imagine a return of mercantilist structures in the
sphere of international trade policy (trade wars), but not as the leitmotif
of the *technological* reconfiguration of capitalism. In our common-sense
understanding, technology represents a source of growing efficiency; it is the
reason why we can have ever more with ever less effort. It is undeniable that
productivity growth is the basis of all economic prosperity. Who would be
able to afford a car made entirely by hand? Likewise, the mercantilist state
of the seventeenth century ultimately sought to control external trade in
order to foster the emergence of a (more productive) domestic manufacturing (or proto-industrial) economy.

Nevertheless, this deep-seated belief in productivity[3] arises out of a
historical situation that is more similar to what Schumpeter described
in *Capitalism, Socialism and Democracy* than today's global digital
economy. While the nexus of technological development, increasing
productivity and prosperity gains can be regarded as fact for the heyday
of Fordism, it becomes much more complicated thereafter. For one
thing, the atmosphere of secular stagnation in the global economy has

understandably fostered great scepticism about the prospect of digitalisation creating productivity gains (Gordon 2016). For another, the mercantilist motive of trading profit stands out among the characteristics of the leading companies of digital capitalism. On the other hand, numerous systematic parallels to the economic logic of mercantilism become visible. In view of the secular stagnation tendencies in the global economy we possibly find ourselves much closer to a situation of 'rigidity, inertia and lethargy', as Braudel described for the 'still elementary economy'. That the leading capitalist enterprises would orientate on trading profit in such a situation is as plausible today as it was in the seventeenth century. So contemporary venture capital assumes the role played in the past by merchant capital, which was also closely interwoven with the state. In the absence of 'real' (productivity-increasing) investment opportunities, both look to trade monopolies to extract profits.

The decisive difference is naturally the question of who the beneficiaries are. Where classical mercantilism operated with the state's blessing and in its interest, digital capitalism is an undertaking of enterprises operating as markets and profiting from the achievements of an investing state (see Chapter 2) but themselves contributing little to general prosperity. Aside from inadequate redistribution via taxation, the most decisive aspect is the application of mercantilist strategies (in modified form). In classical mercantilism, trade is controlled in order to create a competitive domestic market economy: trade profits enable the establishment of manufacturing as the basis of a more productive market economy. The losers from this development were the global economic peripheries, where the trade monopolies often pursued their interests with brute force (Wallerstein 1998 [1980]).

In today's global economy the peripheries of the digital trading giants assume dimensions that the original mercantilism could never have dreamed of. On the other hand, the state no longer derives much benefit from trade profits and no longer acquires resources (profits) to serve the public interest. Instead, the ransacking of the periphery is reproduced in the capitalist centres. Now it is in the process of expanding successively into the world of producers as a whole.

Inequality in privatised mercantilism

With respect to social inequality we are dealing here with four analytically distinct but empirically closely related dynamics: appropriation of public goods, generation of financial risk cascades, extraction of rents from market ownership, and expropriation of labour.

Commodification of public goods

As laid out above, the expansion of the digital economy was based to a staggering extent on the investing state, which enabled the rise of the commercial internet in the first place by funding basic research, investing public venture capital, and providing and expanding infrastructure. One widespread criticism in this connection is that the leading companies of a sector that has profited so enormously from state funding themselves pay so little in taxes. To name but one example, despite profits at record levels, in 2021 Amazon managed to avoid more than US$5 billion in corporate income taxes (Gardner 2022).[4] While the public sector shoulders the initial risks, the profits ultimately accrue almost exclusively to the private sector. Here we are looking at unearned income, where private investors reap the rewards of state risk-taking (Mazzucato 2019). This appropriation of public funds is one of the factors behind the combination of 'private opulence and public squalor' (John Kenneth Galbraith) that has begun to attract criticism, for example in the San Francisco Bay Area (Aisslinger 2016; Morozov 2018; Rötzer 2018; Voss 2018).

Commodification of public goods is also implicated in the development of digital capitalism at an even deeper level. The prime example is the privatisation of telecommunications infrastructure in the OECD economies, which gained momentum in the 1980s. Providers today possess enormous power (Winseck 2017). They certainly embody the appropriation of digital infrastructure by private sector actors, even if they were not destined to become the dominant companies of digital capitalism.

Free-riding on publicly funded infrastructure remains a central aspect of the ongoing expansion of the digital economy. Leading companies have recently shown interest in core sectors of public services. While the expansion of their cloud services rounds off their market functions (see Chapter 4), it also offers the prospect of controlling areas of absolutely central importance for the public sector. The state is expected to invest in digital capitalism's smart city systems – and then communities and other parties are expected to pay for the data they gather. The platforms have been circling the health sector for some years now; Google in particular has persisted despite various setbacks (Landeweerd, Spil and Klein 2013). The provision of hardware and software for American schools is another hotly contested field, where Google and Apple again jostle for market share. Finally the internet platforms, as laid out in Chapter 5, have made growing inroads into the territory of the telecommunications providers, for example by investing in intercontinental cables (Winseck 2017). All these fields represent useful expansions of the socio-technical ecosystems – and they all illustrate, yet again, the leading companies' orientation on state investment and public demand. The next round of that development is beginning, with state programmes promoting AI clusters and the return of industrial policy.

As we see, transforming public wealth into private profit is a core trait of digital capitalism. The process is by no means concluded with the successful consolidation of the digital economy. Digital capitalism boosts inequality if for no other reason than that the public funds channelled into the internet economy (but not returned to anywhere like the same extent) are no longer available for redistributive purposes.

Risk cascades

The beneficiaries of this development are, along with the internet companies, above all the venture capitalists (see Chapter 3). They reap the economic rewards without bearing the risks, employing the risk evasion mechanisms entrenched in the financial sector. This mainly affects, as shown in Chapter 3, the weakest links in the ownership structure. As such the leading companies turn the neoliberal idea of trickle-down economics on its head. The idea that deregulating the financial markets and lowering taxes will cause wealth to trickle down is an axiom of mainstream economics. The financial structure of the digital economy is also based on cascades, but what trickles here is risk. Risk cascading does not end with the weakest investor. Employees are affected in multiple respects by the exit strategies of the tech sector. And every bubble must burst at some point. In the financial world this is the moment when economic risks materialise in financial losses, as occurred around 2000 in the dotcom crash.

One can only speculate about the exact mechanisms of future market corrections. In Germany, where acquisitions have significantly outnumbered flotations in recent years, it must be suspected that the risks hidden in technology firms are increasingly permeating into the rest of the economy and ultimately suppressing wages there.[5] In the case of the American technology sector, extremely highly valued firms are expected to seek IPOs. In such a scenario the risks associated with general market corrections and the loss of the steady flow of private venture capital would potentially also affect workers and other less privileged groups – whether because start-ups find themselves unable to pay salaries or because institutional investors like pension funds experience heavy losses.

And even if online financial capitalism's bets pay off in the medium term, many workers will ultimately lose out. Digitalisation of work and algorithmic management are not going away.

Market rents and the commodification of superabundance

The proprietary market model is the real socio-technical innovation of digital capitalism. There was no historical necessity for this. No technological imperative dictates the social form assumed by the leading companies of the commercial internet. The emphasis is on capitalism. The digital – the technology – is merely the tool of capital seeking to maximise returns.[6]

Proprietary markets are to a great extent *digital* infrastructure. They share the (im)materiality of digital goods: infinitely scalable, non-rival and therefore ultimately superabundant.[7] If we understand meta-platforms as digital infrastructures, they are clearly – like other digital goods – scalable at very low marginal cost. And if proprietary markets are able to provide services to their users (producers and consumers) at practically zero cost, their non-marginal revenue shares can only be understood as unearned income: in other words rents. Power is what businesses operating as markets are primarily capitalising on.

When judging the influence of specific enterprises, competition law generally considers their ability to dictate consumer prices. Is a producer the 'single seller' (Schumpeter 2003 [1942])? Is this reflected in prices determined solely by the monopoly's power? In digital capitalism that approach misses the point. Proprietary markets generate their profits not through overpricing but by 'taxing' market transactions or through secondary use of data (Chapter 3). It is the producers who must pay the fee. In the 'ideal' case – the Google and Apple app stores being the prime examples – the market owners are free to set whatever margins they wish.

In a more general sense the problem is not so much that the market owners' profits are largely unearned. The issue is their appropriation and distribution. Although a certain share of the market ownership rents flows to the platforms' workers as income, the lion's share ends up in the enormous capital reserves of the leading companies. If these resources are put to use at all, then it is generally for further expansion or, increasingly, share buybacks – yet again to the benefit of the investors.

Whether as a direct share of sales or via the detour of advertising revenues, the profits of these trade monopolies are extracted from the producers – meaning from labour. After all, the goods for whose intermediation and distribution the platforms collect their fees have to be produced somewhere. The further the leading companies expand into new product markets, the more parts of the economy are affected by this dynamic. On the one hand, the growing reach of the platforms makes ever larger parts of the labour market dependent on them. On the other, as they expand into the world of ordinary (scarce) things they lose the advantages of producing purely digital goods, which were key to the process of commodifying superabundance.

Expropriation of labour

All in all, the processes described here amount to what we could term an expropriation of labour.[8] Where taxes are converted into private profits the taxpayer is deprived of the fruits of the entrepreneurial state. Workers shoulder some of the central risks of these processes, in the sense that they are much more exposed to the volatility that private venture capital systematically produces (being much less able to diversify their economic risks). Additionally, in lean digital infrastructures sustained profits frequently depend on sacrifices by labour, as seen when cross-subsidisation of pay ends and a company suddenly needs to operate profitably. In these cases investors' profits are ultimately financed through pay cuts. Whether this is successful in the long term is quite another matter. Doubts over the economic viability of this model revolve around the eruptive risks of corporate crisis and speculative bubble-bursting. *Consolidated* proprietary markets, on the other hand, secure the transfer of prosperity from labour to wealth.

Social conflict stalemated

This argument has further implications for the sociological effects of the digital reconfiguration of the economy. Yet again Schumpeter is our compass. In *Capitalism, Socialism and Democracy* he introduces a theory of the origin of entrepreneurship from which he infers hypotheses about the development of capitalism. The origins of the entrepreneurial spirit, as the mainspring of economic modernisation, he shows, lie in the reconfiguration of Western societies at the dawn of the modern age (Schumpeter 2003 [1942], chapter 12). The emergence of a 'bourgeois way of life' – whose origins Schumpeter locates less in inner asceticism (M. Weber 2016 [1904/05]) than, with Georg Simmel (1911), in the representational duties – was, he argues, the basis of the activities of the great entrepreneurial dynasties. Maintaining a bourgeois household – with children, staff and a commensurate residence – provided strong motivation for 'getting things done' (Schumpeter 2003 [1942]: 215).

By the mid-twentieth century Schumpeter saw the prospect of the entrepreneurial function withering away, with the general rise in standard of living, falling fertility rates, the expanding consumerism of the middle classes, and the advent of managerialism. To his understanding, the paradigm of industrial monopoly capitalism was more planning than innovation, its central figure the salaried manager not the entrepreneurial patriarch. This, Schumpeter concluded, would soon rob capitalism of its dynamism.

If we accept the narrative that the leading companies of the commercial internet represent the paradigmatic economic project of our era, what are the implications? I would argue that, although its protagonists insist otherwise, digital capitalism does not represent a revival of entrepreneurialism. Instead, digital capitalism revolves around a coalition between the rentier and the consumer, who form one side of the equation. The other is labour.

Protest and progress

This is an important point, because sociologists view social conflict as the driver of social change. If we want to know what alternatives to the status quo are conceivable, we must first understand this constellation and then the logic of the social conflict ensuing from digitalisation.

Marx, who 'saw the relative development of the productive forces and what he termed the relations of production as the motor of social change' (translated from Nachtwey 2016b: 240), treats this fracture as the heart of the contradictions that ultimately bring about a free society (Bude 2016). Later sociologists have in principle sustained this reading of the connection between social conflict and societal change, although frequently placing greater emphasis on the stabilising role of conflict (Coser 2009 [1956]).

Conflict theory dropped the historical perspective in the course of the twentieth century, turning attention successively to an ever broader spectrum of societal change. By the late 1950s Ralf Dahrendorf was arguing that class conflict in the Marxian sense merely formed a subcategory of social conflict, which he understood as the struggle over power in society (Dahrendorf 1956). At the same time the dominant – and strongly normative – reading survived, under which social conflict plays a progressive role in resolving societal tensions. This perspective on social conflict still shimmers through even in diagnoses that attest a 'regressive' character to contemporary modernity (Nachtwey 2016a).

The concept of 'citizenship' is key. The British sociologist T. H. Marshall argued that social conflict led to progress, which brought with it expanding categories of new (civil) rights: from the eighteenth century individual liberties (freedom of expression, freedom of trade), in the nineteenth century political participation (in particular the expanding franchise) and finally in the twentieth century social entitlements in fields like education and health (Marshall 1950). The expansion of working people's rights and entitlements, above all in the heyday of Fordism, is regarded as a further stage in that development; the sociological literature refers to 'industrial citizenship' (Marshall 1950; Crouch 1998) and 'industrial democracy' (Müller-Jentsch 2009).

Ralf Dahrendorf pointed out that having more rights does not necessarily guarantee greater freedom. Any expansion of 'life chances', he argues, must combine rights with social 'ligatures', understood as ties between individuals and institutions that encourage the realisation of specific rights (Dahrendorf 1986). An adult role model may be important for a child from a working-class family to make use of their right to attend university. A functioning trade union may be crucial for exercising workplace rights.

It is conspicuous that more recent works on contemporary social conflict (see for example Fudge 2005; Schmalz, Liebig and Thiel 2015; Staab 2015; Zhang and Lillie 2015; Nachtwey 2016b) frequently start by observing forms of protest empirically before moving on to employ conflict theory as the frame of interpretation.[9] While such an approach is empirically laudable, it appears to me impractical for the case of digital capitalism. There are certainly numerous examples of disparate protests directed against digital companies. The issues involved include classical labour matters (such as long-running labour disputes in Amazon warehouses), as well as protests over consumer issues and the role of Google and Facebook in restructuring the democratic public sphere.

Many of these conflicts – possibly all – can also be understood as criticism of the power and exploitation described in this volume. However I am not seeking to lay out an exhaustive hermeneutics of such protests (whose conclusion might be exactly that finding). First of all, I would be suspicious of the intention of such an analysis, which would – in the light of the theory's normative implications – boil down to the question of whether the protests are (a) incubators of future alternatives or (b) hopeless lost causes. Both are legitimate political positions. But in the end they are nothing more than opinions about a contingent historical process. I see little point in that, even if I am well aware of the demand for such interpretations. Moreover, and this is by far the more important argument, there are empirical reasons why that approach cannot lead to a proper understanding of digital capitalism.

Capital plus consumer vs. labour: the unlikelihood of a social movement against digital capitalism

If we assume that the central social conflict of digital capitalism pits an alliance of capital and consumers against labour, I would argue that we are dealing with a *stalemated conflict*. That is not to say that conflicts, even social movements, are inconceivable. But I do see strong arguments for outright protest in this connection being unlikely.

The history of social conflict reveals successive metamorphoses of con-stituencies, issues, organisations and social bases (Nachtwey 2016b: 253). There are also structural commonalities, however. The strongest and most persistent movements – the bourgeoisie of early capitalism, the labour movement in liberal capitalism, the new social movements in the welfare state era (Nachtwey 2016b) – felt they were fighting to overturn outdated structures, striving for a better future. They were all children of capital-ist growth phases, and their critique successfully connected political and economic interests. The bourgeois revolutions of the eighteenth century articulated the confidence of a class demanding political rights and liber-ties commensurate to its economic significance. The labour movement of the late nineteenth and early twentieth centuries succeeded in combining economic interests with the struggle for political emancipation. The citi-zens described by Marshall and Dahrendorf also sought political as well as economic rights. It was always about the connection of democracy and economy, the fusion of the spheres of state and labour.

The story does not end with the new social movements and their 'artist critique' (Boltanski and Chiapello 2003) of the 'democratic capitalism' of the post-war era (Streeck 2014). From the 1980s the neoliberal constella-tion introduced a new model of civil rights whose roots can be traced to the initial crisis of Fordism in the early 1970s. Wolfgang Streeck argues that the underconsumption crisis of late Fordism marked the starting point not only of a restructuring of capitalism, but also of a change in the meaning and significance of work and the state (Streeck 2012).

Capitalist enterprises responded to the saturated consumer markets of late Fordism with a systematic individualisation of production, hoping to boost demand by encouraging consumers to replace products more fre-quently. Suddenly everyone was trying to sell – to the very same people who were feeling the first chill winds of neoliberalism in their role as workers.[10]

The elevation of the consumer, Streeck argues, successively transcended the bounds of the consumer goods markets and became the paradigm of a transformation of the public sector and ultimately of politics. Citizens, certainly encouraged by the state, began to see themselves as customers. This transformed 'the nature of politics itself' and led to a new 'politics of consumption', which Streeck saw as characterised by the final demise of the social ligatures that had integrated the citizens of 'democratic capitalism' into the tedious political process (Streeck 2012: 271 ff.).

The political sphere became increasingly irrelevant to the public, or more precisely the basis of its legitimacy shifted: 'The decline of political legitimacy did not, however, stop in the area of service provision. Gradually it extended into the very core of citizenship, where the traditional relationship between citizens and the state became increasingly subject to unfavourable comparison with the relationship between customers and producers in the refurbished post-Fordist markets for consumer goods.' (Streeck 2012: 39). The concept of 'market citizenship' (Fudge 2005) puts the 'expansion of the domain of the market and contraction in social' in a nutshell (Fudge 2005: 646).[11]

Today the conflicts of interest between workers and consumers, engendered by the new politics of consumption, are relatively open and visible. From the perspective of 'consumer citizens' (Streeck 2012), politics and economics are no longer the decisive arenas where life opportunities are distributed. A society whose dominant integration mechanisms are governed by the logic of consumption, one can conclude, not only lacks the social ligatures required to activate collective rights; even the demand for such rights is anaemic.

Thus the social conflict in digital capitalism is fundamentally stalemated: one can separate the roles of consumer and worker in theory, but not in practice. Any political spark, it follows, must overcome not only the habitualisation of the consumer role but also the conflicts within the political subjects, whom digital capitalism subsidises as consumers while systematically expropriating them as workers.[12]

It may be hard to imagine a revolutionary subject of digital capitalism, but that does not mean that change is impossible. An intense political debate addressing various aspects has been under way in Europe for quite some time (see the preface). In the concluding chapter I therefore turn to the political options mapped out by an analysis of regional path dependencies.

Notes

1 What would ever be 'completely new' to a moderately well-read sociologist?

2 Braudel speaks of the anti-market or anti-markets to describe the practice of the most powerful and most profitable companies, which can operate without heed to market prices, or indeed set them themselves.

3 Martin Baethge (2000) spoke in this context of an inherited 'industrialism'.

4 In fact Amazon achieved a negative tax rate of minus 1 per cent: it received money from the taxpayer. The reasons for this were tax rebates, tax cuts introduced by the Trump administration and legal loopholes in the tax system.

5 Given the moderate size of the tech sector in Germany this could play out without particularly extreme effects.

6 Otherwise, if the process was technically inevitable, we would be dealing with 'capitalist digitalism' rather than 'digital capitalism'.

7 I am arguing in general and abstract terms here. The point obviously applies to platforms like app stores and social networks, but is less applicable to a company like Amazon, which has significant fixed capital (warehouses, vehicle fleets, machines, aircraft).

8 In the sense that the four currently dominant profit extraction strategies ultimately withdraw resources from labour and transfer them to private wealth (with corresponding distribution conflicts on the capital side).

9 For an especially impressive example see Nachtwey 2016b.

10 For example Oliver Nachtwey (2016a) defines the neoliberal epoch in Germany as a phase of reduction of social and workplace rights.

11 In this perspective post-Fordism (or the neoliberal constellation) was a phase where ligatures were separated from rights, where the individual customer in the individualised markets of a consumption-based democracy increasingly began to expect 'services' instead of the hard work of political and economic democracy. On the other hand, the growing importance of the social role of the consumer can also be understood as a reaction to stagnant or falling real incomes, the changing role of the state and various dynamics of individualisation.

12 It is therefore conceivable that the conflict within digital capitalism will become more obvious as the cross-subsidisation of consumption by venture capital ends.

7

Conclusion: can there be a European-style digital capitalism?

Are new poles of growth – of profitable accumulation – forming? Are rival states contending to steer the global capitalist political economy in divergent directions? … A bright thread of digital technology runs through all these questions.

D. Schiller 2014

Under the label of 'digitalisation', technological change has been high on the European agenda for more than a decade now. Europe's political elites have been looking for a politico-economic strategy to respond to the expansion of the American and Chinese tech giants in particular, trying to develop their own vision of digital transformation. Proactive and reactive aspects mingle here. A veritable smorgasbord of technological innovation strategies has emerged in the larger European economies, probably most notably around Germany's Industrie 4.0, an initiative launched around 2011 and driven by an opaque complex of business, political and lobbying interests (Schroeder 2017; Schroeder, Greef and Schreiter 2017).

At the supranational level we have seen intense discussion leading to new regulatory initiatives. Most notably, the EU Commission has launched an ambitious package of legislation covering digital competition (Digital Markets Act), digital content (Digital Services Act) and data (Data Governance Act, Data Act). These attempts to regulate the platforms all share an assumption that the successive expansion of technology companies operating as proprietary markets should be contained or even reversed. The Digital Markets Act focusses on abuse of market power by the same companies that I identify as operators of proprietary markets, seeking to prohibit access control and price discrimination harmful to producers. Additionally, attempts to break lock-ins and data control through interoperability and data sharing requirements are cross-cutting issues throughout the EU's platform regulation programme.

While one may generally welcome the political pushback that the regulation of proprietary markets intended by the EU represents, its approach to platform regulation also demonstrates a great lack of historical imagination and, in a sense, the ideological bankruptcy of a political system warped by four decades of neoliberalism. While tech companies have built market-like structures that grant them great power over the overall fate of the economy, European policymakers have largely failed to recognise the opportunities that these mechanisms offer for a democratic and ecological transformation of the economy. Instead their focus is on bringing back *political* control over markets without using this power to achieve anything but a neutral market environment. Through crisis and catastrophe, the neoliberal paradigm persists.

To my mind there are two principal obstacles to progress. Firstly, strategic political thinking is obstructed by an understanding of state and economy that has been utterly perverted by neoliberalism. Secondly, Europe appears to me to be much too slow to recognise the normative position endowed to it – like it or not – by the geostrategic reconfiguration of digital capitalism. To do so inevitably means finally taking leave of neoliberal and geostrategic illusions.

The smoking ruins of neoliberalism

What we are dealing with in the EU's approach to digital capitalism is an attempt to turn the marketisation programme of neoliberalism into a counter-hegemonic movement carried out by political elites. Digital markets are being politicised, abolishing the laissez-faire approach of the past twenty years. At the same time, this politicisation is guided by the very same belief in the market that enabled the digital privatisation in the first place. EU platform regulation is, at least in the context of the global West, the most ambitious and powerful initiative to date against the meta-platforms' privatisation of the markets. However, in its attempt to break the power of big tech, it clings to an ideological framework that the vanguard of digital capitalism has already left far behind.

While one could argue that digital capitalism is essentially a programme of market expansion, and thus neoliberal practice (Birch 2020), proprietary markets actually have little in common with the markets of (neo)liberal economic theory. They represent nothing less than the end of neoliberalism, given the centrality it places on the *neutrality of the market*. In line with the neoliberal mantra, market radicals view 'fair competition' as a precondition for legitimate profits, indeed for a properly functioning economy of any kind. Here 'fair' means that the market should be open to all. Admittedly, the practitioners of neoliberalism have always borne empirical violations of their noble theory with great stoicism. The emergence of a system of proprietary markets means they can now kiss goodbye forever to the fiction of a neutral marketplace.[1] If the system of proprietary markets represents the central capitalist innovation of privatised mercantilism, then it is by nature the opposite of everything neoliberal. We are no longer looking at deviations from the theory: the theory itself has been retired by the leading capitalist elites. Ownership abolishes the market as a neutral institution.

Why, one could object, should we be interested in the *ideas* of neo-liberalism? Its trajectory has always been forged by powerful actors – transnational corporations, the institutional trinity of IMF, WTO and World Bank etc. – that were happy to wield the theory to legitimise their actions, without necessarily paying too much attention to the details. Well, for one thing, left-wing critics have argued for years (and still do today) that neoliberalism rules because it is a 'hegemonic' idea. There are shelves and shelves of publications saying just that, often as not citing Antonio Gramsci (1992 [c.1930]). Hegemony theory is based on the assumption that power is secured more by ideas than by practice. But how can one speak of a hegem-ony of neoliberalism, if the neoliberal doctrine is employed only instrumen-tally in the current transformation of capitalism, while actual developments head in quite the opposite direction? Of course fragments of neoliberal doctrine are still alive and kicking – in management, in economic, fiscal and social policy, and in the EU's platform regulation efforts. Nevertheless, the rise of the proprietary markets has brought forth a different model, one that has, at least in theory, the potential to open up much broader – and more democratic – realms. If neoliberal doctrine was no obstacle to the advent of digital capitalism, why should it continue to obstruct strategic thinking in the political economy? If Europe is to save whatever is left of its social model, it will need to develop an idea of the digital society that goes beyond restoring the market.

Life chances as services[2]

Such a model would have to take into account the existing geostrategic ten-sions that characterise global digital capitalism. The emerging geopolitical confrontation between the United States and China burst into view after the Trump administration ditched the free trade consensus in 2016, imposed a string of new tariffs and blocked acquisitions by Chinese companies.[3] The divide in the commercial internet occurred a good deal earlier and runs much deeper than strategic tariff policy ever could. China began working to separate its internet from the rest of the world years ago, creating a complex system of filters and blocking methods. It was this 'Great Firewall', in con-junction with political pressure on US tech companies, that enabled the rise of the Chinese platforms in the first place. Today, despite the comparatively similar trajectories of their leading companies, China and the United States stand for quite distinct models of digital capitalism. The differences lie less in the economic than in the different models for distributing life chances (Dahrendorf 1986).

Dahrendorf describes life chances as a yardstick of the quality of a society. The underlying idea is that states can be judged by the options they offer their citizens. Life chances are based, as described in Chapter 6, on a combination of rights and social ties (ligatures). The rights to political participation, for example, that were extended to ever broader sections of society in Europe from the nineteenth century, had to be brought to life by political parties and activated within particular ideologies. Rights are by no means the only method for distributing life chances. European feudal societies also granted personal development opportunities, but they did so according to very different criteria of rank and status.

Considering digital capitalism from this angle reveals a specific trend in Western societies.[4] In the historically new domain of the digital, life chances are distributed not as entitlements but according to a logic of capitalist services. Access is granted not on the basis of citizenship, but to those who sign up to the conditions of profit-driven companies.

Yet again we find citizens reduced to their role as consumers. This exacerbates the legitimacy problems of the political apparatuses, which find themselves unable to offer any prospect of prosperity gains through digitalisation, while commercial technologies become ever more seamlessly integrated into their citizens' everyday lives. Not only does the consumer-centred nature of digital capitalism generate no social ties of its own – digitalisation finds itself in increasingly open conflict with democracy (Pfister and Yang 2018).

Digital capitalism Chinese-style

In China a different model appears to be emerging. Rather than distributing life chances as capitalist services, this is a model of social privileges, which the leading companies of Chinese-style digital capitalism also serve.

The poster child of this development is Social Credit Scoring (SCS) (Dai 2018; Jiang and Fu 2018), which has caused outrage in the West without being properly understood. SCS is intended to apply to Chinese citizens and resident foreigners alike (Leigh and Li 2018). Implementation of the basic system is ongoing, but appears patchy (Drinhausen and Brussee 2021). Nevertheless, the system certainly sets out to combine the technical possibilities of information control (big data) with political control ('big brother') and economic management (big profit) (Jiang and Fu 2018).

National platforms for data exchange came into operation in October 2015, to aggregate public data (from the central, regional and local government) with ratings from commercial entities (Alibaba being the most important) (Meissner 2017). They are managed by forty-seven different institutions, led by the State Council, the National Development and Reform Commission (NDRC) and the People's Bank of China (Drinhausen and Brussee 2021). Credit reference systems have proliferated in many parts of the world (Mau 2017) – observers speak of the United States for example as a 'reputation society' (Dai 2018). A person's credit score regulates their access to bank loans, rental housing and other capitalist services. SCS goes a great deal further.

This is not individual companies aggregating or purchasing data and making score-based decisions, but the Chinese 'reputation state' (Dai 2018) defining what is (un)desirable behaviour to regulate access to public services. Proprietary markets provide the blueprint: data is aggregated from an unprecedented number of sources (information control) in order to regulate access to services and opportunities (access control) and steer economic development (price and performance control). Every citizen starts with a base score that is increased by desirable behaviour and reduced by violations. The score is associated with sanctions and rewards. For example foreign travel, use of high-speed trains, business permits and property purchases may be denied.[5] SCS is reported to include means to punish companies and their managers for transgressions such as payment arrears, violations of emission levels and labour safety laws, breaking state investment rules or late delivery by e-commerce companies (Meissner 2017). The catalogue of potential sanctions includes exclusion from public contracts, worse borrowing terms, higher taxes, stopping investment and a prohibition on issuing bonds.

This focus on economic management places SCS in the context of other far-reaching strategies for transforming China's 'state capitalism 3.0' (ten Brink 2016), such as the 'Belt and Road Initiative' launched in 2013 and followed in quick succession by the 'Internet Plus' agenda and the 'Made in China 2025' programme (Butollo and Lüthje 2017; Hong 2017a; H. Shen 2018).[6] From the perspective of critical political economy, all these initiatives are driven not only by China's 'new strength' but above all by the creeping crisis of its model of production. Chinese industry has been struggling for years with chronic overcapacity, great dependency on low-skilled industrial labour, and on foreign investment and key components, as well as corresponding social tensions, especially in the context of industrial labour conflicts (Hong 2017a, 2017b; H. Shen, 2018). In this context the SCS system represents an attempt to manage the economic transformation at the micro level and to keep a lid on the social conflicts provoked by the necessary changes. This places SCS at the heart of the restructuring of Chinese capitalism, where its designated role is to integrate economic and social control.[7] It embodies a configuration of power that differs from the West's digital capitalism, by distributing life chances not as services but according to a logic privileging social conformity. Rather than reducing the citizen to the consumer role, punishments and coercion substitute for social ties.

A society of digital rights

Digital capitalism is not just a machine for producing social inequality, but in a more comprehensive sense a new format of societal power. This model has brought forth two new options for distribution of life chances: one model supplying them as capitalist services and another privileging political and social conformity.

Both versions represent social and fundamentally normative challenges to whatever survives of the legacy of 'social modernity' (Nachtwey 2016a) in post-neoliberal Europe. As the expansive and extractive logic of digital capitalism unfolds in two geostrategically polarised versions, the periphery is left with only two options: to integrate more deeply or to map out its own path (S. Weber 2017: 415 f.). It has been obvious for some time that the political class in Europe – in the digital sphere as elsewhere – is torn between neoliberal patterns, economic interests and inalienable values. In this context digital capitalism exposes the absurdity of neoliberal thinking, the precarity of economic interests and the danger to shared values. Taking the normative goals seriously would mean establishing a good digital society built on civic rights – in opposition to the capitalist services and state privileges models. The thrust of such a countermovement must consist in the politicisation of individual and collective liberty.

Notes

1 Of course market neutrality has always been a fiction in reality.
2 I am indebted to Francesca Bria for the model of services, privileges and rights which I introduce in the following. She laid out the concept at a conference of the Decode project in autumn 2018 in Barcelona.
3 Russia forms a relatively autonomous periphery.
4 Societies whose digital complex is dominated by the leading companies of the commercial internet (the GAFA group and structurally similar firms).

5 Punishments observed in pilot cities included public shaming on billboards for traffic violations, fines for incorrect recycling, and confiscation of a loudly barking dog (Ohlberg, Ahmed and Lang 2017; Liang and Chen 2022).

6 'Made in China 2025' outlines steps to be undertaken by the Chinese state and enterprises to acquire key technologies by 2025. The 'Internet Plus' agenda is ultimately a supplement to 'Made in China 2025' outlining the specific role of the internet in the economic restructuring. The New Silk Road ('One Belt, One Road') comprises international investments by the Chinese state in trade infrastructure projects.

7 Little is yet known about its practicability and possible unintended consequences. For example it is doubtful whether the Chinese government will actually succeed in harmonising data from such diverse public and private sources; apparently much of the public data exists only on paper, which clearly restricts its usefulness for an automated scoring system (Meissner 2017).

Appendix

Table A1 Selection of known Alibaba investment funds

Name (year established)	Available information on size and strategy
Alibaba Capital Partners (2008)	• Investment fund, regarded as Alibaba's 'investment arm' • Investments include Koubei (local services), Kuaidi Dache (ride-hailing app), Twiggle (e-commerce), Xiami (music streaming, closed 2021)
Alibaba Cloud (2009)	• Investment in digital infrastructure and start-ups in the Asia-Pacific region
Alibaba Entrepreneurs Fund (2015)	• Not-for-profit fund investing in young entrepreneurs and graduates in Hong Kong and Taiwan
Alibaba Health Information Technology (n.a.)	• Direct and online distribution of pharmaceuticals and health services
Alibaba Innovation Ventures (n.a.)	• Investments in transport and telecommunications
Digital Media, Entertainment Investment Fund (2006)	• Investment fund for the culture industries • Investment in digital media and the entertainment business • Volume (November 2016): US$1.5 billion
Hainan Alibaba Pictures Entertainment Industry Investment Fund (2016)	• Investment fund for the culture industries • Investment in 'high-quality' film and television projects, especially production, marketing and distribution, new technologies, and 'celebrity resources' • Volume (July 2016): US$300 million • Investors: Alibaba Pictures (US$75 million), Wuhu Gopher (US$225 million)
Shanghai Yunxin Venture Capital Co. (2014)	• Venture capital fund (belongs to Ant Financial) • Investments in IT, transport, culture and media, financial services • Stakes include Jiangsu Yonganxing (bike-sharing), Shunyitong (smart parking)

Table A1 (continued)

Name (year established)	Available information on size and strategy
Taiwan Fund (2015)	• Venture capital fund for start-ups in Taiwan
	• Managed by a subsidiary of China Development Industrial
	• Volume (November 2015): *c.*US$310 million
Yu Le Bao (2014)	• Investment fund for the culture industries
	• Investment in films, television, online games
	• Investors: retail investors can contribute small amounts via smartphone app Taobao -> crowdfunding
Tianhung Yu'e Bao Money Market Fund (2013)	• Money market fund specially designed for Alipay
	• Investment in financial products
	• Marketed through Ant Financial, managed by Tianhong Asset Management Co.
	• Volume (December 2020): US$157 billion; one of China's largest financial institutions
	• Investors (January 2022): more than 500 million
NREAL FUND	• US$60 million investment in augmented reality equipment manufacturer NREAL

Sources: Compiled from ongoing public reporting.

Table A2 Internet platforms: fields of expansion and main rivals

Platform	Core business	Expansion	Main rivals
Apple	Hardware and Software		Samsung, Lenovo, Asus, Microsoft, Amazon, Google, Xiaomi, Fujitsu
		Media: iTunes store, Apple Music, app store, Apple Books and Apple Books Store (e-book reader/store), Apple Music (music streaming), Apple TV+	Google, Amazon Prime Video, Netflix, Hulu, Spotify, Disney+, YouTube Music, Tencent Music, HBO Max, Nook, traditional media companies
		Finance: Apple Pay, Apple Pay Cash, Apple Wallet, Apple Financing	PayPal, Amazon, Google, Samsung, credit card companies, Alibaba, Tencent
		Cloud services: iCloud	Amazon, Azure, Salesforce, Microsoft, IBM, Google, Tencent Cloud, Oracle Cloud, Alibaba Cloud

Table A2 (continued)

Platform	Core business	Expansion	Main rivals
		Smart Home: Apple Homekit, Siri, smart speakers	Amazon, Google, Alibaba
		Education: iPad, Apple Pencil, iCloud, apps	Google, Amazon, Microsoft
		Mobility/travel: Carplay, Apple Maps	Google (Android Auto), Automotive Grade Linux
		Health: Apple Health, Apple Watch	Samsung, Fitbit, Garmin
		AI: Apple Machine Learning Research, Apple Developer	Amazon, Google, IBM, Microsoft, Alibaba
Amazon	E-commerce		Traditional operators like Walmart, supermarkets/retailers, specialised internet retailers, eBay, Alibaba
		Media: Amazon Games Studios (video game development), Prime Video (film streaming), Fire TV, Amazon Music, Amazon Publishing (book publisher), Audible Studios (audio book production), Amazon Studios (film and series production), Amazon Underground (in-app purchases)	Google, Apple, Microsoft, Netflix, Spotify, Tencent, Disney+, HBO Max, Noo, games producers, film studios, television stations, traditional media companies, publishers
		Finance: Amazon Pay, Amazon Coins, Amazon Visa	PayPal, Google, Apple, Samsung, banks, Alipay, Tencent
		Cloud services: Amazon Web Services, Amazon Drive	Microsoft, Google, IBM, Apple, Alibaba, Tencent,
		Hardware/software: Kindle (e-book reader), Kindle Fire (tablet), Fire (phone), Amazon Fire (set-top box), Fire TV (stick (HDMI))	Apple, Kobo, Nook
		Smart home: Amazon Echo (smart speaker), Amazon Alexa	Google, Microsoft, Cisco, Alibaba, Apple

Table A2 (continued)

Platform	Core business	Expansion	Main rivals
		Education: TenMarks, Amazon Ignite, AWS Educate, Amazon Inspire, Prime Student, LMS Integrated Store, Amazon Education Publishing, Amazon Business, Amazon Catalyst	Google, Apple, Microsoft
		Logistics: Amazon Logistics (courier services), Amazon Locker (parcel lockers), Prime Air (air freight, delivery drones)	UPS, Fedex, DHL, Hermes
Alibaba	E-commerce		Amazon, JD.com, eBay, Meituan-Dianping, Baidu, Pinduoduo, Meituan, Shopify, Rakuten, Flipkart
		Media: 9Apps (app store), 9Game (gaming platforms), Aligames (video game production), Damai (ticketing platforms), MaiLive (live events), Maizuo (content creation), Alimusic/Xiami (music streaming), Alibaba Planet (music platforms), Alibaba Pictures (film and series licensing/production), Youku Tudou (online television, video streaming), AliSports, *South China Morning Post*, UC News (news and entertainment), Weibo, Youko, DingTalk for Sports (sports coverage), 88VIP	Tencent, Google, Apple, Netease, Toutiao, ByteDance (TikTok/ Douyin), Chinese newspaper publishers, Amazon Prime
		Communication: Alimail, Aliwangwang (messaging), DingTalk (business communication app), Laiwang (news app)	Tencent, Facebook, Google, Renren

Table A2 (continued)

Platform	Core business	Expansion	Main rivals
		Advertising: on Alibaba platforms, UC Union (traffic monetisation platforms), Focus Media (advertising)	Tencent, Google, Baidu
		Finance: Alipay, MYbank (online bank, lending), Sesame Credit/Zhima Credit (credit scoring), Ant Fortune (asset management app)	Tencent, Apple, PayPal, Google, credit card companies, banks
		Cloud services: Alibaba-Cloud, Aliyun, OBS Cloud	Amazon, Microsoft, Google, Tencent
		Hardware/software: Ali OS (mobile operating system), UC Browser (mobile browser), Shenma (search engine)	Apple, Baidu, Tencent, Google
		Smart home: Ali Genie (personal assistant), Tmall Genie (smart speaker), Ali-Smart (app)	Tencent, Baidu, JD, Apple, Google, Xiaomi, electronics manufacturers (Hisense, LG, Samsung)
		Health: Ali Health (medical products and services)	JD Health
		Mobility/travel: AutoNavi (navigation), Fliggy (tourism), Didi (ride-hailing), Ofo (bike-sharing)	Tencent, Google, Apple
		Offline retail: New Retail Strategy, Hema (supermarkets), vending machines, malls, Sun Art Retail Group	Stationary retail, Walmart, Tesco, Carrefour
		Logistics: Cainiao Smart Logistics Network, STO Express, ZTO Express, YTP Express, BST Express, Air China Cargo	JD Logistics, Amazon
Tencent	Messaging, games		Alibaba, Google, Apple, Amazon, Facebook, Baidu, ByteDance, NetEase

Table A2 (continued)

Platform	Core business	Expansion	Main rivals
		Media: Yingyongbao (app store), WeChat Miniprograms (apps in WeChat), QQ Music (music platforms), QQ Player (media player), China Reading Limited/Tencent Literature (reading platforms), Tencent Comic (anime/manga platforms), Tencent News (news app), QQ.com (online portal for news, e-mail, software, online games, dating), Tencent Pictures (film/celebrity platforms), Tencent Video (video streaming platforms), Now Live (live streaming app), Pitu (photo software), Nextradio, Huya, DouYou (video game sites), 1C Entertainment and other game developers	Alibaba, Facebook, Google, Microsoft, Apple, games producers, Toutiao, Chinese newspaper publishers and television stations, ByteDance (TikTok/Douyin), NetEase, Meituan
		Communication: QZone, 3G QQ (mobile social network), Tencent Microblog, Interest Tribe, Pengyou, QQ Mail, Tencent Questionnaire (survey platforms), Tucao (feedback platforms), QQ Show (virtual avatars), QQ Home (virtual homes), Enterprise WeChat/Weixin (business communication app)	Alibaba, Sina Weibo, Renren
		Advertising: on Tencent platforms	Baidu, Alibaba, ByteDance
		Finance: TenPay, WeChat Pay, QQ Wallet, WeBank (online bank), Tencent Credit (credit scoring system)	Alibaba, PayPal, Apple, Google, Chinese banks

Table A2 (continued)

Platform	Core business	Expansion	Main rivals
		Cloud services: Tencent Cloud	Alibaba Cloud, Amazon, Google, IBM, Microsoft, Oracle Cloud, Apple, Baidu AI Cloud, Huawei
		Software: QQ browser, Tencent Mobile Manager (mobile security software), Tencent PC Manager (online security software), WeChat Search (search engine), Sogou (search engine)	Google
		Education: Tencent Education, Tencent Classroom Intellisense (education platforms), CODING, Study QQ, WeLearning	Google, Apple, Amazon, Microsoft
		Mobility/travel: Didi (ride-hailing), Mobike (bike-sharing), public transport ticketing, AI in Car, Tencent Intelligent Mobility (TIM)	Alibaba, Uber
		Retail: QQ Gen (clothing brand), The Paypers (NFT trading platform)	JD.com
		AI: Tencent AI Lab, Tencent YouTu Lab	Baidu, Alibaba, Google, Amazon, Facebook

Sources: Compiled from company annual reports, websites, press releases and ongoing news reporting (building on Dolata 2015). The table does not claim to be exhaustive. In all cases, and especially the Chinese platforms Alibaba und Tencent, it is difficult to differentiate between investments, acquisitions and fields of expansion. I have therefore concentrated on the areas of greatest strategic significance.

References

Abbate, Janet. 1999. *Inventing the Internet*. Cambridge, MA: MIT Press.

Aglietta, Michel. 2015. *A Theory of Capitalist Regulation: The US Experience*. London and New York: Verso.

Aisslinger, Moritz. 2016. 'Die armen Kinder vom Silicon Valley'. *Die Zeit*, 22 September. www.zeit.de/2016/38/silicon-valley-kalifornien-usa-armut (Accessed May 2022).

Andrae, Anders S. G. 2019. 'Projecting the Chiaroscuro of the Electricity Use of Communication and Computing from 2018 to 2030'. Preprint (February 2019). https://doi.org/10.13140/RG.2.2.25103.02724 (Accessed May 2022).

Aneesh, Aneesh. 2010. 'Globale Arbeit: Algokratische Formen der Organisation'. In *Internationale Arbeitsräume: Unsicherheiten und Herausforderungen, Soziologische Studien*, edited by Esther Ruiz Ben, 55–96. Freiburg: Centaurus Verlag.

AppBrain. 2022. 'Number of Available Applications in the Google Play Store from December 2009 to March 2022', cited from Statista (March 2022). www.statista.com/statistics/266210/number-of-available-applications-in-the-google-play-store/ (Accessed May 2022).

Armbruster, Alexander. 2018. 'Hightech ist nicht im Angebot'. *Frankfurter Allgemeine Zeitung*, 13 March. www.faz.net/aktuell/wirtschaft/diginomics/donald-trump-unterbindet-qualcomm-uebernahme-durch-broadcom-15491452.html (Accessed May 2022).

Arnoldi, Jakob. 2009. *Alles Geld verdampft: Finanzkrise in der Weltrisikogesellschaft*. Frankfurt am Main: Suhrkamp.

Arrighi, Giovanni. 1994. *The Long Twentieth Century*. London: Verso.

Aspers, Patrik. 2015. *Märkte*. Wiesbaden: Springer VS.

Associated Press. 2017. 'Smart Speaker Sales More Than Tripled in 2017'. *Billboard*, 28 December. www.billboard.com/articles/business/8085524/smart-speaker-sales-tripled-25-million-year-2017 (Accessed May 2022).

Attwood-Charles, William. 2019. 'Technology and Control: Institutional Work and Digital Platforms', unpublished manuscript.

Aytay, Ryan. 2017. 'Salesforce and Google Form New Global Strategic Partnership', 6 November 2017, www.salesforce.com/content/blogs/us/en/2017/11/salesforce-google-form-strategic-partnership.html (Accessed February 2023).

Baccaro, Lucio, and Chris Howell. 2017. *Trajectories of Neoliberal Transformation: European Industrial Relations Since the 1970s*. Cambridge: Cambridge University Press.

Baethge, Martin. 2000. 'Abschied vom Industrialismus: Konturen einer neuen gesellschaftlichen Ordnung der Arbeit'. *SOFI-Mitteilungen* 28: 87–102.

Bahl, Friederike, and Philipp Staab. 2015. 'Die Proletarisierung der Dienstleistungsarbeit'. *Soziale Welt* 66(4): 371–88.

Bahrdt, Hans Paul, Horst Kern, Martin Osterland and Michael Schumann. 1970. *Zwischen Drehbank und Computer: Industriearbeit im Wandel der Technik.* Reinbek bei Hamburg: Rowohlt.

Barboza, David. 2016. 'How China Built "iPhone City" with Billions in Perks for Apple's Partner'. *New York Times*, 29 December. www.nytimes.com/2016/12/29/technology/apple-iphone-china-foxconn.html (Accessed May 2022).

Barlow, John Perry. 1996. *A Declaration of the Independence of Cyberspace,* Davos. www.eff.org/cyberspace-independence (Accessed February 2023).

Bartnik, Marie. 2021. 'Amazon a perdu des parts de marché en France'. *Le Figaro,* 17 March. www.lefigaro.fr/flash-eco/amazon-moins-performant-que-le-marche-du-e-commerce-en-france-en-2020-20210317 (Accessed May 2022).

Baumol, William J. 2013. *The Cost Disease: Why Computers Get Cheaper and Health Care Doesn't.* New Haven, CT and London: Yale University Press.

BEA (US Bureau of Economic Analysis). 2018a. 'National Income and Product Accounts. Table 6.16B. Corporate Profits by Industry'. https://apps.bea.gov/iTable/?ReqID=19&step=4&isuri=1&1921=flatfiles&3Place=N#eyJhcHBpZCI6MTksInN0ZXBzIjpbMSwyLDNdLCJkYXRhIjpbWyJDYXRlZ29yaWVzIiwiU3VydmV5Il0sWyJOSVBBX1RhYmxlX0xpc3QiLCIyMzciXV19 (Accessed February 2023).

BEA (US Bureau of Economic Analysis). 2018b. 'National income and product accounts. Table 6.16C. Corporate profits by industry'. https://apps.bea.gov/iTable/?ReqID=19&step=4&isuri=1&1921=flatfiles&3Place=N#eyJhcHBpZCI6MTksInN0ZXBzIjpbMSwyLDNdLCJkYXRhIjpbWyJDYXRlZ29yaWVzIiwiU3VydmV5Il0sWyJOSVBBX1RhYmxlX0xpc3QiLCIyMzgiXV19 (Accessed February 2023).

BEA (US Bureau of Economic Analysis). 2018c. 'National income and product accounts. Table 6.16D. Corporate profits by industry'. https://apps.bea.gov/iTable/?ReqID=19&step=4&isuri=1&1921=flatfiles&3Place=N#eyJhcHBpZCI6MTksInN0ZXBzIjpbMSwyLDNdLCJkYXRhIjpbWyJDYXRlZ29yaWVzIiwiU3VydmV5Il0sWyJOSVBBX1RhYmxlX0xpc3QiLCIyMzkiXV19 (Accessed February 2023).

BEA (US Bureau of Economic Analysis). 2021. 'Updates Digital Economy Estimates – June 2021'. *US Bureau of Economic Analysis.* www.bea.gov/system/files/2021–06/DE%20June%202021%20update%20for%20web%20v3.pdf (Accessed May 2022).

Bell, Daniel. 1973. *The Coming of Post-Industrial Society.* New York: Basic Books.

Benkler, Yochai. 2006. *The Wealth of Networks: How Social Production Transforms Markets and Freedom.* New Haven, CT and London: Yale University Press.

Benner, Christiane, ed. 2015. *Crowdwork – zurück in die Zukunft?* Frankfurt am Main: Bund-Verlag.

Bercovici, Jeff. 2016. 'Peter Thiel is Very, Very Interested in Young People's Blood'. *Inc.,* 1 August 2016. www.inc.com/jeff-bercovici/peter-thiel-young-blood.html (Accessed May 2022).

Beverungen, Armin. 2017. 'Algorithmisches Management'. In *Nach der Revolution: Ein Brevier digitaler Kulturen,* edited by Timon Beyes, Jörg Metelmann and Claus Pias, 52–63. Berlin: Tempus Corporate.

Birch, Kean. 2020. 'Automated Neoliberalism? The Digital Organisation of Markets in Technoscientific Capitalism'. *New Formations: A Journal of Culture/Theory/ Politics* 100: 10–27.

BIS (Bank for International Settlements). 2022. 'Global OTC Derivatives Market'. *Bank for International Settlements.* https://stats.bis.org/statx/srs/table/d5.1 (Accessed May 2022).

Blomert, Reinhard. 2003. 'Kämpfer gegen die Wall-Street: Der ehemalige Chef der US-Börsenaufsicht enthüllt die Vetternwirtschaft an den Finanzmärkten'. *Die Zeit*, 13 March.

Blomert, Reinhard. 2005. 'Das Ende der „neuen Ökonomie": Eine finanzsoziologis che Untersuchung'. *Berliner Journal für Soziologie* 15(2): 179–98.

Blossfeld, Hans-Peter, and Karl Ulrich Mayer. 1991. 'Berufsstruktureller Wandel und soziale Ungleichheit: Entsteht in der Bundesrepublik ein neues Dienstleistungsproletariat?' *Kölner Zeitschrift für Soziologie und Sozialpsychologie* 43(4): 671–96.

Board of Governors of the Federal Reserve System. 2022. 'Nonfinancial Corporate Business; Total Liabilities, Level'. *Federal Reserve Bank of St Louis* (10 March 2022). https://fred.stlouisfed.org/series/TLBSNNCB (Accessed May 2022).

Boes, Andreas, Tobias Kämpf, Barbara Langes and Thomas Lühr, eds. 2018. *'Lean' und 'agil' im Büro: Neue Organisationskonzepte in der digitalen Transformation und ihre Folgen für die Angestellten*. Bielefeld: Transcript.

Boltanski, Luc, and Eve Chiapello. 2003. *Der neue Geist des Kapitalismus*. Konstanz: UVK.

Bourdieu, Pierre. 1982. *Die feinen Unterschiede: Kritik der gesellschaftlichen Urteilskraft*. Frankfurt am Main: Suhrkamp.

Boutang, Yann Moulier. 2011. *Cognitive Capitalism*. Cambridge, UK and Malden, MA: Polity.

Boyer, Robert, and Jean-Pierre Durand. 1993. *L'après-fordisme*. Paris: Syros.

Boyer, Robert, and Michel Freyssenet. 2003. *Produktionsmodelle: Eine Typologie am Beispiel der Automobilindustrie*. Berlin: Edition Sigma.

Braudel, Fernand. 1986 [1979]. *Sozialgeschichte des 15.–18. Jahrhundert*, vol. 2: *Der Handel*. Munich: Kindler.

Braudel, Fernand. 2016 [1976]. *Die Dynamik des Kapitalismus*. Stuttgart: Klett-Cotta.

Braverman, Harry. 1975. *Labor and Monopoly Capital: The Degradation of Work in the Twentieth Century*. New York: Monthly Review Press.

Brinkmann, Ulrich. 2011. *Die unsichtbare Faust des Marktes: Betriebliche Kontrolle und Koordination im Finanzmarktkapitalismus*. Berlin: Edition Sigma.

Broadberry, Stephen, and Mary O'Mahony. 2005. 'Britain's Twentieth Century Productivity Performance in International Perspective'. In *Work and Pay in Twentieth-Century Britain*, edited by Nicholas Crafts, Ian Gazeley and Andrew Newell, 38–57. Cambridge: Cambridge University Press.

Brynjolfsson, Erik, and Andrew McAfee. 2014. *The Second Machine Age: Wie die nächste digitale Revolution unser aller Leben verändern wird*. Kulmbach: Börsenmedien.

Bude, Heinz. 2001. *Generation Berlin*. Berlin: Merve.

Bude, Heinz. 2016. *Wie weiter mit Karl Marx?* Hamburg: Hamburger Edition.

Bundeszentrale für politische Bildung. 2017. 'Börsengehandelte und außerbörslich gehandelte Finanzderivate: Bestand in absoluten Zahlen, weltweit 1993 bis 2016'.

www.bpb.de/nachschlagen/zahlen-und-fakten/globalisierung/52602/finanzderi
vate (Accessed May 2022).

Burawoy, Michael. 1979. *Manufacturing Consent: Changes in the Labor Process
under Monopoly Capitalism*. Chicago: University of Chicago Press.

Butollo, Florian. 2016. 'Die große Mobilmachung: Die globale Landnahme von
Arbeit und die Reservearmeemechanismen der Gegenwart'. In *Kapitalismus und
Ungleichheit: Die neuen Verwerfungen*, edited by Heinz Bude and Philipp Staab,
215–36. Frankfurt am Main: Campus.

Butollo, Florian, and Boy Lüthje. 2017. '"Made in China 2025". Intelligent
Manufacturing and Work'. In *The New Digital Workplace: How New
Technologies Revolutionise Work*, edited by Kendra Briken, Shiona Chillas,
Martin Krzywdzinski and Abigail Marks, Critical Perspectives on Work and
Employment Series, 42–61. London: Palgrave.

Butterwegge, Christoph, Bettina Lösch and Ralf Ptak. 2017. *Kritik des
Neoliberalismus*, 3rd ed. Wiesbaden: Springer VS.

Canalys. 2018. 'Google Beats Amazon to First Place in Smart Speaker Market'.
www.canalys.com/static/press_release/2018/Press%20release%2020230518%20
Google%20beats%20Amazon%20to%20first%20place%20in%20smart%20
speaker%20market.pdf (Accessed May 2022).

Canalysis and Statista. 2022. 'Cloud Infrastructure Services Vendor Market Share
Worldwide from 4th Quarter 2017 to 1st Quarter 2022'. *Statista* (August 2022).
www.statista.com/statistics/967365/worldwide-cloud-infrastructure-services-
market-share-vendor/ (Accessed May 2022).

Caplan, Robyn, and danah boyd. 2018. 'Isomorphism through Algorithms.
Institutional Dependencies in the Case of Facebook'. *Big Data and Society* 5(1):
1–12.

CBInsights. 2021. 'State of Venture: Global. 2021'. *CBInsights*, 12 January. www.
cbinsights.com/reports/CB-Insights_Venture-Report-2021.pdf (Accessed May
2022).

CBInsights. 2022. 'State of Venture Q1'22 Report'. *CBInsights*, 7 April.
www.cbinsights.com/research/report/venture-trends-q1-2022/ (Accessed May
2022).

Cecchetti, Stephen G., Madhusudan Mohanty and Fabrizio Zampolli. 2011. *The
Real Effects of Debt*, BIS Working Paper 352. www.bis.org/publ/work352.htm
(Accessed May 2022).

Cecchetti, Stephen G., and Kim Schoenholtz. 2018. 'Financing Intangible Capital'.
VoxEU, 22 February 2018. https://voxeu.org/article/financing-intangible-capital
(Accessed May 2022).

Cendrowski, Scott. 2015. 'Alibaba Launches Two New Venture Funds'. *Fortune*,
19 November. http://fortune.com/2015/11/19/alibaba-vc-funds (Accessed May
2022).

Chen, Celia. 2018. 'Online Retailer JD.com Follows Amazon's Footsteps with
Own Brand Selling Household Basics'. *South China Morning Post*, 16 January.
www.scmp.com/tech/china-tech/article/2128481/online-retailer-jdcom-follows-
amazons-selling-own-brand-selling (Accessed May 2022).

Chen, Lulu Yilun. 2018. 'The Chinese Unknown That's Making Africa's Phones'.
Bloomberg, 29 March. www.bloomberg.com/news/articles/2018-03-28/this-
chinese-phone-maker-has-taken-over-africa-for-better-and-worse (Accessed May
2022).

Chen, Tingyi. 2017. 'China Mobile Payment Report 2017'. *Walk the Chat*, 25 June 2017. https://walkthechat.com/china-mobile-payment-report-2017 (Accessed June 2019).

Chen, Tingyi. 2018. 'Tencent, One of China's Largest Investment Fund'. *Walk the Chat*, 11 February 2018. https://walkthechat.com/tencent-one-chinas-largest-investment-fund (Accessed June 2019).

Christensen, Clayton M. 1997. *The Innovator's Dilemma: When New Technologies Cause Great Firms to Fail*. Boston, MA: Harvard Business School Press.

Cisco. 2016. *The Zettabyte Era: Trends and Analysis*. https://webobjects.cdw.com/webobjects/media/pdf/Solutions/Networking/White-Paper-Cisco-The-Zettabyte-Era-Trends-and-Analysis.pdf (Accessed May 2022).

Cisco. 2019. *Cisco Visual Networking Index: Forecast and Trends, 2017–2022*. Cisco public white paper. https://twiki.cern.ch/twiki/pub/HEPIX/TechwatchNetwork/HtwNetworkDocuments/white-paper-c11-741490.pdf (Accessed May 2022).

Coser, Lewis A. 2009 [1956]. *Theorie sozialer Konflikte*. Wiesbaden: VS Verlag für Sozialwissenschaften.

Crotty, James. 2007. *If Financial Market Competition is so Intense, Why are Financial Firm Profits so High?: Reflections on the Current 'Golden Age' of Finance* [working paper]. Amherst, MA: University of Massachusetts Amherst.

Crouch, Colin. 1998. 'The Globalized Economy: An End to the Age of Industrial Citizenship?' In *Advancing Theory in Labor Law and Industrial Relations in a Global Context*, edited by Ton Wilthagen, 151–64. Amsterdam: North-Holland Publishing.

Crouch, Colin. 2008. *Postdemokratie*. Frankfurt am Main: Suhrkamp.

Crouch, Colin. 2009. 'Privatised Keynesianism: An Unacknowledged Policy Regime'. *British Journal of Politics and International Relations* 11(3): 382–99.

Cuthbertson, Anthony. 2018. 'Billionaire Trump Supporter Peter Thiel Denies Being a Vampire', *Independent*, 2 November. www.independent.co.uk/life-style/gadgets-and-tech/news/peter-thiel-vampire-donald-trump-life-extension-blood-transfusion-ambrosia-palantir-a8614061.html (Accessed June 2019).

Dahrendorf, Ralf. 1956. *Unskilled Labour in British Industry*. London: University of London.

Dahrendorf, Ralf. 1965. *Gesellschaft und Demokratie in Deutschland*. Munich: Piper.

Dahrendorf, Ralf. 1979. *A New World Order?: Problems and Prospects of International Relations in the 1980s*. Singapore: FEP.

Dahrendorf, Ralf. 1986. *Lebenschancen: Anläufe zur sozialen und politischen Theorie*. Frankfurt am Main: Suhrkamp.

Dahrendorf, Ralf. 2007. *Auf der Suche nach einer neuen Ordnung: Eine Politik der Freiheit für das 21. Jahrhundert*, 4th ed. Munich: C. H. Beck.

Dai, Xin. 2018. 'Toward a Reputation State: The Social Credit System Project of China'. *SSRN*, 24 June. https://ssrn.com/abstract=3193577 (Accessed May 2022).

Davidkhanian, Suzy. 2021. 'US Retail Spending Jumped Nearly 16% This Year Despite Inflation, Supply Chain Woes'. *eMarketer*, 27 October. www.emarketer.com/content/us-retail-spending-jumped-this-year-despite-inflation-supply-chain-woes (Accessed May 2022).

Davis, Leila Emami. 2014. 'The Financialization of the Nonfinancial Corporation in the Post-1970 US Economy'. PhD dissertation, University of Massachusetts, Amherst.

de Grazia, Victoria. 2016. 'The Crisis of Hyper-Consumerism: Capitalism's Latest Forward Lurch'. In *Capitalism: The Reemergence of a Historical Concept*, edited by Jürgen Kocka and Marcel van der Linden, 71–106. London: Bloomsbury Academic.

Deeg, Richard, Iain Hardie and Sylvia Maxfield, eds. 2016. 'What is Patient Capital, and Where does it Exist?' *Socio-Economic Review* 14(4): 615–25.

Deng, Iris. 2019. 'Tencent Says Criticism of Its Dominance in Social Media Is "Groundless" after its WeChat App Blocks Three Rivals'. *South China Morning Post*, 17 January. www.scmp.com/tech/apps-social/article/2182494/tencent-says-criticism-its-hegemony-social-media-groundless-after (Accessed June 2019).

Deutschmann, Christoph. 2001. *Postindustrielle Industriesoziologie: Theoretische Grundlagen, Arbeitsverhältnisse und soziale Identitäten*. Weinheim and Munich: Beltz Juventa.

Dohse, Knuth, Ulrich Jürgens and Thomas Malsch. 1984. 'Vom „Fordismus" zum „Toyotismus"? Die Organisation der industriellen Arbeit in der japanischen Automobilindustrie'. *Leviathan* 12(4): 448–77.

Dolata, Ulrich. 2015. 'Volatile Monopole: Konzentration, Konkurrenz und Innovationsstrategien der Internetkonzerne'. *Berliner Journal für Soziologie* 4: 505–29.

Dolata, Ulrich. 2018. 'Die zweite Reihe – neue Konkurrenz für die Internetkonzerne?' *spw Schwerpunk* 2: 23–8.

Dörre, Klaus, and Ulrich Brinkmann. 2005. 'Finanzmarktkapitalismus: Triebkraft eines flexiblen Produktionsmodells?' *Finanzmarkt-Kapitalismus: Analysen zum Wandel von Produktionsregimen*, special issue of *Kölner Zeitschrift für Soziologie und Sozialpsychologie* 45: 85–116.

Dörre, Klaus, and Bernd Röttger. 2003. *Das neue Marktregime*. Hamburg: VSA.

Dowling, Savannah. 2018. 'Huge Rounds, Heated Competition: How Tencent & Alibaba Are Defining VC in China'. *Crunchbase news*, 21 January. https://news.crunchbase.com/news/huge-rounds-heated-competition-tencent-alibaba-defining-vc-china (Accessed June 2019).

Drinhausen, Katja, and Vincent Brussee. 2021. China's Social Credit System in 2021: From Fragmentation towards Integration. *Merics China Monitor: Report 3*. https://merics.org/de/veranstaltungen/chinas-social-credit-system-2021 (Accessed May 2022).

Duhigg, Charles, and Keith Bradsher. 2012. 'How the US Lost Out on iPhone Work'. *New York Times*, 21 January. www.nytimes.com/2012/01/22/business/apple-america-and-a-squeezed-middle-class.html (Accessed June 2019).

Dunne, Chris. 2019. 'Amazon Has 1,029,528 New Sellers This Year (Plus Other Stats)'. www.feedbackexpress.com/amazon-1029528-new-sellers-year-plus-stats (Accessed June 2019).

Dyer-Witheford, Nick. 1999. *Cyber-Marx: Cycles and Circuits of Struggle in High Technology Capitalism*. Champaign, IL: University of Illinois Press.

Economist. 2018a. 'Steering Group: A Bold Scheme to Dominate Ride-Hailing'. *Economist*, 10 May. www.economist.com/briefing/2018/05/10/a-bold-scheme-to-dominate-ride-hailing (Accessed May 2022).

Economist. 2018b. 'Workers of the World, Log On!: Technology May Help to Revive Organised Labour'. *Economist*, 15 November. www.economist.com/briefing/2018/11/15/technology-may-help-to-revive-organised-labour (Accessed May 2022).

Edwards, Richard C. 1979. *Contested Terrain: The Transformation of the Workplace in the Twentieth Century*. New York: Basic Books.

Elder-Vass, Dave. 2016. *Profit and Gift in the Digital Economy*. Cambridge: Cambridge University Press.

eMarketer. 2019. 'Alibaba, JD.com Lead in China, But a Few Others Are Making Dents, Too'. *eMarketer*, 2 July. www.emarketer.com/content/alibaba-jd-com-lead-in-china-but-a-few-others-are-making-dents-too (Accessed May 2022).

Engels, Anita. 2009. 'Die soziale Konstitution von Märkten'. *Wirtschaftssoziologie*, special issue of *Kölner Zeitschrift für Soziologie und Sozialpsychologie* 49: 67–86. https://link.springer.com/book/9783531157269.

Erikson, Robert, and John H. Goldthorpe. 1993. *The Constant Flux: A Study of Class Mobility in Industrial Societies*. Oxford: Clarendon Press.

Esposito, Elena. 2010. *Die Zukunft der Futures: Die Zeit des Geldes in Finanzwelt und Gesellschaft*. Heidelberg: Carl Auer Systeme Verlag.

European Commission. 2008. 'Antitrust: Commission Imposes €899 Million Penalty on Microsoft for Non-Compliance with March 2004 Decision'. https://ec.europa.eu/commission/presscorner/detail/en/IP_08_318 (Accessed February 2023).

European Commission. 2009. 'Antitrust: Commission Imposes Fine of €1.06 bn on Intel for Abuse of Dominant Position; Orders Intel to Cease Illegal Practices'. https://ec.europa.eu/commission/presscorner/detail/en/IP_09_745 (Accessed February 2023).

Eurostat. 2022a. 'Internet Purchases by Individuals (until 2019)'. *Eurostat*, 30 March. https://ec.europa.eu/eurostat/databrowser/view/isoc_ec_ibuy/default/table?lang=en (Accessed February 2023).

Eurostat. 2022b. 'Internet Purchases by Individuals (2020 Onwards)'. *Eurostat*, 30 March. https://ec.europa.eu/eurostat/databrowser/view/isoc_ec_ib20/default/table?lang=en (Accessed May 2022).

Evans, Benedict. 2017. *The Scale of Tech Winners*. www.ben-evans.com/benedictevans/2017/10/12/scale-wetxp (Accessed June 2019).

Evans, Leighton, and Rob Kitchin. 2018. 'A Smart Place to Work? Big Data Systems, Labour, Control and Modern Retail Stores'. *New Technology, Work and Employment* 33(1): 44–57.

Federal Reserve Bank of New York. n.d. *Quarterly Report on Household Debt and Credit: Historical (pre-2003) Data*. www.newyorkfed.org/medialibrary/media/research/national_economy/householdcredit/pre2003_data.xlsx (Accessed June 2019).

Federal Reserve Bank of New York. 2022. *Quarterly Report on Household Debt and Credit: Quarter 3, 2022*. Center for Microeconomic Data, New York FED. www.newyorkfed.org/microeconomics/hhdc (Accessed May 2022).

Federal Reserve Bank of St Louis and US Office of Management and Budget. 2022. 'Federal Debt: Total Public Debt as Percent of Gross Domestic Product'. Federal Reserve Bank of St Louis/US Office of Management and Budget, 30 March 2022. https://fred.stlouisfed.org/series/GFDEGDQ188S (Accessed May 2022).

Feiner, Lauren. 2019. 'Apple Is Once Again the Most Valuable Public Company in the World'. *CNBC*, 6 February. www.cnbc.com/2019/02/06/apple-is-once-again-the-most-valuable-public-company-in-the-world.html (Accessed June 2019).

Financial Stability Board. 2021. *Global Monitoring Report on Non-Bank Financial Intermediation: 2021*. n.p.: Federal Stability Board. www.fsb.org/wp-content/uploads/P161221.pdf (Accessed May 2022).

Fleischmann, Christoph. 2019. 'Böhm, Hayek, Merz: Der Staat als Diener des Marktes'. *Blätter für deutsche und internationale Politik* 3: 111–18.

Fligstein, Neil, and Luke Dauter. 2007. 'The Sociology of Markets'. *Annual Review of Sociology* 33: 105–28. https://doi.org/10.1146/annurev.soc.33.040406.131736.

Fourastié, Jean. 1954. *Die große Hoffnung des zwanzigsten Jahrhunderts*. Cologne: Bund-Verlag.

Fuchs, Christian. 2010. 'Labor in Informational Capitalism and on the Internet'. *Information Society* 26(3): 179–96. https://doi.org/10.1080/01972 241003712215.

Fuchs, Christian. 2022. *Digital Capitalism: Media, Communication and Society*, vol. 3. Abingdon and New York: Routledge.

Fudge, Judy. 2005. 'After Industrial Citizenship: Market Citizenship or Citizenship at Work?' *Relations Industrielles/Industrial Relations* 60(4): 632–56.

FXSSI. 2022. 'Most Valuable Companies in the World – 2023'. *FXSSI*, 27 July 2022. https://fxssi.com/top-10-most-valuable-companies-in-the-world (Accessed May 2022).

García Martínez, Antonio. 2016. *Chaos Monkeys: Obscene Fortune and Random Failure in Silicon Valley*. New York: HarperCollins.

Gardner, Matthew. 2022. 'Amazon Avoids More Than $5 Billion in Corporate Income Taxes, Reports 6 Percent Tax Rate on $35 Billion of US Income'. *JustTaxes: Institute on Taxation and Economic Policy*, 7 February. https://itep.org/amazon-avoids-more-than-5-billion-in-corporate-income-taxes-reports-6-percent-tax-rate-on-35-billion-of-us-income/ (Accessed May 2022).

Gerig, Austin. 2015. 'High-Frequency Trading Synchronizes Prices in Financial Markets'. *SSRN*, 1 January, 2173247. http://dx.doi.org/10.2139/ssrn.2173247 (Accessed May 2022).

Giddens, Anthony. 1984. *Die Konstitution der Gesellschaft: Grundzüge einer Theorie der Strukturierung*. Frankfurt am Main and New York: Campus.

Giddens, Anthony. 1987. *The Nation-State and Violence*. Volume 2 of *A Contemporary Critique of Historical Materialism*. Berkeley and Los Angeles, CA: University of California Press.

Giersch, Herbert, Karl-Heinz Paqué and Holger Schmieding. n.d. 'Durchschnittliches jährliches Wachstum von BIP, Bevölkerung und Produktivität in der Bundesrepublik Deutschland in den Jahren 1950 bis 1989'. *Statista*. https://de.statista.com/statistik/daten/studie/249644/umfrage/historisches-wachstum-von-bip-bevoelkerung-und-produktivitaet-in-deutschland (Accessed June 2019).

Gin, Willie. 2018. 'Big Data and Labor: What Baseball Can Tell Us about Information and Inequality'. *Journal of Information Technology and Politics* 15(1): 66–79.

Goda, Thomas, and Photis Lysandrou. 2014. 'The Contribution of Wealth Concentration to the Subprime Crisis: A Quantitative Estimation'. *Cambridge Journal of Economics* 38(2): 301–27.

Gompers, Paul A., William Gornall, Steven N. Kaplan and Ilya A. Strebulaev. 2016. *How Do Venture Capitalists Make Decisions?* Cambridge, MA: National Bureau of Economic Research.

Google. 2022. 'Advertising Revenue of Google from 2001 to 2021'. *Statista*. www.statista.com/statistics/266249/advertising-revenue-of-google/ (Accessed May 2022).

Gordon, Robert. 2012. 'Is US Economic Growth Over? Faltering Innovation Confronts the Six Headwinds', NBER Working Paper 18315.

Gordon, Robert. 2016. *The Rise and Fall of American Growth: The US Standard of Living since the Civil War*. Princeton, NJ: Princeton University Press.

Gornall, Will, and Lya A. Strebulaev. 2017. *Squaring Venture Capital Valuations with Reality*. www.nakedcapitalism.com/wp-content/uploads/2017/08/SSRN-id2955455-1.pdf (Accessed June 2019).

Gramsci, Antonio. 1991 [*c*.1930]. 'Vergangenheit und Gegenwart'. In *Gefängnishefte* 2 and 3, *Kritische Gesamtausgabe*, vol. 2, edited by Klaus Bochmann and Wolfgang Fritz Haug, 354 f. Hamburg: Argument.

Gramsci, Antonio. 1992 [*c*.1930]. 'Hegemonie (Zivilgesellschaft) und Gewaltenteilung'. In *Gefängnishefte 6*, vol. 4, edited by Klaus Bochmann and Wolfgang Fritz Haug, 772 ff. Hamburg: Argument.

Grieco, Elizabeth. 2017. 'More Americans are Turning to Multiple Social Media Sites for News'. *Pew Research Center*, 2 November. www.pewresearch.org/fact-tank/2017/11/02/more-americans-are-turning-to-multiple-social-media-sites-for-news (Accessed June 2019).

Gurman, Mark, and Sarah Frier. 2018. 'Facebook Hires a Head of Chip Development from Google'. *Bloomberg*, 13 July. www.bloomberg.com/news/articles/2018-07-13/facebook-hires-a-head-of-chip-development-from-google (Accessed June 2019).

Harvey, David. 1991. *The Condition of Postmodernity: An Enquiry into the Origins of Cultural Change*. Hoboken, NJ: Wiley-Blackwell.

Haucap, Justus, and Ulrich Heimeshoff. 2014. 'Google, Facebook, Amazon, eBay: Is the Internet Driving Competition or Market Monopolization?' *International Economic Policy* 11(1–2): 49–61. https://doi.org/10.1007/s10368-013-0247-6.

Häußermann, Hartmut, and Walter Siebel. 1995. *Dienstleistungsgesellschaften*. Frankfurt am Main: Suhrkamp.

HDE Handelsverband Deutschland. 2021. *Online-Monitor 2021*. Berlin: HDE.

Heeks, Richard. 2017. *Decent Work and the Digital Gig Economy: A Developing Country Perspective on Employment Impacts and Standards in Online Outsourcing, Crowdwork, etc.* Manchester: Centre for Development Informatics, Global Development Institute, SEED, University of Manchester.

Hirsch, Joachim. 1995. *Der nationale Wettbewerbsstaat: Staat, Demokratie und Politik im globalen Kapitalismus*. Berlin: Edition ID-Archiv.

Hirsch, Joachim, and Roland Roth. 1986. *Das neue Gesicht des Kapitalismus: Vom Fordismus zum Post-Fordismus*. Hamburg: VSA.

Hirsch, Lauren, and Michelle Castillo. 2018. 'Amazon Has Big Plans for Alexa Ads in 2018; It's Discussing Options with P&G, Clorox and Others'. *CNBC*, 2 January. www.cnbc.com/2018/01/02/amazon-alexa-is-opening-up-to-more-sponsored-product-ads.html (Accessed June 2019).

Holweg, Matthias. 2007. 'The Genealogy of Lean Production'. *Journal of Operations Management* 25(2): 420–37. https://doi.org/10.1016/j.jom.2006.04.001.

Hong, Yu. 2017a. 'Pivot to Internet Plus: Molding China's Digital Economy for Economic Restructuring?' *International Journal of Communication* 11: 1486–1506.

Hong, Yu. 2017b. 'Reading the 13th Five-Year Plan: Reflections on China's ICT Policy'. *International Journal of Communication* 11: 1755–74.

Höpner, Martin. 2003. *Wer beherrscht die Unternehmen?: Shareholder Value, Managerherrschaft und Mitbestimmung in Deutschland*. Frankfurt am Main and New York: Campus.

Höpner, Martin. 2016. 'Das deutsche Lohnregime und der Merkantilismus'. *Makroskop*, 27 May. https://makroskop.eu/das-deutsche-lohnregime-und-der-merkantilismus/ (Accessed February 2023).

Horrocks, John W. 2017 [1925]. *A Short History of Mercantilism*. New York: Routledge.

Huang, Zheping. 2021. 'China Slashes Kids' Gaming Time to Just Three Hours a Week'. *Bloomberg*, 30 August. www.bloomberg.com/news/articles/2021-08-30/china-limits-minors-to-just-three-hours-of-online-gaming-a-week (Accessed May 2022).

Huber, Joseph. 2015. 'Monetäre Modernisierung: Vom Giralgeld zum Vollgeld'. In *Geld und Krise: Die sozialen Grundlagen moderner Geldordnungen*, edited by Klaus Kraemer and Sebastian Nessel, 291–308. Frankfurt am Main and New York: Campus.

Huws, Ursula, Neil H. Spencer, Dag S. Syrdal and Kaire Holts. 2017. *Work in the European Gig Economy: Research Results from the UK, Sweden, Germany, Austria, the Netherlands, Switzerland and Italy*. Brussels: FEPS (Foundation for European Progressive Studies).

Hwang, Tim. 2018. 'Computational Power and the Social Impact of Artificial Intelligence'. SSRN, 23 March. https://ssrn.com/abstract=3147971 (Accessed June 2019).

IAB (Interactive Advertising Bureau) and PwC (PricewaterhouseCoopers). 2021. *Outlook 2022: The US Digital Advertising Ecosystem*. n.p.: Interactive Advertising Bureau and PwC. www.iab.com/wp-content/uploads/2021/10/IAB-PWC-Outlook-2022-The-Digital-Advg-Ecosystem-Oct-2021.pdf (Accessed May 2022).

IAB (Interactive Advertising Bureau) and PwC (PricewaterhouseCoopers). 2022. *Internet Advertising Revenue Report: Full-Year 2021 Results*. n.p.: Interactive Advertising Bureau and PwC. www.iab.com/wp-content/uploads/2022/04/IAB_Internet_Advertising_Revenue_Report_Full_Year_2021.pdf (Accessed May 2022).

Ingham, Geoffrey. 2004. *The Nature of Money*. Cambridge, UK and Malden, MA: Polity.

International Telecommunication Union. 2022. 'Individuals Using the Internet (% of Population)'. *World Bank*. https://databank.worldbank.org/reports.aspx?source=2&type=metadata&series=IT.NET.USER.ZS (Accessed May 2022).

Iqbal, Mansoor. 2023. 'App Revenue Data (2023)'. *Business of Apps*, 4 May. www.businessofapps.com/data/app-revenues/ (Accessed February 2023).

IT Dashboard. 2019. 'IT Spending FY 2011–2020 ($ billions) – Government-wide'. https://itdashboard.gov/#explore-2019 (Accessed June 2019).

Iyengar, Rishi. 2018. 'Xiaomi Overtakes Samsung in World's Hottest Smartphone Market'. *CNN Business*, 25 January. https://money.cnn.com/2018/01/25/technology/samsung-xiaomi-india-smartphone-market/index.html?iid=EL (Accessed June 2019).

Jacobs, Ben. 2016. 'Peter Thiel, PayPal Co-Founder, to be Delegate for Donald Trump'. *Guardian*, 10 May. www.theguardian.com/us-news/2016/may/10/peter-thiel-paypal-co-founder-to-be-delegate-for-donald-trump (Accessed June 2019).

Jia, Lianrui. 2018. 'Going Public and Going Global: Chinese Internet Companies and Global Finance Networks'. *Westminster Papers in Communication and Culture* 13(1): 17–36.

Jiang, Min, and King-Wa Fu. 2018. 'Chinese Social Media and Big Data: Big Data, Big Brother, Big Profit?' *Policy and Internet* 10(4): 372–92.

Jin, Dal Yong. 2013. 'The Construction of Platform Imperialism in the Globalization Era'. *tripleC* 11(1): 145–72.

Jürgens, Ulrich. 2017. 'Lean Production/Toyotismus'. In *Lexikon der Arbeits- und Industriesoziologie*, edited by Hartmut Hirsch-Kreinsen and Heiner Minssen, 204–7. Baden-Baden: Nomos.

Jürgens, Ulrich, and Martin Krzywdzinski. 2016. *New Worlds of Work: Varieties of Work in Car Factories in the BRIC Countries.* Oxford: Oxford University Press.

Kantor, Jodi, and David Streitfeld. 2015. 'Inside Amazon: Wrestling Big Ideas in a Bruising Workplace'. *New York Times*, 16 August. www.nytimes.com/2015/08/16/technology/inside-amazon-wrestling-big-ideas-in-a-bruising-workplace.html (Accessed June 2019).

Kässi, Otto, and Vili Lehdonvirta. 2016. *Online Labour Index: Measuring the Online Gig Economy for Policy and Research.* Oxford: Oxford Internet Institute.

Kawa, Luke. 2018. 'S&P 500 Hits Tech-Heavy Milestone Last Seen with Dot-com Bubble'. *Bloomberg*, 28 February. www.bloomberg.com/news/articles/2018-02-28/s-p-500-hits-tech-heavy-milestone-last-seen-amid-dot-com-bubble (Accessed June 2019).

Kaziukėnas, Juozas. 2021. 'Marketplaces Year in Review 2021'. *Marketplace Pulse.* www.marketplacepulse.com/marketplaces-year-in-review-2021#gmv (Accessed May 2022).

Kharpal, Arjun. 2017. 'China's Rapidly Growing Smartphone Stars Set Sights on World Domination to Challenge Samsung, Apple'. *CNBC*, 6 March. www.cnbc.com/2017/03/06/china-smartphone-stars-oppo-vivo-huawei-gionee-set-sights-on-world-domination-challenge-apple-samsung.html (Accessed June 2019).

Kharpal, Arjun. 2019. 'Amazon is Shutting Down its China Marketplace Business: Here's Why it has Struggled'. *CNBC*, 18 April. www.cnbc.com/2019/04/18/amazon-china-marketplace-closing-down-heres-why.html (Accessed May 2022).

Kharpal, Arjun. 2021. 'Alibaba, JD Smash Singles Day Record with $139 Billion of Sales and Focus on "Social Responsibility"'. *CNBC*, 11 November. www.cnbc.com/2021/11/12/china-singles-day-2021-alibaba-jd-hit-record-139-billion-of-sales.html (Accessed May 2022).

Kharpal, Arjun. 2022. 'China's Next Regulatory Target – Algorithms, the Secret of Many Tech Giants' Success'. *CNBC*, 7 January. www.cnbc.com/2022/01/07/china-to-regulate-tech-giants-algorithms-in-unprecedented-move.html (Accessed May 2022).

Kirchhoff. 2021. *IPO-Studie 2021.* Hamburg: Kirchhoff-Consult AG. www.kirchhoff.de/fileadmin/static/pdfs/20211209_IPO_Studie_2021.pdf (Accessed May 2022).

Kirchner, Stefan, and Jürgen Beyer. 2016. 'Die Plattformlogik als digitale Marktordnung: Wie die Digitalisierung Kopplungen von Unternehmen löst und Märkte transformiert'. *Zeitschrift für Soziologie* 45(5): 324–39.

Klare, Michael. 1972. *War Without End: American Planning for the Next Vietnams.* New York: Vintage.

Klein, Jodi Xu. 2018. 'Behind US Private-Equity Investors' Growing Appetite for Chinese Start-Ups'. *South China Morning Post*, 5 January. www.scmp.com/news/china/money-wealth/article/2126920/behind-us-private-equity-investors-growing-appetite-chinese (Accessed June 2019).

Klingler-Vidra, Robyn. 2016. 'When Venture Capital is Patient Capital: Seed Funding as a Source of Patient Capital for High-Growth Companies'. *Socio-Economic Review* 14(4): 691–708.

Kloeck, Alexander. 2014. 'Implicit Subsidies in the EU Banking Sector: An Intermediary Report Which is Part of the Forthcoming Study "Banking Structural Reforms: A Green Perspective"'. n.p.: The Greens/EFA Group in the European Parliament. www.greens-efa.eu/files/assets/docs/implicit_subsidies_in_the_eu_banking_sector_study_january_2014.pdf (Accessed February 2023).

Kocka, Jürgen. 2016. *Capitalism: A Short History*. Princeton, NJ: Princeton University Press.

KPMG. 2022a. *Q4'21 Venture Pulse Report – Global Trends*. https://home.kpmg/xx/en/home/campaigns/2022/01/q4-venture-pulse-report-global.html (Accessed May 2022).

KPMG. 2022b. *Venture Pulse Q4 2021*. https://assets.kpmg/content/dam/kpmg/xx/pdf/2022/01/venture-pulse-q4-2021.pdf (Accessed May 2022).

Krippner, Greta R. 2011. *Capitalizing on Crisis: The Political Origins of the Rise of Finance*. Cambridge, MA and London: Harvard University Press.

Krugman, Paul. 1999. *The Age of Diminished Expectations: US Economic Policy in the 1990s*, 3rd ed. Cambridge, MA and London: MIT Press.

Kühl, Stefan. 2002. 'Konturen des Exit-Kapitalismus: Wie Risikokapital die Art des Wirtschaftens verändert'. *Leviathan* 30(2): 195–219.

Kühl, Stefan. 2003. *Exit: Wie Risikokapital die Regeln der Wirtschaft verändert*. Frankfurt am Main and New York: Campus.

Kushida, Kenji E. 2015. 'The Politics of Commoditization in Global ICT Industries: A Political Economy Explanation of the Rise of Apple, Google, and Industry Disruptors'. *Journal of Industry, Competition and Trade* 15(1): 49–67.

Landeweerd, Marcel, Ton Spil and Richard Klein. 2013. 'The Success of Google Search, the Failure of Google Health and the Future of Google Plus'. *International Working Conference on Transfer and Diffusion of IT (TDIT)*. www.researchgate.net/publication/299706856_The_Success_of_Google_Search_the_Failure_of_Google_Health_and_the_Future_of_Google_Plus (Accessed June 2019).

Lange, Ann-Christina, Marc Lenglet and Robert Seyfert. 2016. 'Cultures of High Frequency Trading'. *Economy and Society* 45(2): 149–65.

Langlois, Ganaele, and Greg Elmer. 2019. 'Impersonal Subjectivation from Platforms to Infrastructures'. *Media, Culture and Society* 41(2): 236–51.

Lassalle, Ferdinand. 1862. *Arbeiterprogramm: Über den besonderen Zusammenhang der gegenwärtigen Geschichtsperiode mit der Idee des Arbeiterstandes*. Leipzig: Reclam.

Lee, Min Kyung, and Su Baykal. 2017. 'Algorithmic Mediation in Group Decisions: Fairness Perceptions of Algorithmically Mediated vs. Discussion-Based Social Division'. *ACM Conference*. www.researchgate.net/publication/313738865_Algorithmic_Mediation_in_Group_Decisions_Fairness_Perceptions_of_Algorithmically_Mediated_vs_Discussion-Based_Social_Division (Accessed June 2019).

Lee, Min Kyung, Daniel Kusbit, Evan Metsky and Laura Dabbish. 2015. 'Working with Machines: The Impact of Algorithmic and Data-Driven Management on Human Workers'. *CHI '15 Proceedings of the 33rd Annual ACM Conference on Human Factors in Computing Systems Conference*. www.researchgate.net/

publication/277875720_Working_with_Machines_The_Impact_of_Algorithmic_
and_Data-Driven_Management_on_Human_Workers (Accessed June 2019).

Leigh, Karen, and Dandan Li. 2018. 'How China Is Planning to Rank 1.3
Billion People'. *Bloomberg*, 1 December. www.bloomberg.com/news/arti
cles/2018-12-01/china-s-radical-plan-to-judge-each-citizen-s-behavior-quick
take (Accessed June 2019).

Leisegang, Daniel. 2014. *Amazon: Das Buch als Beute*. Stuttgart: Schmetterling.

Lemke, Tim. 2022. 'What Is the Weighting of the S&P 500? Understanding
the Sectors and Market Caps in the Index'. *The Balance*, 29 March. www.
thebalance.com/what-is-the-sector-weighting-of-the-s-and-p-500-4579847
(Accessed May 2022).

Lepore, Jill. 2014. 'The Disruption Machine: What the Gospel of Innovation Gets
Wrong'. *New Yorker*, 16 June. www.newyorker.com/magazine/2014/06/23/the-
disruption-machine (Accessed June 2019).

Lewis, Michael. 2003. *Moneyball: The Art of Winning an Unfair Game*. New York:
Norton.

Liang, Fan, and Yuchen Cheng. 2022. 'The Making of "Good" Citizens: China's
Social Credit System and Infrastructures of Social Quantification'. *Policy and
Internet* 14: 114–35. https://doi.org/10.1002/poi3.291.

Lin, Ken-Hou, and Donald Tomaskovic-Devey. 2013. 'Financialization and
US Income Inequality, 1970–2008'. *American Journal of Sociology* 118(5):
1284–1329.

LiPuma, Edward, and Benjamin Lee. 2004. *Financial Derivatives and the
Globalization of Risk*. Durham, NC: Duke University Press.

Lovink, Geert. 2017. *Im Bann der Plattformen: Die nächste Runde der Netzkritik*.
Bielefeld: Transcript.

Lund, Susan, Toos Daruvala, Richard Dobbs, Philipp Härle, Ju-Hon Kwek and
Ricardo Falcón. 2013. *Financial Globalization: Retreat or Reset? Global Capital
Markets 2013*. n.p.: McKinsey Global Institute. www.mckinsey.com/featured-
insights/employment-and-growth/financial-globalization (Accessed May 2022).

Magnusson, Lars. 2015. *The Political Economy of Mercantilism*. New York:
Routledge.

Marketplace Pulse. 2022. 'Amazon Percent of Units by Third-Party Sellers:
2004–2022'. www.marketplacepulse.com/stats/amazon/amazon-percent-of-un
its-by-marketplace-sellers-1 (Accessed June 2019).

Marrs, Kira. 2008. *Arbeit unter Marktdruck: Die Logik der ökonomischen
Steuerung in der Dienstleistungsarbeit*. Berlin: Edition Sigma.

Marshall, Thomas H. 1950. *Citizenship and Social Class and Other Essays*.
Cambridge: Cambridge University Press.

Martin, Randy. 2009. 'The Twin Towers of Financialization: Entanglements of
Political and Cultural Economies'. *Global South* 3(1): 108–25.

Mas, Mathilde, et al. 2018. *The 2018 Predict Key Facts Report: An Analysis of ICT
R&D in the EU and Beyond*. Seville: European Commission.

Mason, Paul. 2016. *Post-Capitalism: A Guide to Our Future*. London: Penguin.

Mau, Steffen. 2017. *Das metrische Wir: Über die Quantifizierung des Sozialen*.
Berlin: Suhrkamp.

Mauldin, Alan. 2017. 'A Complete List of Content Providers' Submarine Cable
Holdings'. *TeleGeography*, 9 November. https://blog.telegeography.com/telege
ographys-content-providers-submarine-cable-holdings-list (Accessed June 2019).

Mazzucato, Mariana. 2018. *The Entrepreneurial State: Debunking Public vs. Private Myths in Risk and Innovation*. London: Penguin Books.

Mazzucato, Mariana. 2019. *The Value of Everything: Making and Taking in the Global Economy*. London: Penguin Books.

McFarlan, Warren. 1984. 'Information Technology Changes the Way You Compete'. *Harvard Business Review* 62(3): 98–103.

Meissner, Mirjam. 2017. *Chinas gesellschaftliches Bonitätssystem: Marktregulierung mit Hilfe von Big Data hat weitreichende Folgen für Unternehmen in China*. Berlin: Merics.

Merton, Robert K. 1968. 'The Matthew Effect in Science: The Reward and Communication Systems of Science are Considered'. *Science* 159(3810): 56–63.

Meta Platforms. 2023. 'Annual Advertising Revenue of Meta Platforms Worldwide from 2009 to 2022'. *Statista*. www.statista.com/statistics/271258/facebooks-advertising-revenue-worldwide/ (Accessed February 2023).

Mittal, Mohit. 2017. 'WeChat: The One App That Rules Them All'. *Digital Initiative*. https://digital.hbs.edu/innovation-disruption/wechat%E2%80%8A-%E2%80%8Athe-one-app-rules/ (Accessed June 2019).

Moore, Phoebe V. 2018a. *The Quantified Self in Precarity: Work, Technology and What Counts*. Abingdon: Routledge.

Moore, Phoebe V. 2018b. 'Tracking Affective Labour for Agility in the Quantified Workplace'. *Body and Society* 24(3): 39–67.

Moore, Phoebe V., and Lukasz Piwek. 2017. 'Regulating Wellbeing in the Brave New Quantified Workplace'. *Employee Relations* 39(3): 308–16.

Moreno, John. 2021. 'Google Estimated to be Paying $15 Billion to Remain Default Search Engine on Safari'. *Forbes*, 27 August. www.forbes.com/sites/johanmoreno/2021/08/27/google-estimated-to-be-paying-15-billion-to-remain-default-search-engine-on-safari/?sh=58925619669b (Accessed May 2022).

Morozov, Evgeny. 2018. 'Silicon Valley oder die Zukunft des digitalen Kapitalismus'. *Blätter für deutsche und internationale Politik* 1: 93–104.

Mosco, Vincent. 1989. *The Pay-Per Society: Computers and Communication in the Information Age*. Toronto: Garamond Press.

Müller-Jentsch, Walther. 2009. *Arbeit und Bürgerstatus: Studien zur sozialen und industriellen Demokratie*. Wiesbaden: Springer VS.

Nachtwey, Oliver. 2016a. *Die Abstiegsgesellschaft: Über das Aufbegehren in der regressiven Moderne*. Berlin: Suhrkamp.

Nachtwey, Oliver. 2016b. 'Gibt es einen neuen sozialen Konflikt? Einige sozial-theoretische Überlegungen'. In *Kapitalismus und Ungleichheit: Die neuen Verwerfungen*, edited by Heinz Bude and Philipp Staab, 239–60. Frankfurt am Main: Campus.

Nachtwey, Oliver, and Timo Seidl. 2017. *Die Ethik der Solution und der Geist des digitalen Kapitalismus*, IfS Working Paper 11. Frankfurt am Main: Institut für Sozialforschung.

Nachtwey, Oliver, and Philipp Staab. 2015. 'Die Avantgarde des digitalen Kapitalismus'. *Mittelweg 36* 24(6): 59–84.

Nachtwey, Oliver, and Philipp Staab. 2020. 'Das Produktionsmodell des digitalen Kapitalismus'. *Soziale Welt*, special issue of *Soziologie des Digitalen – Digitale Soziologie?* 23: 285–304. https://doi.org/10.5771/9783845295008-285.

Nechushtai, Efrat. 2018. 'Could Digital Platforms Capture the Media through Infrastructure?' *Journalism* 19(8): 1043–58.

Noss, Joseph, and Rhiannon Sowerbutts. 2012. *The Implicit Subsidy of Banks*, Bank of England Financial Stability Paper 15. London: Bank of England.

O'Connor, Fiona. 2022. 'Amazon Has 1.9 Million Active Sellers Worldwide (Plus Other Stats)'. *eDesk*, 31 January. www.edesk.com/blog/amazon-statistics/ (Accessed May 2022).

OECD (Organisation for Economic Co-operation and Development). 2013. *OECD Communications Outlook 2013*. Paris: OECD Publishing.

OECD (Organisation for Economic Co-operation and Development). 2015. *OECD Digital Economy Outlook 2015*. Paris: OECD Publishing.

OECD (Organisation for Economic Co-operation and Development). 2016. *New Markets and New Jobs*. Paris: OECD Publishing.

OECD (Organisation for Economic Co-operation and Development). 2017a. *Entrepreneurship at a Glance 2017*. Paris: OECD Publishing.

OECD (Organisation for Economic Co-operation and Development). 2017b. *OECD Digital Economy Outlook 2017*. Paris: OECD Publishing.

OECD (Organisation for Economic Co-operation and Development). 2021. 'Value Added by Activity'. *OECD Data*. https://data.oecd.org/natincome/value-added-by-activity.htm (Accessed May 2022).

OECD (Organisation for Economic Co-operation and Development). 2022. 'Narrow Money (M1)'. https://data.oecd.org/money/narrow-money-m1.htm (Accessed May 2022).

Ohlberg, Mareike, Shazeda Ahmed and Bertram Lang. 2017. *Central Planning, Local Experiments: The Complex Implementation of China's Social Credit System*. Berlin: Merics.

O'Neil, Mathieu, and Olivier Frayssé. 2015. *Digital Labour and Prosumer Capitalism: The US Matrix (Dynamics of Virtual Work)*. Basingstoke: Palgrave Macmillan.

Ong, Thuy. 2017. 'Microsoft and Facebook Just Laid a 160-Terabits-per-Second Cable 4,100 Miles across the Atlantic'. *The Verge*, 25 September. www.theverge.com/2017/9/25/16359966/microsoft-facebook-transatlantic-cable-160-terabits-a-second (Accessed June 2019).

Osterhammel, Jürgen, and Niels P. Petersson. 2007. *Geschichte der Globalisierung: Dimensionen, Prozesse, Epochen*, 5th ed. Munich: C. H. Beck.

Ovide, Shira, and Rani Molla. 2016. 'Technology Conquers Stock Market: This Sweep of the Market's Top Rungs Didn't Even Happen during the Dot-com Bubble'. *Bloomberg*, 2 August. www.bloomberg.com/opinion/articles/2016-08-02/tech-giants-form-fab-five-to-dominate-stock-valuation-chart (Accessed June 2019).

Pace, Jonathan. 2018. 'The Concept of Digital Capitalism'. *Communication Theory* 28(3): 254–69.

Palan, Ronen, and Anastasia Nesvetailova. 2014. 'Elsewhere, Ideally Nowhere: Shadow Banking and Offshore Finance'. *Politik* 16(4): 26–34.

Parsons, Gregory. 1983. 'Information Technology. A New Competitive Weapon'. *Sloan Management Review* 24(10): 3–14.

Pasquale, Frank. 2015. *The Black Box Society: The Secret Algorithms That Control Money and Information*. Cambridge, MA: Harvard University Press.

Perez, Bien. 2017. 'Tencent Poised to Rub Shoulders with Apple and Facebook as China's First Entrant to Elite US$500 Billion Tech Club'. *South China Morning Post*, 14 November. www.scmp.com/tech/enterprises/article/2119896/tencent-poised-rub-shoulders-apple-and-facebook-chinas-first (Accessed June 2019).

Perez, Sarah. 2018. '47.3 Million US Adults Have Access to a Smart Speaker, Report Says'. *Techcrunch*, 7 March. https://techcrunch.com/2018/03/07/47-3-million-u-s-adults-have-access-to-a-smart-speaker-report-says/?guccounter=1 (Accessed June 2019).

Pettifor, Ann. 2017. *The Production of Money: How to Break the Power of Bankers*. London and New York: Verso.

Pfeiffer, Sabine. 2014. 'Agile Methoden als Werkzeug des Belastungsmanagements? Eine arbeitsvermögensbasierte Perspektive'. *Arbeit* 23(2): 119–32.

Pfister, Damien Smith, and Misti Yang. 2018. 'Five Theses on Technoliberalism and the Networked Public Sphere'. *Communication and the Public* 3(3): 247–62.

Phillips, Leigh, and Michal Rozworski. 2019. *The People's Republic of Walmart: How the World's Biggest Corporations Are Laying the Foundation for Socialism*. London and New York: Verso.

Piketty, Thomas. 2014. *Das Kapital im 21. Jahrhundert*. Munich: C. H. Beck.

Plantin, Jean-Christophe, and Gabriele de Seta. 2019. 'WeChat as Infrastructure: The Techno-Nationalist Shaping of Chinese Digital Platforms'. *Chinese Journal of Communication* 1(19): 257–73.

Plass-Fleßenkämper, Benedikt. 2017. 'Audi und Volvo haben bald Android an Bord'. *GQ*, 17 May. www.gq-magazin.de/auto-technik/articles/audi-volvo-android-auto-google-apps (Accessed June 2019).

Pocket Gamer. 2022. 'Number of Available Apps in the Apple Store from 2008 to October 2022'. *Statista*, November. www.statista.com/statistics/268251/number-of-apps-in-the-itunes-app-store-since-2008/ (Accessed May 2022).

Polanyi, Karl. 2001 [1944]. *The Great Transformation: The Political and Economic Origins of Our Time*. Boston, MA: Beacon Press.

Pon, Bryan, Timo Seppälä and Martin Kenney. 2014. 'Android and the Demise of Operating System-Based Power: Firm Strategy and Platform Control in the Post-PC World'. *Telecommunications Policy* 38(11): 979–91.

Pongratz, Hans J., and Sarah Bormann. 2017. 'Online-Arbeit auf Internet-Plattformen: Empirische Befunde zum "Crowdworking" in Deutschland'. *Arbeits- und Industriesoziologische Studien* 10(2): 158–81.

Postberg, Christian. 2013. *Macht und Geld: Über die gesellschaftliche Bedeutung monetärer Verfassungen*. Frankfurt am Main and New York: Campus.

PwC (PricewaterhouseCoopers). 2021. *Global Top 100 Companies by Market Capitalisation: May 2021*. New York: PwC. www.pwc.com/gx/en/audit-services/publications/assets/pwc-global-top-100-companies-2021.pdf (Accessed May 2022).

PwC (PricewaterhouseCoopers). 2022. 'Value of Venture Capital Investment in the United States from 2006 to 2021'. *Statista*. www.statista.com/statistics/277501/venture-capital-amount-invested-in-the-united-states-since-1995/ (Accessed May 2022).

PwC (PricewaterhouseCoopers) and CBInsights. 2019. 'MoneyTree™ Data Explorer: Filtered by Sector: Computer Hardware & Services or Electronics or Internet or Mobile & Telecommunications or Software (Non-Internet/Mobile)'. www.pwc.com/us/en/industries/technology/moneytree/explorer.html#/ (Accessed May 2022).

PwC (PricewaterhouseCoopers) and CBInsights. 2021. *MoneyTree™ Report: Q4 2020*. New York: PwC. www.pwc.com/us/en/moneytree-report/assets/pwc-moneytree-2020-q4.pdf (Accessed May 2022).

PwC (PricewaterhouseCoopers) and IAB (Interactive Advertising Bureau). 2021. 'Online Advertising Revenue in the United States from 2000 to 2021'. *Statista*. www.statista.com/statistics/183816/us-online-advertising-revenue-since-2000/ (Accessed May 2022).

PYMNTS. 2022. 'Amazon's Share of US eCommerce Sales Hits All-Time High of 56.7% in 2021'. *PYMNTS*, 14 March. www.pymnts.com/news/retail/2022/ama zons-share-of-us-ecommerce-sales-hits-all-time-high-of-56-7-in-2021/ (Accessed May 2022).

Raffetseder, Eva-Maria, Simon Schaupp and Philipp Staab. 2017. 'Kybernetik und Kontrolle: Algorithmische Arbeitssteuerung und betriebliche Herrschaft'. *Prokla* 187(2): 229–47.

Randewich, Noel. 2017. 'After 17 Years, S&P Tech Index Breaks Record'. *Reuters*, 20 January. www.reuters.com/article/us-usa-technology-stocks/after-17-years-sp-tech-index-breaks-record-idUSKBN1A42O2 (Accessed June 2019).

Reitz, Tilman. 2017. 'Was ist digitaler Kapitalismus?'. *Soziopolis*, 27 July. https://soziopolis.de/lesen/buecher/artikel/was-ist-digitaler-kapitalismus/ (Accessed June 2019).

Richter, Felix. 2020. 'Uber's Blockbuster Growth Comes at a Hefty Price'. *Statista*. www.statista.com/chart/12059/uber-revenue-bookings-and-net-loss (Accessed May 2022).

Rifkin, Jeremy. 2014. *The Zero Marginal Cost Society: The Internet of Things, the Collaborative Commons, and the Eclipse of Capitalism*. New York: Palgrave Macmillan.

Ritter, Jay R. (2022. 'Initial Public Offerings: Updated Statistics'. https://site.war rington.ufl.edu/ritter/files/IPO-Statistics.pdf (Accessed May 2022).

Ritzer, George, and Nathan Jurgenson. 2010. 'Production, Consumption, Prosumption: The Nature of Capitalism in the Age of the Digital "Prosumer"'. *Journal of Consumer Culture* 10(1): 13–36.

Robbins, Lionel. 1932. *An Essay on the Nature and Significance of Economic Science*. London: Macmillan.

Rochet, Jean-Charles, and Jean Tirole. 2003. 'Platform Competition in Two-sided Markets'. *Journal of the European Economic Association* 1(4): 990–1029.

Rolfe, Alex. 2019. 'Chinese Mobile Payments Market Projected to Grow 21.8% to $96.73 Trillion'. *Payments: Cards and Mobile*, 9 January. www.paymentscard sandmobile.com/chinese-mobile-payments-market-projected-to-grow-21-8 (Accessed June 2019).

Rötzer, Florian. 2018. 'Silicon Valley boomt, aber die meisten haben nichts davon'. *Telepolis*, 25 October. www.heise.de/tp/features/Silicon-Valley-boomt-aber-die-meisten-haben-nichts-davon-4203474.html (Accessed June 2019).

Ruttan, Vernon W. 2006. *Is War Necessary for Economic Growth?: Military Procurement and Technology Development*. Oxford: Oxford University Press.

Sahr, Aaron. 2013. 'Von Richard Nixon zur 1.000.000.000.000-$-Münze: Kreditgeld als politische Verknappungsaufgabe'. *Mittelweg 36* 2: 4–31.

Sahr, Aaron. 2016. 'Reichtum aus Feenstaub: Das Free-Lunch-Privileg des Keystroke-Kapitalismus'. In *Kapitalismus und Ungleichheit: Die neuen Verwerfungen*, edited by Heinz Bude and Philipp Staab, 25–44. Frankfurt am Main: Campus.

Sahr, Aaron. 2017a. *Das Versprechen des Geldes: Eine Praxistheorie des Kredits*. Hamburg: Hamburger Edition.

Sahr, Aaron. 2017b. *Keystroke-Kapitalismus: Ungleichheit auf Knopfdruck.* Hamburg: Hamburger Edition.

Sauer, Dieter. 2010. 'Vermarktlichung und Vernetzung der Unternehmens- und Betriebsorganisation'. In *Handbuch Arbeitssoziologie*, edited by Fritz Böhle, Günther G. Voß and Günther Wachtler, 545–68. Wiesbaden: VS Verlag für Sozialwissenschaften.

Sauer, Dieter. 2011. 'Indirekte Steuerung: Zum Formwandel betrieblicher Herrschaft'. In *Macht und Herrschaft in der reflexiven Moderne*, edited by Wolfgang Bonß and Christoph Lau, 358–78. Weilerswist: Velbrück Wissenschaft.

Schaupp, Simon, and Ramon Diab. 2020. 'From the Smart Factory to the Self-Organisation of Capital: "Industrie 4.0" as the Cybernetisation of Production'. *Ephemera* 20(4): 19–41.

Schaupp, Simon, and Philipp Staab. 2018. 'Rekursivität und Horizontalisierung: Das kommerzielle Internet als Vorbild digitalisierter Arbeit'. *Arbeits- und Industriesoziologische Studien* 11(2): 294–307.

Schildbach, Jan, and Claudius Wenzel. 2013. *Bank Performance in the US and Europe: An Ocean Apart.* Frankfurt am Main: Deutsche Bank AG/DB Research.

Schiller, Dan. 1999. *Digital Capitalism: Networking the Global Market System.* Cambridge, MA: MIT Press.

Schiller, Dan. 2011. 'Power under Pressure: Digital Capitalism in Crisis'. *International Journal of Communication* 5: 924–41.

Schiller, Dan. 2014. *Digital Depression: Information Technology and Economic Crisis.* Champaign, IL: University of Illinois Press.

Schiller, Herbert. 1989. *Culture, Inc.: The Corporate Takeover of Public Expression.* New York and Oxford: Oxford University Press.

Schiller, Herbert. 1996. *Information Inequality: The Deepening Social Crisis in America.* New York and London: Routledge.

Schmalz, Stefan, Steffen Liebig and Marcel Thiel. 2015. 'Zur Zersplitterung des sozialen Konflikts in Westeuropa: Eine Typologie nichtnormierter Kämpfe um Arbeit'. *Arbeits- und industriesoziologische Studien* 8(2): 49–66.

Schmidt, Florian Alexander. 2019. *Crowdproduktion von Trainingsdaten: Zur Rolle von Online-Arbeit beim Trainieren autonomer Fahrzeuge.* Düsseldorf: Hans-Böckler-Stiftung.

Scholz, Trebor. 2017. *Uberworked and Underpaid: How Workers are Disrupting the Digital Economy.* Cambridge, UK and Malden, MA: Polity.

Schor, Juliet B., and William Attwood-Charles. 2017. 'The "Sharing" Economy: Labor, Inequality, and Social Connection on For-Profit Platforms'. *Sociology Compass* 11(8): 1–16.

Schor, Juliet B., William Attwood-Charles, Mehmet Cansoy, Isak Ladegaard and Robert Wengronowitz. 2020. 'Dependence and Precarity in the Platform Economy'. *Theory and Society* 49(5–6): 833–61.

Schössler, Martin. 2018. *Plattformökonomie als Organisationsform zukünftiger Wertschöpfung: Chancen und Herausforderungen für den Standort Deutschland*, WISO Diskurs 21/2018. Berlin: Friedrich-Ebert-Stiftung. http://library.fes.de/pdf-files/wiso/14756.pdf (Accessed June 2019).

Schroeder, Wolfgang. 2017. *Industrie 4.0 und der Rheinische kooperative Kapitalismus*, WISO direkt 03/2017. Berlin: Friedrich-Ebert-Stiftung. http://library.fes.de/pdf-files/wiso/13206.pdf (Accessed June 2019).

Schroeder, Wolfgang, Samuel Greef and Benedikt Schreiter. 2017. *Shaping Digitalisation: Industry 4.0 – Work 4.0 – Regulation of the Platform Economy*. Berlin: Friedrich-Ebert-Stiftung.

Schumpeter, Joseph A. 2003 [1942]. *Capitalism, Socialism and Democracy*. London and New York: Routledge.

Schumpeter, Joseph A. 2021 [1934]. *The Theory of Economic Development*. London and New York: Routledge Classics.

Schwarz, Jonas Andersson. 2017. 'Platform Logic. An Interdisciplinary Approach to the Platform-Based Economy'. *Policy and Internet* 9(4): 374–94.

Schwellnus, Cyrille, Andreas Kappeler and Pierre-Alain Pionnier. 2017. *Decoupling of Wages from Productivity: Macro-Level Facts*, edited by OECD. Paris: OECD Publishing.

Shao, Nathan. 2018. 'The Evolution of Mobile Payments in China'. *Medium*, 15 December. https://medium.com/iveyfintechclub/the-evolution-of-mobile-payments-in-china-4a70d38f22f4 (Accessed June 2019).

Shapiro, Aaron. 2018. 'Between Autonomy and Control: Strategies of Arbitrage in the "On-Demand" Economy'. *New Media and Society* 20(8): 2954–71.

Shapiro, Carl, and Hal R. Varian. 1999. *Information Rules: A Strategic Guide to the Network Economy*. Boston, MA: Harvard Business Press.

Shearer, Elisa, and Jeffrey Gottfried. 2017. 'News Use across Social Media Platforms 2017'. *Pew Research Center Journalist & Media*, 7 September. www.journalism.org/2017/09/07/news-use-across-social-media-platforms-2017 (Accessed June 2019).

Shen, Alice. 2018. 'China Pulls Further Ahead of US in Mobile Payments with Record US$12.8 Trillion in Transactions'. *South China Morning Post*, 20 February. www.scmp.com/tech/apps-gaming/article/2134011/china-pulls-further-ahead-us-mobile-payments-record-us128-trillion (Accessed June 2019).

Shen, Hong. 2018. 'Building a Digital Silk Road? Situating the Internet in China's Belt and Road Initiative'. *International Journal of Communication* 12: 2683–701.

Sherman, Len. 2017. 'Why Can't Uber Make Money?'. *Forbes*, 14 December. www.forbes.com/sites/lensherman/2017/12/14/why-cant-uber-make-money (Accessed June 2019).

Simmel, Georg. 1911. 'Die Mode'. In *Philosophische Kultur: Gesammelte Essais*, 29–64. Leipzig: Klinkhardt.

Smith, Adam. 2013 [1776]. *Der Wohlstand der Nationen*. Munich: Anaconda.

Solomon, Brian. 2015. 'The Hottest On-Demand Startups of 2015'. *Forbes*, 29 December. www.forbes.com/sites/briansolomon/2015/12/29/the-hottest-on-demand-startups-of-2015 (Accessed June 2019).

Solow, Robert M. 1987. 'We'd Better Watch Out'. *New York Times*, 12 July.

Soper, Spencer. 2018. 'Amazon's Clever Machines Are Moving from the Warehouse to Headquarters'. *Bloomberg*, 13 June. www.bloomberg.com/news/articles/2018-06-13/amazon-s-clever-machines-are-moving-from-the-warehouse-to-headquarters (Accessed June 2019).

Soper, Spencer, and Mark Bergen. 2018. 'Amazon Tests Ad Tool That Rivals Google, Criteo'. *Bloomberg*, 14 May. www.bloomberg.com/news/articles/2018-05-14/amazon-is-said-to-test-new-ad-that-competes-with-google-criteo (Accessed February 2023).

Sparsam, Jan. 2015. *Wirtschaft in der New Economic Sociology: Eine Systematisierung und Kritik*. Wiesbaden: Springer VS.

Spencer, David A. 2018. 'Fear and Hope in an Age of Mass Automation: Debating the Future of Work'. *New Technology, Work and Employment* 33(1): 1–12.

Spiegel online. 2008. 'EU-Kommission verhängt Rekordbußgeld von 899 Millionen Euro gegen Microsoft'. *Spiegel*, 27 February. www.spiegel.de/wirtschaft/auflagen-aus-bruessel-eu-kommission-verhaengt-rekordbussgeld-von-899-millionen-euro-gegen-microsoft-a-538104.html (Accessed June 2019).

Sprague, Shawn. 2017. 'Below Trend: The US Productivity Slowdown since the Great Recession'. *Beyond the Numbers* 6(2) (US Bureau of Labor Statistics). https://digitalcommons.ilr.cornell.edu/key_workplace/1917/ (Accessed June 2019).

Srivastava, Moulishree. 2021. 'The Rise and Fall of Alibaba in India (Part 1 of 2)'. *KrASIA*, 11 February. https://kr-asia.com/the-rise-and-fall-of-alibaba-in-india-part-1-of-2 (Accessed May 2022).

Srivastava, Shobhit. 2017. 'Q2 2017 Global Smartphones: Chinese Brand Propelling Growth Outside of China'. *Counterpoint*, 2 August. www.counterpointresearch.com/q2-2017-global-smartphones-chinese-brand-propelling-growth-outside-of-china/ (Accessed June 2019).

Srnicek, Nick. 2017. *Platform Capitalism*. Cambridge, UK and Malden, MA: Polity.

Staab, Philipp. 2014. *Macht und Herrschaft in der Servicewelt*. Hamburg: Hamburger Edition.

Staab, Philipp. 2015. 'Personale Herrschaft und die Horizontalisierung des Arbeitskonfliktes'. *Arbeits- und Industriesoziologische Studien* 8(2): 34–48.

Staab, Philipp. 2016. *Falsche Versprechen: Wachstum im digitalen Kapitalismus*. Hamburg: Hamburger Edition.

Staab, Philipp. 2017. 'Souveränität im digitalen Kapitalismus'. *spw – Zeitschrift für sozialistische Politik und Wirtschaft* 220(3):48–54. www.spw.de/jahres register-2017/#218.

Staab, Philipp. 2018. 'Exit-Kapitalismus revisited: Der Einfluss privaten Risikokapitals auf Unternehmensentscheidungen, Marktrisiken und Arbeitsqualität in technologieintensiven Jungunternehmen'. *Leviathan* 46(2): 212–31.

Staab, Philipp, and Florian Butollo. 2018. *Digitaler Kapitalismus: Wie China das Silicon Valley herausfordert*, WISO direkt 03/2018. Berlin: Friedrich-Ebert-Stiftung. https://library.fes.de/pdf-files/wiso/14037.pdf (Accessed June 2019).

Staab, Philipp, and Oliver Nachtwey. 2016. 'Market and Labour Control in Digital Capitalism'. *tripleC* 14(2): 457–74.

Staab, Philipp, and Eva-Maria Nyckel. 2019. *Digitaler Kapitalismus und Unternehmenssoftware: Herrschaft der Betriebssysteme?* WISO direkt 08/2019. Berlin: Friedrich-Ebert-Stiftung. http://library.fes.de/pdf-files/wiso/15536.pdf (Accessed June 2019).

Statcounter. 2022. 'Mobile Operating System Market Share Worldwide: Dec 2019–Jan 2022'. *Statcounter GlobalStats*. https://gs.statcounter.com/os-market-share/mobile/worldwide/#monthly-201912-202201 (Accessed May 2022).

Statcounter. 2023a. 'Social Media Stats Worldwide: Jan 2022–Jan 2023'. https://gs.statcounter.com/social-media-stats (Accessed May 2022).

Statcounter. 2023b. 'Search Engine Market Share Worldwide: Jan 2022–Jan 2023'. https://gs.statcounter.com/search-engine-market-share (Accessed May 2022.

Statista. 2021. 'Number of Users of Alipay and WeChat Pay in China in 2020, with Forecasts from 2021 to 2015'. *Statista*, October. www.statista.com/statistics/1271130/mobile-wallet-user-forecast-in-china/ (Accessed May 2022).

Stern, Alex. 2017. 'Revisiting the Unicorn Club: Get to Know the Newest Crowd of Billion Dollar Startups'. *Medium*, 27 February. https://medium.com/startup-grind/unicorn-club-revisited-e641f9c80e8d (Accessed June 2019).

Stern, Philip J. 2013. 'Companies: Monopoly, Sovereignty, and the East Indies'. In *Mercantilism Reimagined: Political Economy in Early Modern Britain and its Empire*, edited by Philip J. Stern and Carl Wennerlind, 177–95. Oxford: Oxford University Press.

Stern, Philip J., and Carl Wennerlind, eds. 2013. *Mercantilism Reimagined: Political Economy in Early Modern Britain and its Empire*, Oxford: Oxford University Press.

Stone, Brad. 2013. *The Everything Store: Jeff Bezos and the Age of Amazon*. Boston, MA: Little, Brown and Company.

Strategy Analytics. 2021. 'Strategy Analytics: Another Record Quarter for Smart Speakers in 3Q21, Though Supply Chain Woes are on the Horizon'. *Strategy Analytics*, 20 December. https://news.strategyanalytics.com/press-releases/press-release-details/2021/Strategy-Analytics-Another-Record-Quarter-for-Smart-Speakers-in-3Q21-Though-Supply-Chain-Woes-are-on-the-Horizon/default.aspx (Accessed May 2022).

Streeck, Wolfgang. 2011. 'The Crises of Democratic Capitalism'. *New Left Review* 71: 5–29.

Streeck, Wolfgang. 2012. 'Citizens as Customers: Considerations on the New Politics of Consumption'. *New Left Review* 76: 27–47.

Streeck, Wolfgang. 2014. *Buying Time: The Delayed Crisis of Democratic Capitalism*. London: Verso.

Strugar, Milica. 2022. 'Fascinating Amazon Statistics UK Edition [2022]'. *Cybercrew*, 11 March. https://cybercrew.uk/blog/amazon-statistics-uk/ (Accessed May 2022).

Sumits, Arielle. 2015. 'The History and Future of Internet Traffic'. *Cisco Blogs*, 28 August. https://blogs.cisco.com/sp/the-history-and-future-of-internet-traffic?dtid=osscdc000283 (Accessed May 2022).

Summers, Lawrence H. 2013. Speech at the IMF Fourteenth Annual Research Conference in Honor of Stanley Fischer, Washington, DC, 8 November. http://larrysummers.com/imf-fourteenth-annual-research-conference-in-honor-of-stanley-fischer (Accessed June 2019).

Sweezy, Paul, and Paul A. Baran. 1966. *Monopoly Capital: An Essay on the American Economic and Social Order*. New York: Monthly Review Press.

ten Brink, Tobias. 2016. 'Blinde Flecken: Zur makrosoziologischen Analyse nicht-liberaler Kapitalismen im globalen Süden'. In *Kapitalismus und Ungleichheit: Die neuen Verwerfungen*, edited by Heinz Bude and Philipp Staab, 45–62. Frankfurt am Main: Campus.

ten Brink, Tobias, and Andreas Nölke. 2013. 'Staatskapitalismus 3.0'. *dms – der moderne staat: Zeitschrift für Public Policy, Recht und Management* 6(1): 21–32.

Tencent. 2022. 'Number of Monthly Active WeChat Users from 2nd Quarter 2011 to 3rd Quarter 2022 (in millions)', cited from Statista. www.statista.com/statistics/255778/number-of-active-wechat-messenger-accounts (Accessed June 2019).

The Conference Board. 2018. 'Global Productivity on Upward Trajectory'. *The Conference Board*, News Release #6004, March. www.conference-board.org/pdf_free/press/6004%20-%20Productivity%20March%202018.pdf (Accessed May 2022).

Thiel, Peter. 2014. *Zero to One: Wie Innovation unsere Gesellschaft rettet*. Frankfurt am Main and New York: Campus.

Tilley, Aaron, and Priya Anand. 2018. 'Risks for Startups Taking Money from Amazon's Alexa Fund'. *The Information*, 20 February. www.theinforma tion.com/articles/risks-for-startups-taking-money-from-amazons-alexa-fund? (Accessed June 2019).

Uber Investor. 2022. 'Uber Announces Results for Fourth Quarter and Full Year 2021'. *Uber Investor*, 9. February. https://investor.uber.com/news-events/news/press-release-details/2022/Uber-Announces-Results-for-Fourth-Quarter-and-Full-Year-2021/ (Accessed May 2022).

US Securities and Exchange Commission. 2020. 'Form 10-K. Alphabet Inc.'. www.sec.gov/Archives/edgar/data/1652044/000165204421000010/goog-20201231.htm (Accessed May 2022).

Valdez, Jimena. 2022. 'The Politics of Uber: Infrastructural Power in the United States and Europe'. *Regulation and Governance* 17(1): 177–94. https://onlinelibrary.wiley.com/doi/full/10.1111/rego.12456 (Accessed May 2022).

Veblen, Thorstein. 1986 [1899]. *Theorie der feinen Leute: Eine ökonomische Untersuchung der Institutionen*. Frankfurt am Main: Fischer.

Vogl, Joseph. 2011. *Das Gespenst des Kapitals*. Berlin and Zürich: Diaphanes.

Volkswagen. 2020. *Die Zukunft in der Hand: Geschäftsbericht 2020*. Wolfsburg: Volkswagen.

Voß, Günther G., and Kerstin Rieder. 2005. *Der arbeitende Kunde: Wenn Konsumenten zu unbezahlten Mitarbeitern werden*. Frankfurt am Main and New York: Campus.

Voss, Oliver. 2018. 'Obdachlose in San Francisco: Im Schatten des Silicon Valley'. *Tagesspiegel*, 5 November. www.tagesspiegel.de/wirtschaft/obdachlose-in-san-francisco-im-schatten-des-silicon-valley/23353980.html (Accessed June 2019).

Wallerstein, Immanuel. 1998 [1980]. *Das moderne Weltsystem*, vol. 2: *Der Merkantilismus: Europa zwischen 1600 und 1750*. Vienna: Promedia.

Wearden, Graeme. 2022. 'Saudi Aramco Overtakes Apple as World's Most Valuable Company'. *Guardian*, 12 May. www.theguardian.com/business/2022/may/12/saudi-aramco-overtakes-apple-worlds-most-valuable-company (Accessed May 2022).

Weber, Max. 2016 [1904/05]. *Die protestantische Ethik und der Geist des Kapitalismus*, 4th ed. Berlin: Holzinger.

Weber, Steven. 2017. 'Data, Development, and Growth'. *Business and Politics* 19(3): 397–423.

Weise, Elizabeth. 2016. 'Microsoft, Facebook to Lay Massive Undersea Cable'. *USA Today*, 30 May. https://eu.usatoday.com/story/experience/2016/05/26/microsoft-facebook-undersea-cable-google-marea-amazon/84984882 (Accessed June 2019).

Weltz, Friedrich, and Veronika Lullies. 1983. *Innovation im Büro: Das Beispiel Textverarbeitung*. Frankfurt am Main and New York: Campus.

Werner, Richard A. 2014. 'How do Banks Create Money, and Why can Other Firms not do the Same? An Explanation for the Coexistence of Lending and Deposit-Taking'. *International Review of Financial Analysis* 36: 71–7.

West, Joel, and Michael Mace. 2010. 'Browsing as the Killer App: Explaining the Rapid Success of Apple's iPhone'. *Telecommunications Policy* 34(5–6): 270–86.

Wilkens, Andreas. 2004. 'EU-Kommission verfügt Geldstrafe und Produktauflagen gegen Microsoft'. *Heise online*, 24 March. www.heise.de/newsticker/meldung/EU-Kommission-verfuegt-Geldstrafe-und-Produktauflagen-gegen-Microsoft-95941.html (Accessed June 2019).

Windolf, Paul, ed. 2005. *Finanzmarkt-Kapitalismus: Analysen zum Wandel von Produktionsregimen*, special issue of *Kölner Zeitschrift für Soziologie und Sozialpsychologie* 45. Wiesbaden: Springer VS.

Winseck, Dwayne. 2017. 'The Geopolitical Economy of the Global Internet Infrastructure'. *Journal of Information Policy* 7: 228–67.

Wired Staff. 2016. 'Google und Facebook bauen eine Datenautobahn im Pazifik'. *GQ*, 13 October. www.gq-magazin.de/auto-technik/articles/google-und-facebook-bauen-eine-datenautobahn-im-pazifik (Accessed May 2022).

Wired Staff. 2018. 'Google investiert 550 Millionen US-Dollar in JD.com'. *GQ*, 18 June. www.gq-magazin.de/auto-technik/articles/google-investiert-550-millionen-dollar-in-jd-com (Accessed May 2022).

Womack, James, Daniel Jones and Daniel Roos. 1990. *The Machine that Changed the World: The Story of Lean Production*. New York: HarperCollins.

Wood, Alex J., Mark Graham, Vili Lehdonvirta and Isis Hjorth. 2019. 'Good Gig, Bad Gig: Autonomy and Algorithmic Control in the Global Gig Economy'. *Work, Employment and Society* 33(1): 56–75.

Wray, L. Randall. 2012. *Modern Money Theory: A Primer on Macroeconomics for Sovereign Monetary Systems*. Basingstoke: Palgrave Macmillan.

Zenith. 2021. 'Digital Advertising to Exceed 60% of Global Adspend in 2022'. *Zenith*, 6 December. www.zenithmedia.com/digital-advertising-to-exceed-60-of-global-adspend-in-2022/ (Accessed May 2022).

Zhang, Chenchen, and Nathan Lillie. 2015. 'Industrial Citizenship, Cosmopolitanism and European Integration'. *European Journal of Social Theory* 18(1): 93–111.

Zhong, Raymond. 2020. 'In Halting Ant's IPO, China Sends a Warning to Business'. *New York Times*, 6 November. www.nytimes.com/2020/11/06/technology/china-ant-group-ipo.html (Accessed May 2022).

Zimmer, Jameson. 2018. 'Google Owns 63,605 Miles and 8.5% of Submarine Cables Worldwide'. *Broadband Now*, 12 September. https://broadbandnow.com/report/google-content-providers-submarine-cable-ownership (Accessed June 2019).

Zuboff, Shoshana. 2019. *The Age of Surveillance Capitalism: The Fight for a Human Future at the New Frontier of Power*. New York: PublicAffairs.

Zucman, Gabriel. 2014. *Steueroasen: Wo der Wohlstand der Nationen versteckt wird*. Berlin: Suhrkamp.

Index